DEC – 2001

JUDY ALTER

EXTRAORDINARY EXPLORERS
— AND —
ADVENTURERS

Children's Press
A Division of Scholastic Inc.
New York · Toronto · London · Auckland
Sydney · Mexico City · New Delhi · Hong Kong
Danbury, Connecticut

Visit Children's Press on the Internet at:
http://publishing.grolier.com

Interior design by Elizabeth Helmetsie

Library of Congress Cataloging-in-Publication Data

Alter, Judy 1938–
   Extraordinary explorers and adventurers / by Judy Alter
     p. cm. — (Extraordinary people)
   Includes bibliographical references and index.
   ISBN 0-516-21693-7 (Lib. Bdg.)   0-516-27284-5 (Pbk)
    1. Explorers—Juvenile literature. 2. Adventure and adventurers—
     Juvenile literature. [1. Explorers. 2. Adventure and adventurers.]
     I Title. II. Series

G175.A48 2001
910′.92′2—dc21

00-030715

CHILDREN'S PRESS

Contents

33

Marco Polo
First European to
Explore and Introduce
Chinese Culture to Europe
1254–1324

49

Juan Ponce de León
First Western Explorer
to Reach Florida
c.1460–c.1520

61

Ferdinand Magellan
Explorer and Navigator;
Led First Sailing Expedition
Around the World
1480–1521

36

**John Sebastian Cabot
and Sebastian Cabot**
Father and Son Explorers
*John 1450–c.1499
Sebastian Died 1557*

52

Vasco da Gama
Navigator and
Explorer; Opened
Trade Route to China
c.1469–1524

66

Hernán Cortés
Explorer who
Conquered
Mexico for Spain
1485–1547

40

Christopher Columbus
Explored North
American Continent
for Spain
1451–1506

55

Vasco Núñez de Balboa
Explorer Credited with
Claiming the Pacific
Ocean for Spain
1475–1519

69

Giovanni da Verrazzano
Explorer of East
Coast of America
for King of France
c.1485–1528

46

Amerigo Vespucci
Businessman, Navigator,
and Diplomat for
Spain and Portugal
1454–1512

58

Francisco Pizarro
Conqueror of
the Inca people
c.1475–1541

72

Cabeza de Vaca
First Explorer of the
American Southwest
c.1490–c.1560

75

Jacques Cartier
Explorer who
Discovered the
Saint Lawrence River
1491–1557

90

Sir Francis Drake
Second Man to Sail
Around the World
1540s–1590s

105

**René Robert Cavelier,
Sieur de la Salle**
Explored New France,
Now Known as Canada
1643–1687

81

Hernando de Soto
Explorer of the
Southeastern
United States
c.1500–c.1540s

95

Sir Walter Raleigh
Explorer who
Attempted to Settle
the Roanoke Colonies
in North Carolina
1554–1618

108

**Jacques Marquette
and Louis Joliet**
Explorers who Led the
French Expedition to America
*Marquette (1637–1675);
Joliet (1645–1700)*

84

Francisco de Orellana
First European Explorer
to Travel Down
the Amazon River
Died 1546

98

**Samuel
de Champlain**
Explorer of the North
American Coastline;
Founded Québec
1570–1635

112

Vitus Jonassen Bering
Explorer who Proved
that Asia and America
were not One
Continuous Landmass
1680–1741

87

**Francisco Vásquez
de Coronado**
Conquistador; Searched for
the Legendary Seven Cities of
Gold in the American West
1510–1554

101

Henry Hudson
Explorer who
Sought the Northwest
Passage to Asia
1570s–1611

115

Captain James Cook
Pacific Explorer;
First European to
Visit Hawaiian Islands
1728–1778

119

Daniel Boone
Explored Area
Known as Kentucky
1734–1820

134

Sacagawea
Shoshone Indian who
Aided Lewis and Clark
on Their Journey
c.1787–c.1812

147

Charles Wilkes
Explorer who Confirmed
the Existence of an
Antarctic Continent
1798–1877

122

Sir Alexander Mackenzie
Led First Expedition
to Cross America
North of Mexico
Died 1820

137

Davy Crockett
Mountain Man
and Explorer
1786–1836

150

Jim Beckwourth
Mountain Man
and Trapper
c.1798–1866

125

The Franciscan Friars
Roman Catholic Priests from
Spain who Established the
Mission System in California
c. 1769

140

Sir John Franklin
Explorer of the
Arctic Region
1786–1847

154

Joe Walker
Mountain Man and
Explorer of the Region
from the Rockies to Mexico
1799–1876

128

**William Clark and
Meriwether Lewis**
Explored the American
Continent from the Mississippi
River to the West Coast
Clark (1770–1838); Lewis (1774–1809)

145

Hamilton Hume
Settler and Explorer
of Southern Australia
1797–1873

159

Jedediah Strong Smith
Trapper and Trader
in the American West
1800–1832

163

Jim Bridger
Mountain Man
and Explorer of the
Rocky Mountains
1804–1881

182

Sir Richard Burton
Explorer of the Holy
Lands of the Muslims
1821–1890

197

Roald Amundsen
First Man to Reach
the South Pole
1872–c.1928

168

**Chrisopher
"Kit" Carson**
Rocky Mountain
Man and Trapper
1809–1868

186

Robert Edwin Peary
Arctic Explorer;
First Person to Reach
the North Pole
1856–1920

201

**Sir Ernest
Shackleton**
Antarctic Explorer
1874–1922

171

**John Charles
Frémont**
Surveyor and Builder
for the Railroads
1813–1890

190

Matthew Henson
Accompanied Peary
on His First Expedition
to the North Pole
1866–1955

204

**George Mallory
and Andrew Irvine**
Possibly the First Two
Persons to Reach the Summit
of Mount Everest in 1924
*Mallory (1886–1924);
Irvine (1896–1924)*

176

**Dr. David
Livingstone**
Explorer and
Missionary in Africa
1813–1873

193

**Wilbur and
Orville Wright**
First to Fly
Powered Aircraft
*Wilbur (1867–1912);
Orville (1871–1948)*

208

Admiral Richard E. Byrd
Opened the Polar
Regions of the Arctic
and Antarctic to
Modern Research
1888–1957

Hercules

Hercules, one of the most popular Greek heroes, was worshiped at temples all over Greece and Rome. His adventures were celebrated in stories, sculpture, and painting. Was there ever a real Hercules? Probably not, but the myth may have its origins in the life of one extraordinary man.

In the myth, Hercules was the son of the god Zeus and the princess Alcmene, a mortal. (Greek gods were anthropomorphic, which means they looked like humans.) Hera, the goddess of life and the wife of Zeus, was furious at her husband for his unfaithfulness and swore to kill the infant Hercules. She sent two great serpents to destroy him, but the baby strangled the snakes.

So many stories are told about Hercules that it is difficult to trace his adventures in chronological terms. He traveled throughout Greece and Rome, rescuing damsels in distress and fighting immortal and supernatural beings. When he conquered a tribe that had been attacking the people of Thebes, he was rewarded with the hand of a Theban princess—Megara—in marriage. They had three children, but Hera, still determined to destroy Hercules, sent a fit of madness upon him during which he killed his wife and children. The Oracle at Delphi was a priestess who could speak on behalf of the gods. She decreed that Hercules should cleanse himself of the killing by carrying out twelve tasks—known as the Labors of Hercules. The first task was to kill a lion that could not be brought down with any weapon. Hercules stunned the beast with his club and then strangled it. Thereafter he wore the skin of the lion as a cloak and its head as a helmet. He killed a many-headed serpent, captured a stag with golden horns and a giant boar and cleaned thirty years of filth in the Augean stables by making two rivers flow through them. He also brought back the man-eating horses of King Diomedes. Then he captured the cattle of the three-headed monster Geryon, and stole the Golden Apples of the Hesperides. His most difficult labor was bringing back the three-headed dog Cerberus from Hades to the upper world.

Another of Hercules' famed adventures was the killing of the Giants—monstrous gods as tall as mountains. The oracle had told Zeus that he needed the help of a mortal to kill the Giants. Hercules was that mortal. He shot Alkyoneus off Mount Olympus as he was climbing, then dragged him outside Thrace because the oracle said the Giant could not be killed within his own land. Zeus shot a thunderbolt at Porphyrion, who was about to attack the goddess Hera, and Hercules then killed the stunned Porphyrion with his bow and arrow. A war between the Giants and the gods followed, but with the help of Hercules, Zeus was triumphant.

Hercules' famous rescue of Hesione, princess of Troy, illustrates his custom of saving damsels in distress. Hesione's father, King Laomedon of Troy, had cheated the gods Poseidon and Apollo. In revenge, Poseidon—god of the sea—sent a sea monster to devour Hesione. Hercules allowed the monster to swallow him and then killed it from the inside. But when Laomedon cheated Hercules too, the hero raised an army, conquered Troy, and killed Laomedon. He gave Hesione in marriage to Telamon—the father of Ajax—and allowed her to save one Trojan prisoner. She chose her brother, Priam, who became a famous Greek hero.

Hercules' adventures and travels are almost endless. He was so strong and courageous, his deeds were so awesome, and he endured so many hardships, including long imprisonment, that when he died—poisoned by a jealous wife—he was taken to live with the gods on Mount Olympus. There he married Hebe, the goddess of youth.

Odysseus

The name Odysseus has come to stand for someone who wanders the Earth, always wanting to return home. The adventures and hardships of this mythic hero were told in Homer's epic poem, *The Odyssey*.

Odysseus was the king of Ithaca and one of many suitors courting Helen of Troy, the world's most beautiful woman. All her suitors took an oath to support and defend one another, no matter whom Helen chose. When Helen married Menelaus, king of Sparta, Odysseus married Penelope. Later, Paris, son of the king of Troy, stole Helen from Menelaus and took her from Sparta to Troy. All the suitors, bound by their oath, joined together to attack Troy and get Helen back. Odysseus did not want to leave Penelope and Ithaca. He went to war reluctantly.

One thousand Greek ships sailed against Troy, and for ten years they laid siege but were unable to enter the protected city. Then Odysseus came up with a plan. The Greeks constructed a giant wooden horse with a hollow belly and offered it to the Trojans as a symbol of peace. Then the Greek ships sailed away. Troy celebrated, not knowing that a small army of Greeks were hidden in the belly of the horse. When night fell and the Trojans were no longer alert because of their celebration, the Greeks in the belly of the horse slipped out, killed the sentries, and opened the city to the Greeks who had sailed silently back to Troy. All Troy was plundered and its people were killed or taken prisoner. (The saying, "Never trust a Greek bearing gifts," probably comes from this story. And references to Trojan horses still warn us to beware of accepting gifts that may bring problems with them.)

Odysseus set sail for Ithaca but he wandered for twenty years before he reached his home. Many of his adventures are now classic elements of Greek mythology, such as his visit to the land of the lotus-eaters. The lotus was a sweet fruit that caused people to forget their homeland. When his crew ate the fruit, Odysseus had to force them back to their ships.

Next he visited Sicily, the land of the Cyclops. There, the Cyclops Polyphemus, a one-eyed giant and son of the sea god Poseidon, threatened to eat Odysseus. When Odysseus blinded the Cyclops, Poseidon angrily vowed to make the hero's return to Ithaca even more difficult.

Odysseus stopped at the Aeolian Islands, ruled by Aeolus, keeper of the winds and a favorite of the gods. Aeolus entertained Odysseus at lavish feasts and then sent him on his way with a leather bag in which the winds were trapped so that he would have smooth sailing home. Within sight of Ithaca, Odysseus fell asleep. His crew, thinking the bag contained gold, opened it and let loose the winds, which blew them back to the Aeolian Islands. Angrily, Aeolus refused to give Odysseus a fair wind to take him back to Ithaca.

Odysseus sailed on to the island home of the witch Circe. She turned his companions into pigs but when Odysseus threatened her with his sword, she restored them to their natural states. Then she helped Odysseus descend to the underworld to seek advice for returning home.

In the underworld, Odysseus met many famous mythological figures—Achilles; Agamemnon; Ajax; Jocasta, the mother and wife of Oedipus; and Hercules, who was only a ghost because the real Hercules was living on Mount Olympus with the gods.

Odysseus resumed his journey and sailed past the Sirens, whose sweet voices lured sailors to their death. Odysseus wanted to hear the singing of the Sirens but did not want to give in to it. The sorceress Circe had warned Odysseus to fill his companions' ears with wax and have himself bound to the mast. The Sirens' song was so sweet that he begged to be released, but his companions refused.

When his men stole some sacred cattle, Odysseus's ship was struck by a thunderbolt. Odysseus clung to the mast until he came to an island. There, the sea nymph Calypso fell in love with him and kept him prisoner for seven years. She offered him immortality, but he wanted to go home to Penelope and Ithaca so Zeus ordered Calypso to release Odysseus. He made a raft on which he drifted to the shore of the Phaeacians who took him back to Ithaca. After he left, Calypso died of grief.

When he returned to Ithaca, Odysseus found that he was believed dead and Penelope had many suitors. They had spent Odysseus's wealth and eaten his animals. Because she was waiting faithfully for Odysseus, Penelope had made the suitors conditional promises. For example, she said she would marry when she finished weaving a shroud for Laertes, her father-in-law. Every day, she wove the shroud, and every night she unraveled it.

Odysseus returned in disguise, killed all the suitors, and revealed his identity to Penelope. After that, the story is not clear. He left Ithaca and probably took another wife. He may have died of old age or been killed by a son who did not recognize him.

Jason

Jason was not the hero of many adventures, as Hercules and Odysseus were, but he is known for one great deed. He led a band of men known as the Argonauts in the capture of the Golden Fleece. His story is about a quest—a journey in which the hero undergoes many hardships in search of some holy or magical object, like the story of King Arthur and the Holy Grail.

When King Athamas of Thessaly was about to sacrifice his children at the command of the gods, the golden fleece of a flying ram appeared. The boy, Phrixus, and his sister, Helle, escaped on the back of the ram, but Helle fell off into the ocean and drowned at Hellespont. Phrixus rode the ram to a land called Colchis where he was welcomed by Aeites, son of the god Helius and brother of the witch Circe. Phrixus gave him the Golden Fleece, which was then placed high in a tree and guarded by a dragon that never slept.

Jason was the son of Aeson, a Greek king of Iolcus. His uncle, Pelias, seized the throne from Aeson. When Jason claimed the right to rule, Pelias challenged him to regain the Golden Fleece from Colchis, a distant country. The goddesses Hera and Athena helped Jason build a great ship and gather an army of 50 heroes to go with him. The ship was the Argo, and the heroes were known as Argonauts. One of the Argonauts was Hercules, but he left the ship before they reached Colchis because he had to finish his Labors.

The Argonauts had many trials during their journey to Colchis. First they stopped at an island inhabited by women who had offended Aphrodite. The goddess had caused them all to have an unpleasant odor, so that their husbands left them. In return, the women murdered their husbands. The Argonauts stayed several days with these women. After sailing past the Hellespont, a narrow strait, the expedition was attacked by a sea monster, which Jason killed. During a dark night, they sailed in the wrong direction, entered a city's harbor and were mistaken for raiders. In the Black Sea, they killed Harpies, winged monsters who were stealing food from the blind seer Phineus. Then they came to the clashing rocks—rocks that floated on the surface and occasionally clashed together with a force that crushed anything between them. To get past these rocks, the Argonauts released a dove. When it flew between the rocks, they clashed together. When the rocks opened again, the Argonauts sailed through. Then they were attacked by Stymphalian birds—the man-eating birds Hercules had earlier defeated. The Argonauts drove them away by shouting and beating their swords on their shields. The seer Idmon was the first Argonaut to die, killed by a wild boar; then Tiphys, the pilot, drowned, and another pilot had to be chosen.

In Colchis, the king agreed to give Jason the Golden Fleece if he passed several tests. He had to harness fire-breathing bulls to a plough, plant dragons' teeth in the earth, and then defeat the armed men who immediately sprang from the ground. The king's daughter, Medea, a sorceress, fell hopelessly in love with Jason. With Medea's help, Jason completed these tasks. The

Argonauts took the Golden Fleece and returned to Iolcus, pursued by the angry Colchians.

The return trip was also filled with adventure. The Argonauts encountered Circe, were saved from the Sirens by Orpheus, and from a giant who threw boulders at them by Medea. With the gods' help, they figured out how to get the Argo from a lake into the sea.

At last they returned to Iolcus. Medea killed King Pelias who had seized the throne from Jason's father. Jason was exiled but returned to kill Acastus, the son of Pelias who had taken the throne. In his heroic pursuits, Jason was always aided by Medea or Hera. He lived in Corinth with Medea and they had two sons. But when Jason fell in love with another woman, Medea killed the woman, the king who was the woman's father, and her own two sons. Because Medea, as an immortal being, could not be punished, Jason was banished from Corinth.

Gilgamesh

King of Erech and Adventurer

Gilgamesh was the fifth king of Erech after the Great Flood. When he was a young man, his city was held under a long siege by its enemies, but he recaptured it and proved to be a strict ruler. To distract his attention, citizens brought Enkidu, the wise man, who became Gilgamesh's close friend. The two went to the mountains to bring cedar back to the temples of the city, having asked the god Shamash to help them subdue Humbaba, the giant guardian of the forest. Humbaba, defeated, asked for mercy, but Enkidu refused. The gods decided that either Enkidu or Gilgamesh must die; Enkidu was chosen, and Gilgamesh was left alone.

Gilgamesh then went in search of the wisdom of his fathers. His adventures included slaying a lion, whose skin he frequently wore (see Hercules). He also met Scorpion Man on Mount Mashu, and crossed the ocean to meet Utanapishtim, the wise man who told him the story of the Flood. He then returned home, presumably to rule his people in peace and wisdom.

It is fairly certain that Gilgamesh was an actual king of Erech in Sumer. The daring deeds of many men were attributed to Gilgamesh.

Alexander the Great

Explorer and Conqueror
356 B.C.—323 B.C.

Alexander the Great of Macedonia was probably the first recorded explorer and conqueror in the history of Western civilization. Considered one of the world's greatest military geniuses, he conquered much of what was then known as the civilized world—Greece, Egypt, Asia Minor, and Central Asia (now the countries of Algeria, Libya, Egypt, Afghanistan, Saudi Arabia, Iran, and India). He developed new forms of warfare, including the use of elephants in battle. He founded over seventy new cities and spread the Greek, or Hellenistic, culture throughout the lands he conquered. Greek culture is considered one of the three threads of what we now call Western civilization along with Roman culture and Christianity.

Born in Pella, the ancient capital of Macedonia, in 356 B.C., Alexander was the son of Philip II, king of Macedonia, a brilliant ruler and warrior, and

Olympias, a princess of Epirus in western Greece. Philip II not only fought with his enemies—he fought with his wife and finally divorced her in 337. History suggests that Alexander's mother was overprotective and that mother and son had a close and complicated relationship. However, young Alexander grew up fearless and strong. At the age of twelve, he tamed a great horse that no one else could ride. He named the stallion Bucephalus and rode it as far as India on his campaigns. When the horse died in India, Alexander built a city on the spot and named it Bucephala.

Alexander was well educated as a young man. When he was thirteen years old, he studied under Aristotle who introduced him to the world of arts and sciences. But by the age of sixteen he was fighting battles to protect Macedonia and subdue its enemies.

In the summer of 336 B.C., his father was assassinated and Alexander became king at the age of twenty. Because he was the one who gained the most from his father's death, he was suspected of the killing, but he firmly established his authority and executed everyone he thought to be involved in his father's murder, including his father's most recent wife and her infant daughter. He then began a campaign to invade the Persian Empire. A priestess proclaimed him invincible, and he apparently came to believe the prophecy.

To chronicle Alexander's many marches and campaigns on the way to Persia would take several volumes. It is hard to locate the countries he conquered on modern maps, but the extent of his conquest and the ferocity of his campaigns cannot be exaggerated. Once he allegedly marched over 400 miles (640 kilometers) in eleven days and nights. At the end of his march, when the Thebans refused to surrender, he burned down their city. About 6,000 people were killed, and 8,000 others were sold into slavery. Alexander was ruthless.

In the Battle of Issus in what is now northeastern Syria, although his troops were badly outnumbered, he held back a reserve force. This was a first in military history. He conquered the leader, King Darius III, who fled. It is said that when Alexander, known for living modestly, entered Darius's luxurious tent with its golden bath and silk carpets, he said, "So this is what it means to be a king."

In 332 B.C., Alexander conquered Egypt, where he was welcomed as a liberator. He founded the city of Alexandria, then marched on toward Mesopotamia and Persia. By 330 B.C. he was called the "Lord of Asia," and his Asian coins bore the term *King*. By 327 B.C. he was in India, and by 325, after great hardships in the desert, he had conquered Persia.

Alexander never returned to Macedonia, though he sent an army there to keep the peace, and forged a union between the Persians and the Macedonians. In 323 B.C., at the age of thirty-three, he became mysteriously ill and died in Babylon after ten days of fever. He apparently became ill after a huge feast and to dull his pain, he drank more "unmixed wine." Some suggest he was poisoned. He was given divine honors in Egypt and through-out the Greek world.

Alexander is remembered for his military genius and the political skill with which he managed the countries he conquered. Why was he driven to conquer? Probably for glory.

Pytheas

Greek Explorer
Fourth Century B.C.

The discoveries and contributions to knowledge made by Pytheas, a Greek explorer, were outstanding, considering that he lived in the fourth century B.C. Trained as a mathematician and astronomer, he discovered that gravity controls the tides of the ocean, and he pioneered the use of the sun and stars in navigation. He made a remarkable voyage that took him around Britain and he was probably the first man to sail into the waters of the Arctic Ocean. Pytheas was the first explorer to be included in the history of mankind, which was just beginning to be kept in written form by the Greeks.

Pytheas was Greek, living in Massalia, a Greek colony near what is now the French city of Marseilles. At that time, the Carthaginians controlled the trade routes of the Mediterranean Sea. They discouraged the Greeks from sailing into the Atlantic Ocean by describing it as a place of dangerous whirlpools and dreadful monsters. As a scientist, Pytheas knew that these tales were not true, but he also knew that the Carthaginians would not allow him to sail through the Strait of Gibraltar. However, when Carthage was at war with Rome, it left the Strait, and Pytheas seized the chance to escape.

Pytheas sailed north along the shore of Spain, then northeast along the coast of France into the English Channel. He landed in what is now the county of Kent in England and marched across England to Cornwall, a difficult

*A map showing the land of Thule,
first described by Pytheas*

journey through swamps and forests. There he encountered the Celtic people, who had an ancient agricultural civilization. In Cornwall, Pytheas studied the underground mines from which the natives took iron, tin, and gold for their own use and for European traders.

Pytheas returned to his ship and steered north along the western coasts of England and Scotland, apparently landing at Unst, or Muekle Flugga, the most northerly of the Shetland Islands. Here, the natives told him of a place called Thule (now Iceland), some 600 miles (965 km) northwest. Pytheas sailed north until he was stopped by the ice pack, but he was almost certainly the first European to cross the Arctic Circle and see that land in summer when daylight lasts for twenty-four hours. Instead of returning directly home, Pytheas explored the Baltic Sea and the shores of Ireland.

Finally back in Massalia, Pytheas described his journey in a book he called *On the Ocean*. Books were then copied by hand, and the few copies made of *On the Ocean* disappeared before the time of Christ. For 100 years, scientists praised Pytheas, but by the time of Christ, scientists said that the world north of Scotland was a solid block of ice. As for Pytheas, they said he imagined his fantastic journey. Pytheas' reputation was in tatters until the Vikings settled Iceland and Greenland and proved that his journey was not only possible but probable.

In 1893, Sir Clements Markham of London's Royal Geographic Society reconstructed Pytheas's long voyage and announced that his findings were correct. So his reputation was repaired—some 2,000 years after his journey.

Hoei-shin

Chinese Explorer of North and South American Continents
Fifth Century A.D.

The first explorer to discover the North and/or South American continents was probably a Buddhist monk from China named Hoei-shin. Writing in the emperor's record of events for the year A.D. 499, Hoei-shin reported that he had recently returned from a country he called Fusang, because it had so many fusang trees. These trees, he reported, provided paper, cloth, and wood for the residents. The people had no iron but had much gold, copper, and silver. He described houses "built of wooden beams" and a people who had a written language, no "fortified or walled places," no weapons, and no war. There was little crime and only two prisons in the entire country. Hoei-shin also described domestic animals that have been identified as oxen and reindeer.

Hoei-shin even suggested he might not have been the first Asian to visit this new land. The people, he reported, had not lived according to the laws of Buddha until 458. At that time, monks from the kingdom of Kipin in China had arrived and taught the people the religion of Buddha. Thus, he wrote, the monks "changed their manners."

In the mid-eighteenth century, a French scholar who studied Chinese history discovered Hoei-shin's manuscript and shared it with others. Some scoffed that the Chinese could not possibly have made it across the wide Pacific Ocean in their small boats, probably no more than open rowboats.

But traveling from China to North America, the boats could have followed the coast of Siberia, crossed the narrow Bering Sea, and then followed the Aleutian Islands to the tip of Alaska. In that long journey, they would have been out of sight of land only briefly.

Others suggested that the Chinese were not interested in exploration because they believed their own country held all that is worthwhile. They even called it the Celestial Empire. People beyond its borders were considered inferior and could teach the Chinese nothing. But Buddhist monks, like Hoei-shin, traveled to spread their religion, going to Japan, for instance, where they persuaded the people to embrace Buddhism.

Scholars have made various suggestions about the location of Fusang. It could be almost anywhere from Alaska to Mexico or even Peru. Because Hoei-shin recorded such an advanced civilization and because he referred to the king of this empire as "Ichi," it seems likely that he had reached the Inca Empire, later destroyed by the Spanish. However, if his description of reindeer was accurate, he was probably much farther north.

After this manuscript came to light, some scholars looked for evidence that would help them locate Fusang. Some went to China and studied Chinese texts. They found many stories inspired by Hoei-shin's report, some that sounded truthful and others that were obviously fantasy. Other researchers went to North and Central America to look for relics that would prove the presence of the Chinese explorers. A group inspecting the coast of California found small statues of Buddha buried in the ground. Hoei-shin had reported that he and his fellow monks carried similar statues to Fusang.

In the late 1800s, two American experts on China wrote books about Hoei-shin's expedition—*Fusang* by Charles G. Leland (1875) and *An Inglorious Columbus* by Edward F. Vining (1885). Although details of his voyage are sketchy at best, Hoei-shin is believed to have reached North America about 1,000 years before Columbus and 500 years before the Vikings.

Brendan the Navigator

Irish Explorer
Sixth Century A.D.

Saint Brendan was born in what is now County Kerry, Ireland, in about A.D. 486. Raised by a priest of the Roman Catholic Church, he became a monk, then a priest, and finally an abbot. One of Ireland's most important saints, he founded several abbeys and monasteries and helped to bring order to the disorganized Celtic Church. However, history remembers him more for his fantastic descriptions of sea voyages than for his saintly deeds.

Brendan claimed to have been visited by an Irish monk who told him of a land across the ocean. Intrigued, Brendan decided to search for this Land of Promise. He built a boat of ox hides tanned with oak bark and stretched over an ash framework. In case repairs were needed, he stowed extra ox hides and grease aboard. He also took seventeen monks and supplies for forty days.

They had been at sea fifteen days when high winds blew them onto an island, where a dog led them to a settlement. A meal was prepared and waiting for them, but they saw no human beings. Brendan and his party stayed on the island three days and always found food waiting for them, though they saw no one.

Next they landed at the Island of Sheep, where they found not only flocks of sheep but streams full of trout. After resting, they sailed on to a completely barren white island—nothing at all grew on it. When they camped and began to build a fire, the island began to move, gently at first and then with more force. The monks rushed back to their boat and pushed off, watching in horror as the "island" swam away, their fire still burning. They had camped on Jaseonius, a large white whale.

The Paradise of Birds was their next stop, an island that was home to every kind of bird. One small bird told Brendan that his voyage would last seven years instead of the forty days for which he had prepared.

After three months, the exhausted monks reached an island already inhabited by an order of monks who lived under a rule of silence. However, the abbot broke the silence long enough to tell Brendan that they had lived there eighty years without trouble or illness. When Brendan's party moved on, one of their group stayed with the silent order and thus was absent when they reached what Brendan described as the "edge of Hell." They could see fiery furnaces from which ran rivers of gold fire, and giant demons threw fire at them. During this attack, one of the monks fell overboard and was never seen again.

Brendan's party left the edge of Hell and sailed on, only to be chased by a bad whale and then saved by a friendly whale. Sometimes the sea was so clear and calm that they could look straight down and see fish lying in a circle, head to tail. When Brendan sang to the fish, they circled the boat to listen. But at other times, storms and high winds tossed the tiny boat around. Once they saw a huge crystal pillar in the sea. It was covered with a wide-meshed net and so tall that they could not see the top of it. When they sailed closer, they could see that the pillar extended down into the water as far as it did upward. It took them three days to sail around it.

Finally they reached the Land of Promise where a young man acted as their guide. They explored the outer edges of the land, but a wide river prevented them from seeing the entire land. On their return voyage to Ireland, they again met Jaseonius the whale, and this time he towed the boat from the Paradise of Birds to the Island of Sheep.

Although the story of Brendan's journey sounds like a fantasy, it was so popular in the Middle Ages that many versions existed. In 1959, an American scholar named Carl Selmer published a single comprehensive version. For many years, critics dismisssed Brendan's voyage as impossible and suggested that Brendan did not reach North America but may have reached the Canary Islands—if he had even sailed at all. They argued that such a small boat could not possibly travel from Ireland to North America. But in the 1960s, another American named Tim Severin did extensive research into Brendan's trip, studying maps and charts and prevailing winds and currents. Severin decided to prove that the trip was possible by duplicating it.

He built a boat like the one Brendan had built and called it the *Brendan*. With friends, he set sail from Galway, Ireland. They soon found that Brendan had been correct about the seaworthiness of ox hide tanned with oak bark. They also learned that many of the landmarks Brendan described made sense to voyagers in a small boat. The coast of Iceland probably did seem like the edge of Hell because of its many active volcanoes, and an iceberg does look like a crystal column. After wintering in a port, the party reached the coast of Newfoundland, proving that Brendan's fantastic journey was not an impossibility. Severin described this voyage in his book, *The Brendan Voyage*.

Leif Eriksson and the Vikings

Scandinavian Explorers of the North American Continent
Tenth Century A.D.

For years no one was sure whether northern Europeans had reached the American continent before Christopher Columbus arrived there. Colorful tales were told of huge redheaded, bearded men who sailed in massive wooden ships from the Scandinavian countries—Norway, perhaps Sweden, and probably Iceland—to the northern coasts of what is now Canada. They were called *Vikings,* an Icelandic word meaning "exploring." And they were believed to have discovered a beautiful and rich land they called Vinland, meaning "wine land." But the Vikings left no history, no permanent settlements, and no way to be sure where they had actually been.

In 1963, archaeologists found evidence of Viking homes on Newfoundland, the easternmost province of Canada, thereby proving that the Norsemen—"men of the north"—did sail to the Americas, probably before

A.D. 1000. Their "Vinland" was probably the land we know today as Newfoundland.

The Vikings traveled in warships and slightly larger vessels known as *knorr*—boats about 76 feet (23 meters) long and 17 feet (5 m) across at their widest point. They were driven by both wind and oarsmen and could travel easily in fairly shallow water. The ships were of beautifully carved oak, and the sails were brightly decorated with multicolored stripes. A *knorr* had additional half-decks fore and aft and room for a settler to store provisions and tether cattle and horses.

The first Norseman we know much about is Erik the Red. He and his father moved from Norway to Iceland because the father was suspected of murder. Iceland was then largely settled, and Erik married Thjodhild there. But the Vikings were fighting men, and Erik once again was involved in disputes that cost human lives. His slaves sent a landslide on another man's house. The man's relatives then killed the slaves and, in anger, Erik killed the man's relatives. Erik was banished from the community and after several more battles, he was escorted from Iceland. He left saying he would sail west to look for the land that others had reported sighting.

Erik sailed to Greenland and remained there a long time, moving over the land. After three summers and winters, he returned to Iceland but was attacked and defeated by his old enemies. He decided to colonize the new land he'd found and call it Greenland. He sailed for Greenland with twenty-five ships of colonists, but only fourteen arrived at their destination. However, Erik had strong men with him and they established a colony on Greenland.

Erik and Thjodhild had two sons, Thorvald and Leif. Thorvald stayed with his parents in Greenland, but Leif sailed for Norway. Strong winds blew his ship off course and into the Hebrides Islands off northwest Scotland. Leif stayed there for a summer and met a young woman named Thorbunna. Leif believed she had supernatural powers, but he resisted when she wanted to leave the Hebrides with him. She told him she would bear him a son who would journey to Greenland. Years later, the boy, Thorgils, did go to Greenland, and Leif accepted him as his son.

Leif went to Norway, where he was commissioned to spread Christianity in Greenland, and then he returned to his home. Earlier voyagers, however, had told the king of Norway of great and beautiful lands to the west that they had seen but had not landed on, and there was great interest in exploration. Leif bought a ship, gathered a crew, and asked Erik the Red to go with him. Erik declined, because he was too old.

Leif and his crew came to a rocky land with many glaciers. Leif named it *Helluland* (Flat Rock Land). They sailed on and discovered a low, wooded land with wide stretches of beach and soft slopes from the water to the mainland. Leif called this *Markland* (Forestland) and took to the waters again, this time landing on an island to the north. This land had sweet dew on the grass, and they anchored in a shallow lake. Deciding to spend the winter there, they built larger houses. This, Leif decided, was a land of plenty—more salmon than they could eat, food for cattle, no frost in winter, and grass that did not wither. Leif's men found vines and grapes there, so they called the country *Vinland*.

Families from Greenland established a colony on Vinland, and an infant boy named Snorri seems to have been the first white child born in what is now America. But after two winters, hostile natives—either Native Americans or Inuit, whom the Vikings called *Skraelings* (savages)—forced the settlers to leave.

On the voyage back to Greenland, Leif rescued a party of stranded sailors. In return, they gave him their ship's rich cargo. He gained both wealth and honor, and thereafter was known as "Leif the Lucky."

The Norse explorations of the New World were complex and the truth is uncertain, although in recent years more and more documents have been found. But the stories of Erik the Red and Leif the Lucky give us a flavor of the life and times of these early, bold explorers.

Marco Polo

First European to Explore and Introduce Chinese Culture to Europe
1254–1324

Marco Polo was the first to bring extensive knowledge of China and its culture to Europe. Although European merchants had traveled to China over what was called the "Silk Road" for the Chinese silk that was brought back, Marco Polo was the first to thoroughly describe his travels—the culture and people he had known. He called his book *The Description of the World*.

Polo was born in Venice in 1254, the son of Nicolò Polo, a merchant who, with his brother, traveled to Constantinople, crossed the Black Sea, and went to Russia to trade. On the way home, the brothers, Maffeo and Nicolò, found their way blocked by a war. In 1265, taking a roundabout way, they found themselves in the court of Kublai Khan of China. The Khan requested that they return to Europe and then bring 100 missionaries to China to convert his people to Christianity. He also asked for Holy Oil from the lamp kept burning over Christ's sepulchre in Jerusalem.

The brothers returned to Italy, where Marco's mother had died. The boy was now a young man of seventeen. In 1271, when Maffeo and Nicolò returned to China, they took Marco with them. They were unable to bring 100 missionaries—the two assigned to accompany them deserted out of fear for their lives—but they did have letters from the pope, and they went to Jerusalem to obtain the Holy Oil. Their rugged and difficult journey back to the court of Kublai Khan took 3 years and passed through many exotic lands.

Marco Polo soon won the Khan's favor and became his loyal servant. For seventeen years, Marco served as regional ambassador, traveling throughout China and reporting on the lands he saw. Maffeo and Nicolò apparently stayed behind at the Khan's winter and summer palaces in Peking and Shangtu.

After spending almost twenty years in the service of Kublai Khan, the three Polos decided to return to Venice. The Khan was aging and no successor had been named; the Polos feared being caught in rebellions that might follow the leader's death. Also, they were homesick for their own country and their families. The Khan, however, refused countless requests to grant them passage home, because he didn't want to lose his trusted advisors.

Then a Persian princess died. She had willed that a Mongol princess marry her husband and take her place. The Khan decided to let the Polos accompany the chosen princess to Persia and then return to their homeland. So he finally gave them permission to leave. They set sail from the coast of China in 1292, reaching Venice in 1295.

Marco Polo, his father and his uncle had been gone for twenty-three years. Marco was now forty-one years old. Their friends and family did not recognize them because their clothes were tattered after their long journey and because they spoke with a strange accent.

Marco Polo never returned to China. In 1298 he was the captain on a Venetian galley that was captured in a battle between Venice and Genoa.

Taken prisoner by the Genoese, he was jailed, and while in prison, he dictated an account of his travels to a fellow prisoner named Rustichello. The book was copied by hand for distribution—mass printing did not exist at that time—so there are many versions, translations and reconstructions of his book.

Polo's book is not a direct account of his own travels. Instead, it contains historical observations and detailed descriptions of cultures and geography from Constantinople to Japan and from Siberia to Africa, including some places he never actually visited. There are descriptions of cities, architecture, inhabitants, races, languages, and governments. Polo describes the way people lived, what they ate and how they dressed as well as their religious customs, trading practices, plants, animals, and crafts. Because of the detail in his descriptions, he has been called "the father of modern anthropology."

Europeans, however, found crocodiles and coconuts too strange to believe, and they refused to accept the idea that any civilization was older and more advanced than their own. "It's a Marco Polo," became a way of saying something was exaggerated, a product of imagination rather than observation. On his deathbed in 1324, at the age of seventy, Marco Polo said, "I have not written down the half of those things which I saw." He knew that no one would believe him.

Marco Polo's book has been widely used since the thirteenth century. Christopher Columbus studied it before making his first voyage to the New World. And in the nineteenth century, explorers verified his travels. After almost six centuries, Marco Polo's book was finally accepted as fact, not fiction. Indeed, his book made further explorations into China possible— and it remains a valuable source for studying early Chinese history.

John Sebastian Cabot and Sebastian Cabot

Father and Son Credited with Re-discovering Newfoundland Off the East Coast of Canada
John (1450–c.1499); Sebastian (died 1557)

As an explorer, John Sebastian Cabot (left) is often overlooked, partly because little is known about his life, and partly because his son, Sebastian, took credit for the elder Cabot's discoveries. Today John Cabot is credited with discovering—or rediscovering—Newfoundland, off the east coast of Canada. Cabot, like Columbus, believed he had landed in Asia. However, he had landed in North America, and his discovery is significant because England used it as the basis for its claim to all of North America.

John Cabot was born Giovanni Caboto in Genoa, Italy, around 1450. As a young child, he moved to Venice where, in 1476, he married and was active in business. Cabot, interested in the spice trade, learned navigation and mapmaking as well as geography. Unfortunately, the geography of the day was mistaken. When he heard that Columbus had reached the Indies by sailing west, Cabot determined to find a western route himself. Since Spain had funded Columbus, it would be unlikely to support Cabot's mission. He believed that the shortest way to the Indies would be to sail west and north—the distance around the Earth being less the farther north one was from the equator.

Since he knew that ships had been leaving the port of Bristol in England to explore the Atlantic Ocean, Cabot appealed to the king of England, Henry VII, for support. Henry, who had refused to help Columbus, now eagerly sanctioned an expedition. Cabot had not asked the king for money, because the merchants of Bristol, eager to secure Indian spices, were outfitting his trip. To avoid trouble with Spain and Portugal, Henry granted Cabot the right to explore all lands at the same latitude as England—lands directly west of England. But he was told not to venture south.

Cabot outfitted his ship at Bristol, then the second-largest seaport in England and a well-known trade center. He sailed on May 2, 1497, in one small vessel, the *Matthew,* with eighteen men. The *Matthew* was under 70 feet (21 m) long. Some English traders may have gone along, as well as John's son, Sebastian, but Sebastian was not in a position of command as he later claimed.

Cabot landed on the eastern coast of North America in late June. Some scholars claim he landed on the coast of Labrador or "New Found Land"; others believe it was Nova Scotia or Cape Breton Island, both part of Canada today. In any case, he and his men were the first Europeans to touch the mainland since the Vikings. Cabot went ashore and claimed the land in the name of the English king. Later Cabot's crew described the land as "forested" and reported seeing no occupants but noting signs of human habitation, such as farm animals, fishing traps, and the kind of needle used to make fishing nets. Fearing the natives might be hostile, the men returned to their ship and spent the next month cruising along the coast. Finding abundant fishing there, they never went ashore again.

Convinced he had found the northeastern corner of Asia, Cabot returned to England. Henry VII was so pleased he gave Cabot a small reward of ten pounds and the rank of admiral. He was now a hero, called "The Great Admiral" and praised for having reached Cathay (China).

In 1498, Henry VII approved a second expedition—Cabot now intended to reach *Cipango* (Japan) and the Spice Islands. The king provided one ship, and four others were provided by merchants from London and Bristol. The fleet almost immediately ran into a gale, and one ship had to go back to Ireland. After that, the fate of the voyage is uncertain. Scholars believe the ships became separated at Newfoundland, and some may have been lost at sea. The remaining ships sailed south along the coast.

Cabot himself never returned from this voyage, although for a long while it was thought that he was among the survivors who returned in 1499. A manuscript discovered in the late 1930s testifies that he died at sea. However, his son, Sebastian, was among those who returned to England.

After Cabot's second voyage, the English lost interest in exploration. The country had a newfound friendship with Spain that it didn't wish to risk. Also, people were beginning to realize that Cabot had not reached Asia but had landed on an unknown land mass—the New World—which had neither spices nor silks. They did not yet realize the wealth of the fishing grounds off Newfoundland. Each year English ships brought back catches of fish that more than repaid the merchants of Bristol for their investment in Cabot's voyages.

No general history of Cabot's voyages was written at the time, and no log-books survived. In a contemporary source best known as *Hakluyt's Voyages,*

Sebastian Cabot wrote that his father died at the time of Columbus's voyages and that Henry VII sent him, the son, to discover the Northwest Passage to Asia. Finding no such passage, he sailed back down the coast to "that part of this firm land which is now called Florida," where his supplies ran out, forcing him to return to England. Soon his father was forgotten and Sebastian was seen as a hero, which he was not. He was, however, a good navigator, mapmaker, explorer, and businessman. He was also the medieval version of a wheeler-dealer and a con man.

When King Henry VIII ascended the throne of England, he showed no interest in exploration. As a result, Sebastian Cabot transferred his loyalty to Spain and spent years with the Spanish navy, hoping for a voyage west. In 1517, Charles I appointed him Pilot Major of Spain, but this was not enough for the greedy Sebastian. In 1520 he tried to negotiate a trip with England, even though it was in direct conflict with the interests of Spain, his current employer. In 1526, his secret intact, Spain sent him to South America, where he reached the coast of Brazil and explored Argentina's *Rio de la Plata*. The expedition was marked by lost ships, mutinous sailors, hostile natives, and lack of food. Back in Spain four years later, he was tried for abusing his men and disobeying orders and found guilty, but he was pardoned by Charles I. For several years he worked on a new map of the world; published in 1544, it quickly became a guide for other mapmakers.

In 1547, Sebastian was offered a post in England and returned to Bristol to take charge of England's maritime affairs. Although he was too old to go to sea, ships under his command reached Russia and established new trade agreements. However, until the day of his death in 1557, Sebastian dreamed of reaching Cathay. And, like his father, he died without having fulfilled his dream.

For 300 years, scholars gave Sebastian full credit for the voyages his father had made. Then, in the 1800s, documents that revealed the truth were uncovered. John Cabot finally received the recognition he deserved.

Christopher Columbus

Explored North American Continent for Spain
1451–1506

Christopher Columbus is one of history's most famous figures, probably one of the first explorers American children learn about. In our mind's eye, we see Columbus and his men bravely sailing across the unknown seas in those three famous ships—the *Nina,* the *Pinta,* and the *Santa María*—to discover the North American continent for Queen Isabella of Spain. We have cities named Columbus and Columbia in Ohio and South Carolina, for example, we have the District of Columbia, and we sing "Hail, Columbia." On the 400th anniversary of Columbus's arrival in America, the United States held an international world's fair called the Columbian Exposition.

But there is another side to the Christopher Columbus story. He did not actually "discover" America—millions of people were already living in North and South America when he arrived. And he was not the first

European to set foot on these shores—the Vikings beat him and, probably, so did Portuguese sailors who landed in Puerto Rico around 1484. Also, Columbus turned out to be a ruthless leader and a poor governor. For this he spent time in chains and was returned to Spain in disgrace after his third voyage. At sea, Columbus was a strong leader; on land, he was not. At his death, he was an object of scorn and ridicule rather than seen as a great explorer enjoying the world's praise and a great reputation.

Cristoforo Colombo was born in the seaport of Genoa, Italy, in 1451. His father, Domenico Columbo, was a weaver who traded with the sailing ships that docked in the small city. From his earliest years, Columbus, as we call him, was fascinated by the ocean. His first experience at sea probably came when he went on a trade mission for his father. By his early twenties, he was a seaman, sailing from Genoa to England.

On one voyage, the ship he was on was attacked and Christopher was thrown into the sea. Clinging to an oar, he swam and rested for 6 miles (10 km), until he washed up on the shore of Portugal. Because Portugal was then the seafaring center of Europe, many people from Genoa lived there. His brother, Bartholomew, was living in Lisbon, working as a mapmaker. The Genoans welcomed young Columbus and cared for him until he recovered. Living in Portugal for several years, Columbus learned both Portuguese and Spanish, as well as navigation and map-reading. He became skilled at trading, and he learned to write so that he could keep records on long voyages. In 1477 he sailed to England; in 1484, he was made commander of a ship.

Columbus dreamed of reaching Asia—the trading source for silks and valuable spices such as pepper, as well as gold and jewelry—by sailing west rather than east. At that time, Europeans went to Asia by a long and difficult caravan route across deserts controlled by Arabs and Turks. Because Columbus knew the Earth was round, he was sure he could reach Asia by going west. But he was badly misinformed about distance. A famous geographer told

The ships of Columbus: the Nina, *the* Pinta, *and the* Santa María

him that the islands we know as Japan were only 3,000 miles (4828 km) from the European coast.

Columbus went to King John II of Portugal, but the king's navigators rejected the idea, believing the Earth was much larger than Columbus said. They also believed that, without charts or maps, Columbus would disappear on the open ocean—taking with him the money Portugal had invested to outfit his ships. Columbus then went to France, England, and, finally, to King Ferdinand and Queen Isabella of Spain. Jealous of the Portuguese, Spanish royalty was interested but had no money. Columbus waited six years, selling maps and charts to support himself. Finally in 1492, the queen decided to borrow against her jewels to support the exploration. Columbus went to the port of Palos to prepare his ships. He was then more than forty years old.

The *Nina* and *Pinta* were caravels, a new kind of ship that was small and light enough to explore shallow waters, but strong enough to cross the ocean. Each carried twenty-five sailors. The *Santa María* was bigger and heavier and had a crew of forty. They sailed on August 3, 1492. The people of Palos were certain they would never see these men again.

Today, we would find those ships cramped and uncomfortable. Sailors slept wherever they could and there was no water for shaving or bathing. Cooking was done on an open fire and the food was always the same—hard biscuits, tough salty beef, bland beans, and any fish they could catch. They had no fruits or vegetables, and their drinking water soon developed a green scum on the top.

To steer his course across the uncharted waters, Columbus had to know the time as well as the ship's direction and speed. He used an hourglass to measure time, a compass to determine direction, and he guessed at speed by watching articles float by. Columbus kept two logbooks. The first, which he showed the men, made the distance seem much shorter. The second, kept secret, showed the correct distances. Columbus knew they had sailed too far from Spain to turn back, but he also knew they would soon run out of food and water. In October, he told the crew they had come 2,000 miles (3,218 km); in reality, they had sailed more like 4,400 miles (7,080 km). When the sailors became nervous and threatened mutiny, Columbus calmed them with promises of great wealth.

On October 12, 1492, they spotted land and went ashore on one of the small islands of the Bahamas. They were at least 400 miles (643 km) southeast of Florida. Columbus named the island San Salvador and claimed it for the king and queen of Spain. (The actual site of the landing is still in dispute among historians. Among others, Grand Turk Island of the Turks & Caicos island chain claims the honor, which would make sense since it is one of the easternmost islands in the Caribbean.) When the native people on this island, probably the Arawak, came to greet the explorer, Columbus named them Indians—because he was sure he had reached the Indies. When Columbus set sail again, he took a few Arawak with him as guides. The party next landed at what is now Cuba. Convinced he had landed on Asian shores, Columbus expected to find gold immediately. When he did not find it on Cuba, he sailed on to Hispaniola, where the natives did have gold and shared it generously.

On Christmas Day, the *Santa María* ran aground. Supplies were salvaged, and the ship was abandoned, but Columbus had to leave twenty men behind when he sailed for Spain. The party landed on Spanish shores on March 15, 1493, and Columbus was honored with gifts, titles, and great praise. Suddenly, he was the most famous man in Europe. Ferdinand and Isabella were so pleased they sent out another expedition.

This time, Columbus had seventeen ships and more than 1,200 men. When they reached Hispaniola they learned that the Spaniards they had left behind had been killed, apparently for stealing from the natives and forcing them into hard labor. Elsewhere on the island, Columbus founded the colony of Isabella and settled it with more than 1,000 men. He sailed again to Cuba, always looking for signs of Asian culture—pagodas, arched bridges, and other architectural signs. Convinced that he had reached the mainland of the Indies, he sailed for Hispaniola but became so sick at sea that he had to be carried ashore. There he learned that many men in the colony had died, and others were sick. The remaining Spaniards had angered the natives by demanding food. Columbus immediately made matters worse. He executed a few natives, sent thousands to Spain to be sold as slaves, and demanded a monthly tribute of gold from those left behind. In 1496, he returned to Spain—where tales of his cruelty had preceded him—with a crew of fifty half-starved Spaniards and a handful of naked Indians, but no gold, spices, or silks.

In spite of the disaster of his colonization, Columbus persuaded Isabella and Ferdinand that he had found Asia, and at last they granted him yet a third voyage. They thought that since he brought back a little gold, there must be more where it came from. Columbus set sail in 1498. The colony at Hispaniola had fallen apart under the cruel direction of Columbus's brothers, Bartholomew and Diego, who had executed seven rebellious Spaniards. When word reached Spain of the state of things at the colony of Isabella, the king and queen sent a trusted advisor to investigate. The royal commissioner seized Columbus's gold and property, charged him with crimes, and had him bound in chains to return to Spain for trial. The captain of the ship offered to remove Columbus's chains, but he refused. He gambled that Isabella and Ferdinand would feel guilty seeing him in chains and would therefore allow a fourth voyage. He was right. By 1502, his property and titles—except governor—had been restored to him, and he was ready to go to sea once more. He called this the "High Voyage."

This time, Columbus reached the coast of Central America. He was sure there would be a passage through to the sea which he had been told was on the other side of the mountains, but he never found it. At the site of the present Panama Canal, he sailed within 40 miles (64 km) of the Pacific Ocean and the gateway to Asia. But the voyage was difficult, with heavy rains and hostile Indians. After a year, the ships were leaking, riddled with the holes of wood-eating worms and insects. Columbus sailed for Jamaica and ordered the ships unloaded. He sent some sailors to Santo Domingo to return to Spain on other ships and requested that the governor send a ship for him and his remaining men. The governor, delighted at Columbus's difficulties, delayed, and it was another year before Columbus could set sail for Spain. He returned in November 1504, but this time there was no hero's welcome. Queen Isabella lay dying, and Ferdinand had no interest in exploration or riches.

Columbus never went to sea again. He had a small amount of gold—not nearly enough in his eyes—and he was convinced he had reached the Indies, but people doubted him. He died on May 20, 1506, alone and angry. But, whatever his accomplishments and his weaknesses, Columbus will always be the man who "discovered" America. Authentic replicas of Columbus's ships on his first voyage—the *Nina*, the *Pinta*, and the *Santa María*—are are now permanently docked in the harbor at Corpus Christi, Texas.

Amerigo Vespucci

Businessman, Navigator, and Diplomat for Spain and Portugal
1454–1512

Amerigo Vespucci was an Italian-born business-man, navigator, and diplomat who sailed for both Spain and Portugal. He discovered Brazil, explored the Atlantic shores of South America, and was one of the first Europeans to set foot on the mainland of the New World. Today he is remembered because he lent his name to two continents— North and South America.

Vespucci was born into a large family in Florence, Italy, in 1454. In his twenties, he accompanied one of his uncles to Paris as a secretary. When he returned to Florence, he handled business transactions for Lorenzo di Pier Francesco Medici, a member of the ruling family of Florence. In 1489, his work for Medici took him to Seville, a port city in Spain. Vespucci liked Seville and found it more peaceful than Italy, where people were constantly involved in political quarrels. When he returned to Florence, he found that the Medici were being accused of wrongdoing, and even various members of the Vespucci family quarreled over their guilt or innocence. Vespucci quit his job and returned to Seville.

He went into partnership with an elderly banker and developed a reputation for honesty and reliability. One of his clients was Christopher Columbus, who was then preparing for his first voyage across the ocean. Columbus returned from his first voyage in triumph, but after the second voyage King Ferdinand and Queen Isabella had questions about the way he had handled the colony he established at Hispaniola, and about his failure to bring back gold.

In 1496, Ferdinand invited Vespucci to join an expedition across the Atlantic. Wanting to be fair to Columbus and disregard gossip spread by his enemies, Ferdinand sent Vespucci, known to be an admirer of Columbus but also known to be honest, to observe and check on the famous explorer. Vespucci's partner had died and his banking firm had been closed, so he was free to go on the voyage.

Little is known about Vespucci's first voyage, other than that he left Spain in May 1497 and returned in October 1498. The expedition sailed around Cuba, demonstrating that it is an island and not part of the mainland, as Columbus said. They also explored the waters off Costa Rica, Nicaragua, Honduras, and Mexico. Because Vespucci described the customs and homes of people in these regions, it is generally assumed that he was among the first Europeans to set foot on the mainland of South America. Vespucci, who had no previous experience at sea, returned from this voyage ready to command his own ship. His report to the king supported Columbus, and the king sent Columbus on two additional voyages.

Vespucci sailed again in the spring of 1499, captain of one of the three or four ships in an expedition. Over the next two years, he mapped much of the shore of South America, studied pearl fisheries near Venezuela, developed new and important navigational techniques—and discovered Brazil.

By treaty, Brazil was in an area that belonged to Portugal, not Spain. Vespucci's discovery of it brought him to the attention of King Manuel I of Portugal, who urged Vespucci to move to Portugal. The explorer's next two voyages were made under the Portuguese flag. On the first of these, he made probably his most important discovery. Until then, Columbus had reported, and it was generally believed, that the strange land across the Atlantic was part of the Asian continent. Vespucci discovered that he was looking at a separate landmass, and he called it the "New World."

Vespucci reported this in a letter to his former employer, Lorenzo di Pier Francesco de Medici. The letter, called *Mundus Novus (New World)* was published and translated throughout Europe. It came to the attention of a German mapmaker, Martin Waldseemüller, who made a new map from this information. On it he printed "Americi," his spelling of Vespucci's first name. The name caught on, and people began calling the New World "America."

Vespucci made one more trip for Manuel and then returned to Seville, where King Ferdinand named him pilot major, the equivalent of today's secretary of the navy. As part of his responsibilities, Vespucci created a college where young men could study navigation. Today, we would call it a naval academy. Vespucci wanted the academy to be his legacy to the world, but the legacy of the name America is infinitely greater. Amerigo Vespucci died in Seville in March 1512.

Juan Ponce de León

First Western Explorer to Reach Florida
c. 1460–c. 1520

Ponce de León was the first Westerner to reach Florida. According to legend, he was searching for the magic fountain of eternal youth when he discovered Florida. More likely, he was looking for more gold, slaves, and land.

This Spanish explorer was born somewhere about 1460 in Santervas de Campos, the son of a military hero. He came from a noble family and probably served as a page in the royal court as a boy. In 1493, still a young man, he set sail for the New World, accompanying Columbus on his second voyage.

Shortly after 1500, he took part in the conquest of eastern Hispaniola (now the Dominican Republic), and in 1508 he discovered gold on the island of San Juan (now Puerto Rico) and conquered the island. When he was made governor of the island in 1509, he made a fortune in gold, slaves, and land.

From the Arawak Indians of the West Indies, Ponce de León kept hearing tales of a wonderfully rich island called Bimini, said to be north of Cuba. Supposedly, a fountain in Bimini had the power to cure illness; anyone who drank from that fountain would stay healthy and young forever. Spanish folklore said that the "Water of Life" in "The Garden of Eden" was in the Far East, and at that time, Europeans thought of North America as the Far East.

In 1512, Ponce de León was commissioned to conquer and colonize Bimini. With three vessels, he sailed northeast through the Bahamas, and sighted the Florida peninsula, which he believed to be another island. He probably landed near present-day St. Augustine. He is thought to have landed in late March, during the Easter season, so he named the flat "island" with beautiful flowers *La Florida* for the Easter feast—*Pascua Florida*. His explorations of this "island" took him south to the Florida Keys, which he called *Los Matrires* because of their rocks. He then traveled up the western or Gulf Coast of Florida, and sailed around Cuba. For unknown reasons, at this point he sailed southwest, landing on Mexico's Yucatan Peninsula. Putting ashore long enough to fix the sails on his ships, he named this land Bimini, but his dreams of a magic fountain were again disappointed. However, with that short visit, Ponce de León got the credit for discovering the Empire of Mexico. He returned to Puerto Rico in September 1513, only to find the country in revolt. After restoring order there, he returned to Spain.

The king of Spain commissioned Ponce de León to conquer the Carib, the people who lived in the Lesser Antilles (Cuba, Puerto Rico, Hispaniola, and Jamaica), and to conquer and colonize the "isle" of Florida. His 1515 campaign against the Carib was unsuccessful, but he spent the next several years discovering more lands in the Caribbean. Some say he discovered the Leeward Islands, which extend from Puerto Rico to Martinique and include Turks & Caicos. But he did not colonize these islands as the king had commissioned him.

Then he sailed for Florida with two ships, 200 men (including priests who were to convert the natives to Catholicism), fifty horses, and assorted farm implements. He probably landed near Sanibel Island in south Florida. Immediately upon landing, his party was fiercely attacked by Indians. Ponce de León was severely wounded by an arrow and, although taken to Cuba for treatment, died of his wounds.

However, the legend continues to this day. Some say the reason so many people retire to Florida is because they are still looking for Ponce de León's "fountain of youth."

Vasco da Gama

Navigator and Explorer; Opened Trade Route to China
c. 1469–1524

Portuguese navigator and explorer Vasco da Gama opened a trade route to China for his country and all of Europe. He also established Portuguese colonies in India, the land of spices and treasures.

Little is known about da Gama's early life. He was probably born about 1469 in the south of Portugal, where his father was a mayor. By the 1480s, da Gama was in the service of King John II, called "John the Perfect." Young da Gama was praised by John the Perfect for knowing everything there was to know about the sea and knowing how to get things done efficiently.

In 1488, another Portuguese navigator, Bartolomeu Dias, was the first to sail around the Cape of Good Hope, Africa, but his expedition failed to reach India because of a mutiny among his crew. John the Perfect knew, however, that if one ship could reach the Indian Ocean, others could follow to trade for spices and other precious goods at Calicut and other ports on the

Indian coast. They could also carry the Christian message to heathen parts of the world. Before he could get a second expedition together, however, the king died and Manuel I took the throne of Portugal. He immediately announced that he would send the fleet to seek passage to India and made da Gama chief navigator. It would be a dangerous mission because they would sail into ports dominated by the Moors (followers of the faith of Islam, considered enemies of Catholics).

Da Gama and 176 men sailed on July 8, 1497, on three sailing vessels—the *Saint Raphael,* the *Saint Gabriel* and the *Berrioh*—and a ship carrying supplies and food. The storeship carried stone pillars to be set up wherever the voyagers landed, to show that Christians had been there and to establish Portuguese claims in Africa. The expedition stopped twice—once on the African mainland and once at the Cape Verde Islands. It then sailed west toward South America in order to avoid the turbulent waters of the African coast. Dropping back south, it anchored in the Bay of St. Helena, 200 miles (321 km) north of the Cape of Good Hope.

On shore, the fleet encountered natives called Hottentots who were frightened of the newcomers until the sailors gave them trinkets and supplies. They found the same people days later when they had rounded the Cape of Good Hope and landed on the southern shores of what is now South Africa. The Hottentots were always friendly.

Da Gama followed the African shore north to Mozambique, where Arab merchants had established trading centers. The ruler of Mozambique was angered when he learned the voyagers were Christians, and da Gama sailed on before his fleet was attacked. At Mombasa, they again met hostility and were forced to bombard the waterfront with rock-throwing cannons before they could sail away.

At Malindi, then the largest east African port, the sultan had apparently heard of the power of da Gama's guns. He gave the expedition food and supplies and got them the most knowledgeable pilot in that part of the world. The elderly Ibn Majid guided the Portuguese across the Arabian Sea to the city of Calicut. Da Gama had accomplished his mission in 314 days.

Zamorin, the Hindu king of Calicut, welcomed the trade opportunities bought by the Portuguese fleet, but he could not afford to offend the Arab merchants who had traded in his city for years. The Arabs persuaded Zamorin that da Gama was a spy and that his letter from King Manuel was a forgery. Zamorin imprisoned da Gama and three of his men but released them in a few days when da Gama's brother, Paul, made threats against the city. By the time Vasco da Gama left Calicut, he had won Zamorin over, and he took cinnamon, cloves, ginger, nutmeg, pepper, and precious stones back to Portugal. Zamorin also sent several ambassadors to the court at Lisbon.

The trip back was difficult, however. An epidemic of scurvy so weakened the crew that one ship had to be sunk—there were not enough men left to sail it. Fierce storms separated the remaining two ships, and Paul da Gama died of tuberculosis.

When da Gama returned to Lisbon in September 1499, he was hailed as a hero. On his next journey to India, he did not go as an explorer but rather as a conquistador leading warships. With naval bombardment, he took over Calicut and other trading centers along India's eastern coast. On his third journey to the East in 1524 he was the Spanish viceroy of his country's possessions in India. Vasco da Gama died in the city of Cochin on the coast of India in 1524.

Vasco Núñez de Balboa

Explorer Credited with Claiming the Pacific Ocean for Spain
1475–1519

Although he is credited with claiming the Pacific Ocean for Spain, Vasco Núñez de Balboa was always scheming and always in trouble. In the long run, his schemes—and his enemies—caught up with him.

In 1500, he had sailed from Spain to Hispaniola, expecting to find treasure-houses of gold. Unfortunately, someone got the gold before him, and Balboa was forced to turn to farming, which he was not very good at. He was deeply in debt and, to avoid paying, stowed away on a ship leaving for Columbia in South America where a man named Ojeda had established a colony. Balboa, then in his thirties, hid himself in a barrel on board the *Barbara* with his favorite dog, a bloodhound. When the ship was a few days out at sea, Balboa and the dog came out of hiding. The captain, Martin Enciso, threatened to put him off on a desert island but the expedition needed every able-bodied man so he pardoned Balboa.

Arriving in Columbia, they found Ojeda's colonists starving to death. The survivors were taken on board, and, at Balboa's suggestion, the *Barbara* sailed for Darien, a colony on the Isthmus of Panama where they thought gold might be found.

Balboa began plotting to replace Enciso, and his scheme worked so well that the captain was forced onto a ship returning to Spain. Balboa then became governor and captain-general of Darien. Although the Indians were hostile, Balboa made friends with them. They helped him build a town, and they worked in his fields and gold mines. Balboa learned much from the natives about the lands around the isthmus. The Indians were scornful of the Spaniards' greed for gold, and one day, in disgust, a chief said, "If gold is what you want, I can tell you where to find a land where people eat and drink from golden dishes." The Indian said this land of plenty lay to the south and could be reached by crossing "the narrow place" and going out into the great sea or, as he called it, the "Blue Ocean."

Balboa thought he had finally found the passage through the American continent that so many others had looked for. He gathered together an expedition of almost 200 Spaniards along with hundreds of Indian porters and guides. Among the Spaniards was a man named Francisco Pizarro, who eventually became Balboa's trusted lieutenant.

Crossing the "narrow place" was not as easy as the Indians had suggested. The Indians forgot to mention that two mountain ranges had to be crossed but they did say the crossing was a six-day march. However, it took Balboa's expedition three long weeks. During that time they suffered greatly from the heat—they were wearing armor! Also, hostile Indians shot poisoned arrows at them, although they had brought vicious dogs with them for protection. They were also plagued with yellow fever, and, worst of all, ants. When a man became sick with the fever, they bound his hands and feet and left him, but they later found that the ants had picked the bodies clean in a few hours. After that, when a man became sick and crazed with fever, they judged it kinder to kill him.

Only sixty-nine Spaniards survived to reach the ocean in September 1513. Still wearing his armor, Balboa waded in and claimed the water for Spain, calling it the *Mar del Sur* (South Sea). (It was later renamed the Pacific Ocean.) Balboa then returned to Darien and did not try to reach the lands to the south.

Meanwhile, back in Spain, Enciso told the king of Balboa's schemes against him, and of the kingdom of gold the Indians had described. The Spanish court was swept with gold fever, and a fleet of 1,500 adventurers departed for Darien. The expedition was headed by Pedrarias Davila, but included Enciso. Unknown to Balboa, the king had appointed Davila as governor of Darien in Balboa's place.

When they arrived in Darien, Davila, a cruel man, overworked the Indians until they died by the thousands. Balboa sent a letter to the king of Spain, begging him to stop the brutal treatment of the natives, but Davila found out about the letter and never forgave Balboa.

Balboa, meanwhile, was still plotting to reach the land of gold to the south. He was building two ships for his expedition, when word came that Davila wanted to see him at the nearby town of Acla. Davila claimed to need advice on business matters, and Balboa left at once for Acla. Outside the town, soldiers led by Francisco Pizarro arrested him. When Balboa asked what was going on, Pizarro simply smiled and led him to jail.

In 1519, Balboa was given a one-day "trial" with a foregone conclusion and sentenced to death. He was beheaded in the public square of Acla that very day. One of Davila's men poisoned the bloodhound who had shared Balboa's adventures with him. In Balboa's honor, Panama named its currency, the balboa, after him.

Francisco Pizarro

Conqueror of the Inca People
c. 1475–1541

Francisco Pizarro was the cruel conquistador who helped in the plot against Balboa. He has gone down in history as the conqueror of the Inca people of Peru, the land of gold that Balboa himself had tried to reach.

Growing up in Spain, Pizarro was a poor man—a keeper of pigs. In his mid-twenties, to escape the poverty of his life, he became a soldier. In 1502, he went to the New World, and in 1513, he joined Balboa's expedition from Panama in search of the Inca gold. With Balboa, he was one of the first Europeans to see the Pacific Ocean.

Pizarro had enough land in Panama to lead a comfortable life, but his dreams of great wealth never left him. In 1524 and 1526 he led expeditions south. On his second trip, he was welcomed by a rich Inca group on the coast of Peru and brought back enough gold to prove that the legends of Inca treasures were true. When the governor of Panama refused to authorize another expedition, Pizarro went to Spain to seek the king's permission. In 1529, the king authorized the expedition and named Pizarro governor of any lands he discovered. Pizarro had a partner, Diego de Almagro, who became jealous of the great honors given Pizarro by the king. Like Balboa before him, Pizarro had made a traitorous ally.

In 1530, Pizarro, then nearly sixty, sailed southward with an army of almost 200 men, including 27 horsemen, and 2 small cannons. In Peru, he climbed the Andes mountains to the land of the Incas. The Inca Empire covered some 2,000 miles (3,200 km) and was crisscrossed by great highways and bridges. No carriages ever traveled on these huge structures because the Inca, for all their gold and wealth, did not know about the wheel.

When Pizarro threatened the Inca and won several small battles, their emperor, Atahualpa, surrendered the city of Cajamarca. Atahualpa thought he had trapped the Spaniards in this city, but, as it turned out, Atahualpa was the one who was trapped. Pizarro invited Atahualpa and his leaders into the city square for a talk. Atahualpa was accompanied by 4,000 men—courtiers, high priests, army leaders, and guards—surely enough to ensure his safety. As the Inca entered the square, Pizarro and his men hid behind buildings and walls. The Inca met only a priest and an interpreter. The priest told them to surrender to Spain and give up the worship of false gods. Atahualpa then angrily threw the priest's Bible to the ground, and the Spaniards attacked. With cannons and soldiers on horseback, they cut the Inca down. The leaders of the Inca were all killed, and Atahualpa was taken prisoner. Pizarro promised the young emperor freedom if the Inca would fill a large room with gold and two smaller rooms with silver. The Inca brought 13,265 pounds (6,000 kilograms) of gold and 26,000 pounds (12,000 kg) of silver to Pizarro, who then killed Atahualpa anyway. Pizarro's conquest of Peru was easy—the Spaniards marched through the country destroying temples and stealing gold ornaments and vessels. The people of Peru had no leaders and no army so they offered no opposition. In 1533, the Spaniards took over the capital city of Cuzco.

The Inca army did not rise against this conqueror, it simply fell apart. Pizarro and his partner Almagro tried to build an empire, attempting to conquer neighboring Chile. When that attack failed, Pizarro and Almagro blamed each other. In 1538, Pizarro's men killed Almagro, and in 1541, Almagro's men killed Pizarro. Pizarro died as he had lived—by treachery and the sword. He is one of the conquistadors who gave Spanish explorers such a bad name in the New World.

Ferdinand Magellan

Explorer and Navigator; Led First Sailing Expedition Around the World
1480–1521

Ferdinand Magellan is counted among the world's great navigators and explorers because he led the first expedition to sail around the world, thereby proving the world was round. Unfortunately he died on that journey, but his sailors completed it without him. He was the first to sail though the waterway now known as the Strait of Magellan, between South America and Tierra del Fuego.

Magellan was Portuguese, born into a noble family in about 1480. As a boy, he served as a page in the royal court. But when Magellan heard of Christopher Columbus's voyage, he wanted to devote his life to the sea. The Portuguese king at that time, Manuel, was not interested in sea exploration and refused the young man's requests to leave the court and sail. But in 1499 when Vasco da Gama returned to Portugal from India, his ship loaded with riches, King Manuel took more interest. In 1504 he sent twenty-two fighting ships to the Far East to explore, trade, and conquer. They were ordered to chase Arab traders from the African coast and establish Portuguese bases on the Indian coast. Magellan was on one of those ships. The ships won two battles with the Arabs and then took over the Malay Peninsula. Magellan fought bravely in these battles and was wounded twice. He was promoted to captain.

By 1512 Magellan was back in Lisbon, Portugal. When he heard that Portugal was fighting in Morocco, North Africa, across the Strait of Gibraltar, he joined the battle. This time he was wounded so severely that he limped for the rest of his life. After the battle Magellan was charged with making a huge profit on the sale of captured livestock. Too proud to defend himself, he was discharged by the king and denied a pension. The king had believed the rumors. Magellan swore revenge on King Manuel and Portugal, the country he felt had betrayed him.

Magellan knew the theories that Columbus had sailed not to Asia but to a new land, and that two large bodies of water lay to the west between Europe and Asia. He believed that Asia lay beyond that second body of water. Much earlier Pope Alexander VI had drawn a line down the middle of a map of the Atlantic Ocean and decreed that non-Christian lands to the east belonged to Portugal, while those to the west belonged to Spain. Magellan thought he could avoid crossing the pope's line by sailing westward to Asia. He would find this route for Spain and thereby have revenge on Portugal. The major problem would be to find a route through the Americas—so named for Amerigo Vespucci, the Italian navigator who proclaimed the existence of the New World.

Magellan convinced the Spaniards that such a passage could be found. They were impressed by his war record and by the fact that Portugal, which had also denied Columbus, had turned him down. King Charles I of Spain agreed to send Magellan in search of the second ocean. He gave him five ships, about 270 men, and a promise that Magellan could share in any profits from the voyage. Magellan and his five ships—the *Victoria*, the *Santiago*, the *San Antonio*, the *Trinidad*, and the *Concepción*—sailed on September 20, 1519.

The ships reached Brazil in December 1519, but the journey was far from peaceful. The Portuguese had bribed some of Magellan's officers to start a mutiny. Magellan quickly put down this rebellion. In Brazil, the ships were harbored in the bay where Rio de Janeiro stands today, and the crew enjoyed tropical fruit and friendly people. After several months, Magellan ordered his ships southward. Threatened by a storm, they sought shelter in a bay that proved to be the mouth of Argentina's Rio de Plata, but not the passage Magellan sought. Still farther south, they reached Antarctic regions, with icy winds and heavy fog. They spent five months in the Bay of St. Julian waiting for better weather.

A second mutiny erupted on April 1, when rebellious sailors seized the *San Antonio* and two other ships. Once again, Magellan reacted quickly, attacking the *San Antonio*. All three ships were soon under his control again. In August, they saw seals and penguins, which the sailors called "wingless ducks." Magellan named this land *Patagonia*, meaning "big foot," because of the size of the people who lived there. When Magellan tried to capture two natives—7 feet (2 m) tall, they said—a fight broke out and one of Magellan's men was killed. Magellan and his ships quickly moved on. At the lower end of the Santa Cruz River, the *Santiago*, a small ship, was stranded on a sandbank and destroyed by a storm, although the crew jumped to safety. The other ships were in great danger but survived.

By the time the storm subsided, it had carried the ships into an east-west channel. It was October 1520, and Magellan had finally found the strait he sought. The ships spent five weeks in what we now call the Strait of Magellan, enduring cold, storm, and rough waters. Under cover of night, the

Magellan and his men explore the strait connecting the South Atlantic and the South Pacific oceans.

crew of the *San Antonio* deserted and sailed for Spain, but Magellan would not turn back. On November 28, 1520, the three remaining ships passed into a great body of calm water. Magellan knew he had reached the second ocean, and he named it *Pacific* meaning "peaceful."

The ships were low on provisions, but the sailors were sure they would find islands where they could stock up on fresh supplies. They sailed endlessly through open water with no sight of land, month after month. The men ate wormy biscuits, rats, and even sawdust and leather. Some died of scurvy, a disease caused by the lack of vitamin C, which is usually found in fresh fruits and vegetables.

On March 7, 1521, Magellan and his men came to the island we call Guam. The natives were not friendly, and after killing several Indians,

Magellan's crew stocked up on supplies—vegetables, bananas, coconuts, fish, and pigs—and hastily left. On March 16 they reached the islands later named the Philippines in honor of King Philip II of Spain. Magellan claimed the islands for Spain and began converting the natives to Christianity. He was so pleased with the Indians who became Christians that he offered to fight their enemies on the island of Mactan. Magellan's men were outnumbered but thought their guns and armor would win the day. Unfortunately, they were wrong. The islanders drove the sailors back to their ships, and Magellan, covering their retreat, was killed.

The remaining crew members set sail again. Apparently they knew the Indonesian islands and how to get home from there. They spent several months on these islands, loading their ships with spices, but when they reached the coast of Africa, they dared not land because the area was controlled by the Portuguese. In May, they rounded the Cape of Good Hope at the southern tip of Africa, but by now only one ship remained. They had burned the *Concepción* because they did not have enough men to sail it and, the *Trinidad*, overloaded with spices, sank. Only the *Victoria* remained, and it was leaking badly.

On September 8, 1522, the *Victoria*, commanded by former mutineer Sebastian del Cano, returned to Spain. Of the 270 men and five ships that had left more than three years earlier, only one ship and 18 men returned. But the *Victoria* had done something no ship had ever done before—it had sailed around the world. That voyage opened the entire world to navigation. And though Magellan didn't live to enjoy the triumph, his name was forever written in history.

Hernán Cortés

Explorer who Conquered Mexico for Spain;
Introduced the Horse to the North American Continent
1485–1547

Hernán Cortés was the explorer who conquered Mexico with gunpowder and steel in the name of Spain. Perhaps more importantly, he introduced the horse to the North American continent.

The governor of Cuba had chosen Cortés to find out the truth about the rumors of great riches and vast empires in South America. But, before he could sail, his enemies convinced the governor that he was a traitor, and an order went out for his arrest. Cortés moved from place to place to avoid capture, and finally, in February 1519, set sail from Havana with 11 ships and 600 men. His mission was to gain glory and riches for Spain—and for himself. The expedition landed in Yucatán on April 22, 1519, fully prepared for battle. The Tlaxcalan people's only weapons were arrows, spears, and swords of sharpened volcanic glass while the Spaniards had crossbows, guns, and horses. The Tlaxcalan, who had never seen a horse, thought a man on horseback was one monstrous creature and were thoroughly terrified.

A young Tlaxcalan woman who could speak the languages of inland Mexico became Cortés's interpreter. She told Cortés of a great empire in the inland mountains, ruled by the warlike Aztecs. Cortés built a town—Veracruz—and began learning all he could about the Aztecs. He burned all his ships so that his men could not rebel and desert.

Montezuma received Cortés warmly, believing him to be an ancient Aztec god.

Old legends of the Aztecs made Cortés's conquest easier. The Aztec believed that long ago a god named Quetzalcoatl had come from across the water to their land with several other gods. These gods all had white faces and wore beards. They were gentle and kind rulers but the people turned against them and drove them away. Quetzalcoatl said that someday he would return and punish the country for its wickedness. The people believed that Cortés was Quetzalcoatl, and that he had returned for vengeance. Even Montezuma, the Aztec emperor, believed this legend. In his fear and bewilderment, he sent gifts of gold and silver to Cortés. This was a serious mistake—the gifts only proved to Cortés that he was within reach of the great riches he wanted.

Cortés led an army of 415 men toward Tenochtitlán, the Aztec capital. Along the way he enlisted the support of the Indian people by promising to free them from Montezuma. The expedition spent weeks climbing the mountains above the capital city. When they looked down on it, they saw an amazing sight—a city set in the middle of a large lake, with great temples, broad avenues, brightly dressed people, and causeways linking many islands. They knew they were looking at an advanced culture.

Montezuma, still believing that these strangers might be gods, welcomed them into his city and gave them palaces to live in. Cortés pretended friendship, but when he heard rumors that the Aztec leader was planning an attack, he seized and imprisoned Montezuma.

Meanwhile, the governor of Cuba sent armed men to Veracruz to arrest Cortés. Cortés took a small force of men, hurried back to Veracruz, and defeated the governor's troops. Then he returned to Tenochtitlán, only to find that his soldiers were fighting with the people. The Spanish soldiers, horrified by the bloody sacrifices of the Aztecs, had broken up a religious festival and turned the Aztec temple into a Christian Church. The Aztecs now surrounded the Spaniards and held them captive.

Cortés urged Montezuma to walk out and calm the crowd, but the people's anger was so great that they stoned Montezuma. He died three days later. Then, on June 30, 1520—known as the *Noche Triste* (Night of Sorrow)—the people attacked the Spaniards, killing many and forcing the others to flee. Only about 100 people, including Cortés and his Indian interpreter, escaped.

Cortés was still determined to get the gold. He built up another army of loyal Indians and again marched against Tenochtitlán. This time, he cut off all supplies to the city, and after three months the Aztec defenders, weakened by death and starvation, surrendered. On August 13, 1521, Cortés marched triumphantly into what was left of Tenochtitlán. He built Mexico City on its ruins. As governor of Mexico—or "New Spain" as it was called—he made slaves of the Aztecs and took all their wealth.

The Spaniards even fought among themselves for money and power in the New World. In 1528 and again in 1540, Cortés had to return to Spain to defend his honor after enemies brought charges against him. About to return a third time, he died in 1547 at the age of sixty-two.

Giovanni da Verrazzano

Explorer of the East Coast of America for King of France
c. 1485–1528

Giovanni da Verrazzano, an Italian who sailed for the king of France, is best known for exploring the east coast of America and being the first to sail into New York Harbor. He was born in Italy, probably around 1485, but moved to France as a young man to pursue a career at sea. Before his famous voyage, he made several trips to the Mediterranean and may have visited Newfoundland.

In the 1520s, the east coast of America was virtually unmapped. Explorers had been to Newfoundland to the north and Florida to the south but knew little about the waters and land in between. King Francis I of France chose Verrazzano to lead an expedition to explore this territory. Verrazzano sailed from France in 1524.

Verrazzano left with four ships but two were shipwrecked shortly after departure and the third was sent back to France with wealth gathered from raids on the Spanish coast. Only the flagship, *La Dauphine*, crossed the Atlantic. Verrazzano had a crew of fifty men, including his mapmaker brother, Girolamo.

The ship touched land in March near Cape Fear and sailed south a short distance, then turned north and anchored well out at sea. Verrazzano sent a small craft ashore, and their meeting with the natives was pleasant. He described them as a large, handsome people resembling Saracens, with dark skin, thick black hair, and strong bodies.

Verrazzano continued north to the Outer Banks of Carolina. He believed that the water beyond these islands—Pamlico Sound—was the Pacific Ocean and that North America at this point was no more than a narrow isthmus. The 1529 world map made by Girolamo da Verrazzano showed North America divided into two parts and connected by a narrow piece of land on the east coast. This "sea of Verrazzano" erroneously remained on maps for almost a century.

La Dauphine next stopped at a place Verrazzano called Arcadia but which may have been Kitty Hawk, North Carolina, and then sailed north into New York Harbor, anchoring in the narrows that are now named for him and are now Verrazzano Narrows Bridge. He described the Indians here as friendly and quite similar to those he had met in the south. A sudden rising of the wind forced an early return to the ship, but Verrazzano recorded his impression that the land had riches, including minerals in the hills surrounding the harbor.

He sailed north, discovering Block Island, which he called Luisa, and sailing into Narragansett Bay. Once again he described the natives—the Wampanoag—as friendly. But he disliked the Abnake of Maine, who were, in his opinion, crude and barbarous. Verrazzano returned to France on July 8, 1525, or 1526.

The Verrazzano Narrows Bridge

He made two more voyages. In 1527 he sailed for Brazil to cut logwood, a valuable wood then called brazilwood. When his men mutinied and ordered him to return to France, he relied on their ignorance of navigational skills and continued to sail to Brazil. His backers made a good profit from the wood he cut.

In 1528 he again set out to cut logwood, this time landing in Florida and then sailing south along the lesser Antilles. At one of these islands (possibly Guadeloupe), he went ashore in a small boat to greet the natives, not realizing that instead of being friendly and ready to trade they were the cannibalistic Caribs. They killed and ate him before the eyes of his horrified brother who watched from the ship—too far away to send help or use gunfire.

Cabeza de Vaca

First Explorer of the American Southwest
c. 1490—c. 1560

The Spanish began to move into the American Southwest in the 1500s. Although others had gone before him, a conquistador named Álvar Núñez Cabeza de Vaca, an aristocrat whose family name meant "head of a cow," is generally called the first explorer of the American Southwest. He was also the first to write about the land, its people and their customs, and its animals and plants. Cabeza de Vaca recorded his experiences in the Southwest before the land was invaded by many European explorers, before horses were introduced, and before the Native American people were devastated by European diseases. But he got to the Southwest by mistake.

In 1527, second in command under Pánfilo de Narváez, he left Spain with about 300 men on five ships. They were supposed to claim all the land around the Gulf of Mexico for Spain. The Spaniards had maps of North America—the New World, as they called it. But the maps were based on guesswork and they contained many mistakes. For instance, one map was fairly accurate about the way the land curved around the water in the Gulf of Mexico, but it called that body of water the Sea of the North.

The expedition landed first in the Caribbean, then in Cuba, and finally in Florida. At one point, the party was pounded by the strongest storm they had ever seen—a hurricane. A small party went ashore where they fought Indians, sickness, and hunger, and then they could not find their ships again. Finally they built five flatboats out of logs and horsehide and sailed west. Three of the boats capsized, and the men on them were lost.

The two remaining boats, at most 100 men, including Cabeza, went aground at San Luis Island, near present-day Galveston Island in Texas. They managed to swim to the mainland, where some Indians tried to help them. But the Indians were themselves starving. One by one, the explorers died of starvation, malnutrition, and disease. Some wandered off and were never seen again. Eventually there were only four left—Dorantes, Castillo, Esteban the Moor, and Cabeza.

These four Spaniards traveled through the Southwest with the Indians, living on buffalo, deer, and prickly pear. Cabeza found that he could trade seashells for food with inland Indians, and all four found that the Indians believed they had healing powers. The men made the sign of the cross over patients and may also have included native practices in their "healing." Apparently, they were successful enough to avoid being attacked. At times they were treated as slaves, though, and they frequently suffered from malnutrition and exposure.

In 1536, after wandering for more than eight years and 6,000 miles (9,655 km), the four survivors came upon a party of Spaniards. At that time, the four were accompanied by about 600 Pima Indians who had befriended them. The Spaniards, who were hunting slaves, had to be dissuaded by Cabaza from enslaving those who had been good to him. The Indians had even given the four many gifts, including five arrowheads made of a green stone, probably malachite. The Spaniards, after agreeing not to bother the Indians, directed Cabeza and the others to Mexico City, where they were welcomed as conquering heroes. The viceroy of Mexico, a man named Mendoza, questioned Cabeza at length about the legendary Seven Cities of Gold. The explorer repeated over and over that the land he had crossed had no such glorious treasures. But he did repeat rumors he'd heard of a wealthy tribe to the north. Acting on the gossip, Mendoza sent Francisco Vásquez de Coronado to explore the land, so indirectly Cabeza was responsible for the next wave of Spanish exploration of the Southwest. By August 1537, ten years after his departure, Cabeza was back in Spain. He was later appointed governor of Río de la Plata (present-day Paraguay).

Cabeza's importance is that he remembered what he saw and later published his impressions. He was the first to give the Spanish information about the New World—the horror of hurricanes, new animals such as buffalo and opossums, the food, the houses, and the customs of the Indians. He called buffalo "cattle" and said they tasted better than Spanish beef. He found evidence—horseshoe nails, buckles, and other metal items—that Spaniards had already been in the territory. He proved that the American West was land, not a vast body of water as the Spaniards had thought. And, finally, he brought his king a map. But, like the American Indian picture-writing, it was not a map like those we use today. In spite of his errors, Cabeza was an important explorer.

Jacques Cartier

Explorer who Discovered the Saint Lawrence River
While Looking for the Northwest Passage
1491–1557

Jacques Cartier, the explorer who discovered the St. Lawrence River while looking for the Northwest Passage to Asia, was born in 1491 on the rocky island of St. Malo, off the coast of France. Little is known of his childhood, but St. Malo was famous for its seamen, and no doubt Cartier learned the ways of the sea at an early age.

When John Cabot discovered Newfoundland in 1497, he reported that the fishing ground there had abundant codfish. St. Malo fishermen began to cross the Atlantic to fish the waters—the French people ate a great deal of fish. Cartier may have gone on one or more of those expeditions, though we have no definite evidence. It is known that he once sailed across the southern Atlantic to Brazil in a Portugese ship. But Cartier was accustomed to the northern Atlantic with its cold temperatures, fierce storms, and dangerous tides. He apparently never returned to South America.

In October 1533, King Francis I of France commissioned Cartier to sail to Newfoundland and search the waters for the Northwest Passage. In the thirty-six years since John Cabot had discovered Newfoundland, Spanish and Portugese crews had tried and failed to find the passage in this area but no one from France had tried.

The businessmen of St. Malo thought Cartier was mad to plan a voyage to this dangerous area where many sailors were afraid to travel. Besides, they didn't want him to use the ships and sailors they needed for their businesses. They made it impossible for Cartier to get either ships or a crew, until the king declared that no merchant could outfit a fleet until Cartier had equipped his.

Cartier and his crew of about sixty sailed in April 1534 in two small wooden vessels with wide, square sails. They had enough supplies to last until fall. Within twenty days, the strong Atlantic winds blew his ships to the coast of Newfoundland. After navigating around icebergs, he headed north into the unknown regions—the home of hideous monsters and fire-spitting demons, according to medieval legend.

The tip of Newfoundland is separated from the coast of Labrador by the Strait of Belle Isle. Cartier entered the strait, turning west. Once again the sailors had to dodge the icebergs floating out to sea in the spring thaw. Cartier explored Labrador but found little except rocks, stunted trees, and moss. This, he wrote in his logbook, was probably the land God gave to Cain.

By June 10, the ships had reached the harbor of Brest (now called Bonne Esperance), 90 miles (145 km) from the Atlantic and the last port Europeans were familiar with. The party remained there for a week, stocking up on food and freshwater while Cartier explored the region. Then they headed south, along the west coast of Newfoundland and into the Gulf of the St. Lawrence—although Cartier had no idea that he was in the mouth of one of the world's great rivers.

He had only primitive instruments—a compass, a cross-staff and an astrolabe. The astrolabe was used to determine the latitude—or north-south position—of a ship, but it was liable to errors of up to 300 miles (483 km) in rough weather. Longitude—the east-west position—could not be determined accurately because the exact time is an essential part of the equation, and Cartier had only hourglasses to keep time. Accurate chronometers would not be available for another 200 years.

Cartier named the places he passed—Brion Island for the admiral of France who had helped him secure his commission; Cape Savage in honor of a lone Indian who stood there watching; Cape Hope, because he could see highlands in the distance and miles of water between them that he thought was the Northwest Passage; and *Chaleur Bay* (Bay of Heat) because of the hot weather. He encountered Indians who were primitive but generally friendly. Cartier took two young Indians, Taignoagny and Dom Agaya, the sons of a chief, on board his ship, intending to take them back to France so that they could learn French and serve as interpreters on another voyage.

Cartier had discovered Canada, although he didn't know that either. However, he claimed the land in the name of the king of France by planting a huge cross there. He also didn't know that he crossed the point where the St. Lawrence meets the Gulf, and, by turning north toward land, he missed an opportunity to explore the southern St. Lawrence. He may have turned north because it was time to think about returning to France. He had not brought enough provisions for his crew to spend the winter in this wild country so the expedition sailed for home. Surviving a fierce Atlantic storm, they arrived in St. Malo in September.

Although the king of France was disappointed that Cartier had not brought back gold, he agreed to a second voyage to find the Northwest

Passage. Once again the merchants of St. Malo stopped Cartier until Admiral Brion of France granted him first choice of ships and crew. This time Cartier took three larger ships, a crew of 100 men, and enough provisions to last fifteen months. With him were Taignoagny and Dom Agaya, the two Indian boys he had brought back from the first voyage.

Cartier named the bay or gulf he had previously found in honor of St. Lawrence, because his ship was there on St. Lawrence's feast day. Then he sailed into what he thought was a sea, a large body of water he had seen before but did not explore because time was limited. The two Indian boys told him it was not a sea but a river, and no one had ever seen its source. Cartier realized that the river must be very long, the world must be bigger than was ever imagined, and China must be very far away. Cartier headed west, upriver.

Expedition members were overwhelmed with the beauty of the land and the abundance of wildlife. Taignoagny and Dom Agaya introduced them to the Indians of the area and educated the Frenchmen about the local tribes and their organization. When the two boys were reunited with their families, there was great joy. Their village was near what is now the city of Québec, some 800 miles (1,287 km) inland from the Atlantic. From there, Cartier sailed toward present-day Montreal, leaving a crew behind to build winter quarters at Québec.

He arrived at what is now Montreal. The Indians called it *Hochelaga*, meaning "place where the river is obstructed." Cartier called the hill *"Mont Réal"* (Mount Royal). He was welcomed by hundreds of Native Americans who apparently thought he was a god who would drive harm away. Cartier still thought the river might lead to Asia, but it could not be used for trade because of the rapids. However, winter was approaching, and it was time for him to return to the fort at Québec.

Wintering near the village of Taignoagny and Dom Agaya, Cartier was aware of deepening discontent among the Indians. Soon a great sickness

This beautifully drawn map commemorates Cartier's arrival in Canada.

struck both the Indians and the French. Almost all of Cartier's men became ill and about half of them died. Today we know the disease was scurvy, caused by a lack of fresh vegetables. Some sailors were saved by a brew made by the Indians, from evergreen branches.

Once again, Cartier had to return to France. He had discovered nothing more than a river and a wilderness, but he knew the river was important. He decided to take the Indian chief Donnacona back to France this time, but since the chief would not go willingly, he was tricked and captured. Also captured were Taignoagny, Dom Agaya, and six other Indians. Cartier promised to bring the captives back within a year—but as it turned out, none of them ever saw Canada again. Then Cartier sailed for France, discovering the Cabot Strait, a shortcut to the Atlantic Ocean. He reached St. Malo in July 1536.

War between France and Spain kept the French king from authorizing a third voyage. Cartier proposed a plan for colonizing Canada, but the king hesitated. Portugal sent spies to mislead the French king, and Francis I was soon persuaded it would be a good idea to delay the third voyage. Finally in 1540, Cartier received his commission. He planned to take five ships, but once again the local merchants prevented him from getting ships and men. The king was tired of the whole subject. At last Cartier sailed in May 1541.

Records of his third voyage are incomplete, in terms of the waters he explored and his deteriorating relations with the Indians. The Indians were angry because he had not brought back the people he had promised to return, and they began to distrust Cartier. Several tribes combined to plan a war against the French. No record indicates if there was any real fighting, but, with winter approaching, Cartier set sail again for France. Once again he had not found the riches he believed lay to the west. The king of France lost interest in Canada altogether.

When Cartier brought the Indian chief Donnacona to France, the chief gave interviews in which he described lands of great richness as well as pygmies and one-legged men who supposedly inhabited the lands Cartier never reached. Cartier had kept careful logs of his journeys and drawn accurate charts. But sixteenth-century men were more inclined to believe the fantastic tales of demons than Cartier's factual descriptions. The explorer lived out his life in St. Malo, occasionally consulted by mapmakers and geographers who understood the importance of his discoveries. His account of the voyages was published in 1545 but he was not given the recognition he deserved. He died in 1557.

Hernando de Soto

Explorer of the Southeastern United States;
Discovered the Mississippi River
c. 1500—c. 1540s

De Soto was one of the most famous Spanish gold-seekers. His major contribution to history was his exploration of the southeastern United States and the discovery of the mighty Mississippi River. Chronicles of his expedition tell about advanced native cultures, although de Soto apparently did not recognize the strengths of these Indian tribes. However, his expedition contributed important information to sixteenth-century knowledge about the New World.

Born in the province of Extremadura, Spain, around 1500, and intended, by his parents, for a career in the law, de Soto dreamed only of exploration and the riches it would bring. At the age of nineteen he sailed for the New World with Pedrarias Dávila, governor of what is now Panama. In 1523, he joined Francisco Pizarro in the conquest of Peru and his share of the stolen

Peruvian treasures made him a wealthy man. After returning to Spain and marrying Dávila's daughter, he persuaded the king of Spain to appoint him governor of Cuba and Florida. For years, captive Indians had told tales of a land that was wealthier than Mexico or Peru, and de Soto hoped to find it. In 1538, with 1,000 men—soldiers, noblemen, and shopkeepers who all wanted to be rich—he sailed from Spain to Cuba and established head-quarters in Havana. But his sights were set on Florida.

On May 30, 1539, de Soto led 600 men ashore to begin his search for gold at what is now Tampa Bay on the west coast of Florida. They marched north to Georgia, then west along the Alabama River to Mobile Bay. The Indians were hostile because of de Soto's cruel and ruthless treatment. He often tortured the chiefs in an effort to learn where gold and riches could be found. As a result, Indians frequently attacked the expedition. In its most bloody battle, fought near Mobile Bay, about seventy Spaniards were killed and many more, including de Soto, were wounded.

Another time, when the Spaniards attacked a group of fleeing Indians, one revealed himself as Juan Ortiz, a Spaniard who had been held captive for twelve years. De Soto allowed Ortiz to join his party, knowing his language skills with the natives would be useful.

After the battle at Mobile Bay, de Soto rested for a month before moving his men west. They reached the Mississippi River, near what is now Memphis, Tennessee, in May 1541. Apparently, de Soto failed to realize the significance of the river he had found—he wanted gold. After building boats, the party crossed the river and continued westward until they reached what is now northeastern Oklahoma. There they turned southeast again.

But de Soto found no riches. The natives he met valued freshwater pearls, seashells, copper, and mica—they had no gold or precious minerals. More than half of de Soto's men had died, and many others were seriously ill. Most of the horses had died, too. De Soto was even more discouraged than his men.

As he led them back to the Mississippi River, de Soto fell ill and died. His men buried him in the great river he had discovered. One account says that they covered him in rocks because of their great hatred for him.

De Soto left a trail of destruction and disease behind him that changed the lives of the American Indians of the region. The tribes that survived his march eventually became known as the Five Peaceful Tribes: the Creek, Choctaw, Chickasaw, Cherokee and Catawba.

Francisco de Orellana

First European Explorer to Travel Down the Amazon River
Died 1546

Spanish explorer Francisco de Orellana was the first European to travel down the Amazon to the point where it empties into the Atlantic. But his story is one of hardship . . . and greed.

While still a young boy, Orellana crossed the Atlantic to join Spain's armies in the New World. After fighting in Central and South America and taking part in the Spanish seizure of what are now Peru and Ecuador, he founded a settlement on the Pacific coast of Ecuador. Orellana named the town Santiago de Guajaquil. He was managing its affairs when he learned that his cousin, Gonzalo Pizarro, governor of the province, was planning an expedition to the interior of South America to look for cinnamon trees. These trees were valuable for their spice, and Indians had described a great grove of them to Pizarro.

Orellana was an ambitious man who longed to govern a province in the New World. He believed that the king of Spain would look with favor on him if he helped Pizarro find the cinnamon trees. Pizarro agreed to accept his cousin on the expedition if Orellana supplied soldiers. Orellana returned to Guajaquil to get 23 men, but when his party reached Pizarro's headquarters at Quito, he learned that Pizarro had already left with 220 armed Spaniards and 4,000 Indians.

Friends in Quito advised Orellana against trying to catch up with his cousin. They said the Indians had been known to lie and the trees might not even exist. Also, it was too dangerous for such a small party to venture into the jungle beyond the mountains. Many men had already died looking for the legendary city of gold called El Dorado. But Orellana was determined . . . and greedy.

He and his men forged eastward, fighting off Indian attacks and hoarding their small food supplies. By the time they found Pizarro, they had only their swords and shields and the clothes on their backs. Pizarro and his men were in no better shape, however. Many of the Indians had died, and the food supplies were gone. Pizarro was desperate enough to name Orellana second in command.

If they went ahead, the entire expedition might starve; but returning to Quito meant giving up their chance at great wealth. The two leaders chose riches. While Orellana took charge of the camp, Pizarro and a small group went east to find the trees. Instead of a large grove, they found only a few scattered trees, so far apart they were useless. Some time later, Orellana and the forces he led met with Pizarro near a mountain stream called Coca. Again, they faced a dilemma. Returning to Quito in their weakened state would be dangerous—they had robbed every Indian village along the way and could count on hostility from the Indians. Yet many of the men were too sick to go on.

Orellana proposed to take the two brigantines—the small sailing ships they had built for use on the Coca—and look for food downriver. He took sixty-four men with him, including Father Gaspar de Carvajal, whose journal is the only firsthand account of the trip. They sailed for eight months, with little food, meeting sometimes friendly and sometimes hostile Indians, until they reached the point where the Amazon flows into the Atlantic in what is now Brazil.

Orellana did not discover the Amazon. That had been done in 1500 by Vicente Yáñez Pinzón, who was looking for El Dorado. He called the river "Sweet Sea." The Amazon begins almost 4,000 miles (6,400 km) to the north in the Peruvian Andes and is the second-longest river in the world. At its widest, it is 7 miles (11 km) across. Without falls or rapids, it is easily navigated and is still a major trade route today.

According to Father Carvajal's account, the party was attacked at one point by a band of "very large and very tall" women. The Spaniards remembered the tales of a tribe of women called Amazons who allowed no man into their country and fought against the Greeks in the Trojan War. They named the river *Amazon* after these women, though today we suspect that the warriors who attacked Orellana were actually men with their long hair braided around their heads.

Orellana returned to Spain with the survivors of his party, including the wounded Father Carvajal. Here he learned that Pizarro, who had eventually made it back to Quito, had written to the king of Spain claiming that Orellana had deserted him and left his men to starve. Carvajal countered that Orellana's party nearly perished from hunger until they caught the strong current of the Napo, which connects the Coca and the Amazon. They were simply not strong enough to fight the current and travel upstream; their only choice was to continue on.

King Charles I of Spain was apparently not impressed with Pizarro's charge. But he still took two years to make up his mind about Orellana's request to return to the Amazon. Permission was finally granted, and Orellana returned in December 1545. However, he was unable to locate the main channel going northward. In 1546, when Indians attacked and killed seventeen of his men, Orellana died of grief and exhaustion.

Francisco Vásquez de Coronado

Conquistador; Searched for the Legendary Seven Cities of Gold in the American West
1510—1554

Coronado was a Spanish conquistador. His name is traditionally associated with the search for the legendary Seven Cities of Gold in the American West.

Born in Salamanca, Spain, about 1510, Coronado sailed to Mexico at the age of twenty-five and distinguished himself by putting down an Indian revolt near Mexico City. When Antonio de Mendoza, viceroy of Mexico, began to hear rumors of distant Indians to the north who had turquoise, emeralds and other valuable gems, he chose Coronado to lead an exploration of the north. He made Coronado the governor of New Galicia, a region in northwest Mexico from which the young conquistador could oversee and send out expeditions.

First, Coronado sent out a discovery party led by a Franciscan friar named Marcos de Niza with a guide known as the Moor Esteban. Marcos left in the spring of 1539 and soon heard Indian tales about Cíbola, a land of seven rich cities. Even hostile Indians and the execution of some members of his party, including Estéban, did not change Marcos's determination to find Cíbola. After locating what he thought was the first of the seven cities, Marcos turned back to Mexico—for he was ordered to find but not enter the cities. Although he had found no evidence of gold, he had heard many fantastic stories of great wealth. Back in Mexico, the stories grew through Marcos's re-telling.

Throughout Mexico, men volunteered to join the army that Coronado would take to Cíbola. He accepted 240 cavalrymen and 60 foot soldiers as well as 800 Indians and 1,000 pack animals. They left New Galicia in February 1540. A scout reported that Indians told him of much turquoise in Cíbola but that there was no metal.

Coronado pushed on. Leaving the main body of his army to follow more slowly, he made a difficult crossing of what is now Arizona, then entered New Mexico. The expedition had traveled more than 1,000 miles (1,600 km) when they came to what they thought was the first of the seven cities. It was a Zuni pueblo, or village, unimpressive and certainly not as wealthy as Marcos had de-scribed. The soldiers turned on Marcos in anger, and Coronado sent him back to Mexico City in disgrace. Coronado then asked the Zuni Indians to swear loy-alty to the king of Spain, a request they answered with a shower of arrows. The soldiers charged, killing about a dozen Indians, and then conquered the pueblo.

Coronado and his scouts visited more pueblos, distributing trinkets to the Indians, who were generally friendly. At one pueblo, they took a Pawnee Indian captive. He had been a captive of the Zuni, nicknamed "Turk" by the Spanish. Turk promised to lead the party to Quivera, rich in gold, silver, and fabrics. Actually, he intended to lead them to Pawnee country, his home in the northwest.

With winter approaching, Coronado wanted better quarters than tents. He ordered the Indians of a nearby pueblo to get out and to leave behind the provisions they had stored for the winter. The Indians obeyed, but their feelings about the Spaniards were changed. When a soldier attacked an Indian woman, the Indians attacked the Spanish. After the fighting, the Spanish executed all Indian men not killed in the battle.

More battles followed. The Spanish laid siege to the Moho, a pueblo near the Rio Grande. Once again, the Spaniards slaughtered their victims.

Coronado's march then took him into what is now the Panhandle of Texas, with Turk still leading the way and deliberately misguiding Coronado. Finally realizing he was off course, Coronado turned his surviving army northeast and took Turk along in chains to prevent his escape. When they came to the first city of Quivera, they found only a cluster of grass huts with yapping dogs, naked children, shy women, and men in primitive dress. For twenty-five days, Coronado wandered throughout Quivera (the land of today's Wichita Indians), finding nothing but small villages. Turk confessed to his deception and was executed.

Coronado headed back to Mexico City but wintered near Tiguex, a friendly pueblo near present-day Albuquerque, New Mexico. When spring came, he led his army to New Spain, leaving behind several friars to teach the Indians the true religion. Many soldiers deserted on the march, until fewer than 100 soldiers marched into Mexico City with their leader.

Coronado had been as far north as Kansas, had claimed all of the American Southwest for Spain, and had discovered great fertile lands. One of his exploration parties were the first Europeans to see the Grand Canyon. But none of that mattered to Spaniards, greedy for gold. Coronado lost his reputation as well as his personal fortune and died in obscurity in Mexico City on September 22, 1554, at the age of forty-four.

Sir Francis Drake

Second Man to Sail Around the World; His Ship, The Golden Hind, *Was the First English Vessel to Make that Journey 1540s–1590s*

Sir Francis Drake was the second man to sail around the world, and his ship, the *Golden Hind,* was the first English vessel to make that journey. But Drake is better remembered as the hero of the battle that stopped the Spanish Armada's attack on England and the most famous of England's privateering adventurers. (A privateer was a privately owned vessel equipped for war that was commissioned by a country to fight and harass its enemies; at that time, the enemy was Spain.)

Drake was born in the early 1540s in Devon, England. He was the son of a sailor who left the sea and supported his family of twelve sons by reading the Bible and preaching to seamen. At a time when Catholicism ruled the world, Edmund Drake raised his sons to be fierce Protestants, and the family suffered both poverty and persecution because of their religion.

Young Francis Drake loved the ocean and probably went to sea at the age of ten, which was not unusual for the sons of poor families in those days. He so pleased the captain he worked for that when the older man died, he left his ship to Francis. The young man was then sixteen. Drake went into partnership with his cousin, Sir John Hawkins, known as the founder of the English slave trade. (At that time, slave trading was not considered shameful, and Hawkins was said to be a good man.) The two stole captured slaves from Portuguese ships and literally forced Spanish colonies in the New World to buy these slaves. On his third trip, Drake commanded the *Judith* in an unsuccessful attempt to capture and collect slaves in Africa.

In September 1568, Hawkins and Drake anchored off San Juan de Ulua, an island in the harbor of Veracruz in New Spain. Hawkins sensed trouble—the Spaniards were too polite. After agreeing to allow the English to repair their ships in the harbor, the Spanish attacked them. The English were overwhelmed, and Drake sailed his ship out of the harbor under cover of darkness. Hawkins, commanding the *Minion*, had to leave men behind in Mexico to lighten the ship's load. Even then, the *Minion* barely made it back to Plymouth Harbor in England with 15 men. Drake brought back 55 men. The expedition had sailed with 400, so losses were great. The sailors left behind in Mexico were captured and turned over to the Inquisition—Spain's organization for enforcement of Catholicism, known for its extreme cruelty.

From that moment on, Francis Drake hated the Spanish, and his urge for revenge was great. In 1572, he sailed to the Isthmus of Panama (now the Panama Canal) and stole thirty-four tons of silver ingots from the Spanish, treasure which he brought back to England. But Drake's fame and fortune came from his 1577 voyage around the world. With five ships, he was supposedly on a trading expedition to Egypt's Nile River. But when he reached Africa, he admitted that the Pacific Ocean—via the Strait of Magellan—

was his true destination. The sailors in his crew were angry because they had not signed up for such a trip. Many still believed that the Strait contained sea monsters and demons. On a less superstitious level, they knew that it was the world's most treacherous waterway. Drake, however, intended to raid Spanish settlements on the western coast of South America. On this journey, he changed his ship's name from the *Pelican* to the *Golden Hind,* in honor of a supporter who had a golden deer on his coat of arms.

The ships, now reduced to three, made it through the strait without difficulty but ran into terrific storms in the Pacific Ocean. One ship went down with all hands aboard. Another turned tail for England. Finally, the *Golden Hind* was able to sail on. For 5 months Drake raided Spanish settlements, including Valparaiso, Lima, and Arica—and captured Spanish ships. Drake was not a violent and bloody pirate—neither the Spanish nor the Indians were intentionally injured. Finally the *Golden Hind,* with twenty-six tons of silver, sailed to an inlet north of present-day San Francisco, now called Drake's Bay, where the crew made repairs on the ship.

Drake had intended to sail home back through the Strait of Magellan, but he knew the Spanish would be waiting there. Instead, he decided to sail to England by way of India, where he loaded up on spices. When Drake sailed into Plymouth Harbor, Queen Elizabeth I of England was displeased with her privateer for stirring up trouble with Spain. The Spanish were asking for his head and calling him *El Draque* (the Dragon). But Drake brought the queen gifts of gold and silver and jewels. In addition, the royal share of loot from the trip paid off the queen's foreign debts and ensured that she would not need to borrow money for another year. The queen knighted Drake, and all England went wild over the national hero—a commoner who was now Sir Francis Drake and had achieved fame and fortune.

By the 1580s, Spain and England were clearly headed for war. In 1585, Queen Elizabeth commissioned Drake to take 2 navy ships, 23 privateers, and 2,300 men to attack the Spanish colonies. In Santo Domingo, Hispaniola, the Cimaroon Indians helped the English. The Cimaroon had been enslaved by the Spanish and were filled with hatred for those who had made slaves of them. Drake destroyed Santo Domingo and then Cartagena and, finally, burned and sacked St. Augustine, Florida, before returning to England.

The Spanish wanted revenge. They began to organize the Spanish Armada, a huge fleet of ships designed to invade and conquer England. Sent to stop the Armada, Drake invaded Spain first, attacking and destroying the ships in the Cadiz harbor and displaying his military brilliance. Once again, he returned home with a huge treasure. However, the Armada re-formed and assembled at Lisbon, Portugal, in the spring of 1588.

Spain's ships were much bigger and taller, but the English had more ships, and they were more efficient. England prepared for the expected invasion. Although the country had no army, it had 50,000 volunteer infantry and 10,000 cavalry, all organized to defend its shores.

The Armada appeared on July 29, 1588. Sailing up the English Channel, the Armada was attacked in one sea battle after another. While they were anchored near Calais, France, where troops were supposed to get on board, the English sent fireships—empty hulks loaded with flammable materials and gunpowder—downwind, destroying or disabling many Spanish ships and causing others to flee in panic. The huge Battle of Gravelines, named for the French town closest to the action, took place on August 8. The English fleet, commanded by Lord Charles Howard, succeeded in driving the Armada up the Scottish coast and into the North Atlantic, where it disintegrated. Ships separated, and some, badly damaged, literally fell apart. Many were shipwrecked off the coast of Ireland, where the native population killed the survivors. Only 10,000 of the original 30,000 men returned to Spain. The country lost 63 of its fleet of 130 ships and those that survived were badly damaged. The loss bankrupted Spain. The English lost fewer than six ships and only a few hundred men.

The 1588 defeat of the Armada was Drake's moment of glory. After that, his missions met only failure. Spain immediately began rebuilding the Armada and Drake's 1589 attempt to destroy the fleet in its own harbor once again met with disaster. His ships limped home, having suffered heavy losses of men and having stolen no treasure. The queen, displeased, punished Drake by removing him from action for six years. He returned to being the mayor of Plymouth and was frustrated by his disgrace.

In 1595, the queen called Drake out of retirement to lead an expedition with Sir John Hawkins to the Caribbean. Enmity immediately developed between the two men. Against Hawkin's advice, Drake insisted on attacking the Canary Islands, an attack that failed. An attack on San Juan de Puerto Rico also failed, and raids on a few coastal town yielded little value. At the Panama Isthmus, foot soldiers brought with the expedition were so defeated by the jungle that they vowed never to return. The fleet sailed for Nicaragua and Honduras, said to be rich ports, but Drake was a sick man, bedridden with dysentery.

One day he rose from his bed and insisted on being dressed in his armor so that he could die "like a soldier." A servant helped him dress and put him back to bed, where he died peacefully. Like many captains, Drake carried his own lead coffin on his ship. He was buried at sea, and his drum, used to signal so many attacks, gave the final salute.

All England mourned his death, and all Spain celebrated. Spain sent three more unsuccessful Armadas to England—defeated mostly by weather—before signing the Treaty of London in 1604. By then, both Queen Elizabeth I of England and King Philip II of Spain were dead, but the legend of Sir Francis Drake lives on. He is, for the English and the world, a symbol of courage and persistence in times of danger.

Sir Walter Raleigh

*Explorer who Attempted to Settle
the Roanoke Colonies in North Carolina
1554–1618*

Although he is now considered an Elizabethan hero, England's Sir Walter Raleigh was in trouble in England for much of his life and always at the center of bitterness between Catholics and Protestants. As an explorer, he is best remembered for attempting to settle the Roanoke Colonies in North Carolina in 1585 and 1587. (The capital of North Carolina today is named Raleigh.) He never set foot in North Carolina but he did visit both Ireland and South America, where he also had interests.

Raleigh grew up in an England ruled by the Catholic Queen Mary I, called Bloody Mary for her harsh persecution of Protestants. A friend of the Raleigh family, Agnes Prest, was put to death, and Raleigh's own father barely escaped being killed by hiding in a church tower. Understandably, the young man grew up with a hatred of the Catholic Church. When the Protestant

Queen Elizabeth I ascended the throne of England, Raleigh felt free to express his feelings.

Briefly educated at Oxford, Raleigh went to fight the French Huguenots in 1569 and may have been at the Massacre of St. Bartholomew in 1572. When his half-brother, Sir Humphrey Gilbert, received a patent from Queen Elizabeth to "discover and take possession of any remote, barbarous and heathen lands not possessed by any Christian prince or people," Raleigh joined Gilbert on what became a unsuccessful pirate raid against the Spanish. The English were turned back in defeat. Raleigh was party to a second unsuccessful expedition and then led a company of soldiers sent to suppress a rebellion in Ireland. He succeeded there through massacre and assassination.

Back in England, Raleigh became a favorite of Queen Elizabeth I, who granted him money and land, including 40,000 acres (16,000 hectares) in Ireland taken during his defeat of the rebellion. He introduced the potato as a staple crop there and tried to grow tobacco, both brought from the New World. Many people in England disliked Raleigh because he was a favorite of the queen, and they resented the way he had built his personal wealth. Although he claimed to have England's interests at heart in matters of exploration and colonization, many thought he was more concerned about his own money.

In the 1580s, Sir Humphrey Gilbert sailed to Newfoundland. He planned to dispose of the "surplus" population of England—such as prisoners and beggars—by sending them to Newfoundland, and eliminating the native population. However, Gilbert lost his life on this voyage, and Raleigh had Gilbert's patents renewed in his own name. His ship, *The Raleigh,* took possession of Virginia. He named the colony after Elizabeth, the "Virgin Queen", and she in return knighted him—Sir Walter Raleigh—and made him Lord and Governor of Virginia. He sent settlers to colonize Roanoke Island, but they failed to prosper and many returned to England aboard one of Sir Francis Drake's ships. One theory is that Raleigh sent them as a means of discovering gold and silver in the new land. Raleigh sent a second colony, with women and children in the group, to the New World, but this colony simply disappeared. Raleigh claimed to have lost 40,000 English pounds, and the fate of the colony remains a mystery.

By the late 1580s, Elizabeth had a new favorite at court—the Earl of Essex—and Raleigh was given no more grants or favors. The queen forbade him to join expeditions against Spain and to the Azores. He was recalled from yet another expedition when the queen discovered he was in love with one of her ladies-in-waiting. (They were married in 1592 and had a happy life together in spite of royal disapproval.)

In 1595, Raleigh set out in search of gold again. He did not find it, but his account of his trip, *The Discoveries of Guiana*, is a fine narrative of Elizabethan adventure. In 1596, he commanded a triumphant expedition against Cadiz, Spain. But the death of Queen Elizabeth I was his downfall. The estates and privileges given to him by the queen were taken from him, and he was falsely accused of plotting against King James I, a Catholic who succeeded Elizabeth. Raleigh spent thirteen years imprisoned in the Tower of London, although now public opinion had turned and he was a hero to the mostly Protestant population of England. While in the Tower, he wrote his *History of the World*.

Released, he returned to Guiana, but his expedition was unsuccessful, and his son, Walter, was killed in a battle with the Spanish. Spain complained bitterly, and Raleigh knew that he would be executed when he returned to England. At the Spanish ambassador's insistence, Sir Walter Raleigh was beheaded on October 29, 1618.

Raleigh has been called a genius, an idealist, a pirate, a statesman, a scientist, a writer, a gentleman, and a rogue. Probably, in true Elizabethan fashion, he was all of those things. Legend has it that his ghost appears at Sherborne Castle, given to him by Queen Elizabeth, every September 20 (St. Michael's Eve).

Samuel de Champlain

Explorer of the North American Coastline;
Known as the "Father of New France"; Founded Québec
c. 1570–1635

Now known as the "Father of New France" (Canada), Samuel de Champlain was an explorer whose accomplishments were overlooked for centuries. He founded Québec, the first permanent colony in Canada, explored the North American coastline as far south as Cape Cod, discovered Lake Champlain, and served as governor of New France.

Little is known about his childhood. He was probably born about 1570 in Brouage, a seaport in the south of France. His father was a captain in the merchant marine, and young Samuel was raised as a devout Catholic. He showed an early skill for drawing. In 1586, when Champlain was in his teens, the Huguenots—French Protestants—laid siege to Brouage. When he was in his twenties, he fought to drive Spanish invaders from France. When they were finally turned back, Champlain was without a home or a job. He went to sea, sailing to Mexico where he spent time in Mexico City. He was distressed by the Spanish treatment of the Indians in Mexico. The Indians were treated as slaves and forced to convert to Christianity under threat of death. Later, this experience dramatically affected his relations with the Algonquin Indians of Canada.

King Henry IV of France, grateful for Champlain's service during the war and for the notes and records he brought back from his transatlantic journey, gave him a small income and a title of nobility (indicated by the *de* in his name). In 1603, Champlain went on a fur-trading expedition to North America as a geographer and record-keeper. France owned Canada at that time but had never developed a permanent trading post or settlement there.

Champlain and his party, under command of Francois Gravé, usually called Pont-Gravé, landed on the St. Lawrence River. They immediately made friends with the Algonquin Indians, who promised cooperation if the French would help them defeat their traditional enemies, the Iroquois. France's traditional enemy, the English, were then aligned with the Iroquois and thus a long-standing enmity was established.

Champlain returned to Canada in 1604 and explored much of the coast of present-day Massachusetts; when he went again in 1608, he established the settlement of Québec where, with difficulty, the first settlers survived the harsh Canadian winter. In 1609, Champlain's attempt to open the Canadian interior for settlement led to war between the Algonquin and the Iroquois. The badly outnumbered Algonquin were triumphant only because Champlain and two of his officers stepped from behind trees holding long rifles. The Iroquois had never seen "thunder sticks" and were terrified by their murderous efficiency. They fled, and the triumphant Algonquin pledged loyalty to France.

When Champlain returned to France in 1610, he married a woman much younger than himself. In 1611, he left her behind to return to Québec. His wife joined him in Canada in 1620. Accustomed to the glamour of Paris, she took an instant dislike to Québec and left four years later. She never returned. On his 1611 trip, Champlain tried to establish Port Royal (Montreal) and secured Indian permission to explore the country. He could not, however, raise the funds needed to establish a trading post. Year after year, and voyage after voyage, Champlain argued for more men and supplies for Canada, but his pleas were ignored. In 1624, Québec had a total population of only fifty-one.

In 1626, Champlain returned to Canada with six Jesuit priests and the backing of Cardinal Richelieu, chief minister to King Louis XIII of France. Champlain was now recognized as a leader in Canada. Two hundred settlers were sent there, along with supplies, but the English, at war with France again, seized both the settlers and the supplies. The following year, they demanded the surrender of Québec. The French, low on supplies and with not enough men, had no choice. Champlain was taken to England in 1629 as a prisoner but returned to France in 1632.

Champlain made his last trip to Canada in 1633. Finding Québec in ruins, he immediately began to rebuild the city and to renew his friendship with the Indians. More settlers arrived—this time wealthy French nobles came with land grants from the king, and new settlements were established. Champlain, now governor of New France, was in control.

Samuel de Champlain fell ill and died on December 25, 1635. For many years afterwards, the French still did not realize how important Canada was, and Champlain's contributions were not recognized. Today, historians acknowledge that modern Canada, with its riches and resources, owes much to Samuel de Champlain.

Champlain left four books that recorded his explorations and adventures: *Des Sauvages; Les Voyages du Sieur de Champlain; Voyages and Discoveries Made in New France, from 1615 to 1618;* and his most famous, *Treatise on Seamanship and Duty of a Good Navigator.*

Henry Hudson

*Explorer who Sought the Northwest Passage to Asia;
Explored Hudson River, Hudson Bay, and Hudson Strait
1570s–1611*

Henry Hudson came late in the age of exploration but, like so many before him, he sought the Northwest Passage to Asia. Today, several waterways bear his name—the Hudson River, Hudson Bay, and Hudson Strait. One of America's most famous fur-trading companies also used his name—the Hudson's Bay Company.

Documented information on Henry Hudson's early life is not available, but historians presume that he was born in London in the early 1570s. At that time, an alderman in London named Hudson helped start the Muscovy Company, the trading and exploration business for which Henry Hudson later sailed. Alderman Hudson may have been the explorer's grandfather.

The Muscovy Company hired Henry Hudson in 1607 to find a new route to the Orient. Hudson had a new theory; he believed that the shortest route to Asia would be directly over the North Pole. On May 1, never imagining the ice cap he would meet, Hudson sailed on the *Hopewell*. It was a difficult journey, because of the extreme cold and fog as well as the small size of the ship and the harsh waters of the Arctic Ocean. He sailed to Greenland and turned northeast to the islands that Dutch explorers had named Spitsbergen. Here the sailors saw seal, walrus, and whales; on land they found deer, geese, and clear spring water. Hudson mistakenly assumed that the same sun that warmed these islands melted the ice around the North Pole. Twice he was blocked by walls of ice, and finally he returned to London in September, defeated but not hopeless.

When he reported the sighting of whales, the Muscovy Company sent sailors to Spitsbergen, and England's whaling industry was born. Whale blubber was used to make soap, fuel for oil lamps, and grease for carriage wheels. Whalebone was used in women's corsets. In 1608, the Muscovy Company sent Hudson on a second voyage. This time he traveled northeast, along the northern coast of Russia. Hudson reinforced the *Hopewell's* hull with extra wood and installed a stronger, thicker mast.

By late June, the ship had reached an island called Novaya Zemlya and was once again blocked by land and ice. Hudson turned the ship west, planning to sail to North America. When the crew realized they were not returning to England, they threatened mutiny and forced Hudson to sign a paper saying he was returning home of his own free will. Hudson gave in, and probably lost his superiors' respect for not enforcing his authority over the crew. The Muscovy Company dismissed Hudson.

Hudson made his next voyage for the Dutch East Indies Company. He was sent back to the island of Novaya Zemlya. Hudson took many of the men who had sailed with him earlier, including his first mate Robert Juet. However, his contract required him to take Dutchmen as crew, and since he did not speak Dutch, he let someone else hire the men. They sailed on the *Half Moon*, a ship even smaller than the *Hopewell*.

The weather was bad, the crew fought among themselves, and the ship did not reach Norway's northern coast until May. When Hudson proposed that they abandon their original plans and sail to North America, the crew agreed, imagining warmer weather. They reached the Canadian coast in less than a month and sailed southward, but the crew stole from the Indians they met along the way, endangering everyone. Hudson made no effort to control his men. In August, the *Half Moon* was as far south as Cape Hatteras, North Carolina, and turned northward. Hudson was searching for a waterway connecting the Atlantic and Pacific Oceans. He tried Chesa-

The Half Moon *arrives in the Hudson River.*

peake and Delaware Bays and decided they were dead ends. Then he sailed into the harbor of what we now call the Hudson River. Sailing upriver, the crew again clashed with local Indians and this time took two hostages for protection, although the men later escaped. When the river narrowed, Hudson suspected he had not found the longed-for Northwest Passage. A small boat sent ahead confirmed his fears. Hudson wanted to spend the winter in North America but the crew wanted to go home to England. Once again, Hudson gave in to his crew.

In England, King James I heard of Hudson's discoveries while sailing for another country and, in anger, had him arrested. He threatened to bring the explorer to trial for treason. A group of Englishmen went to the king to protest that sailing for another country was not against the law. They convinced James I to allow Hudson to sail again for England—and then they raised the money for a ship and a crew.

On his fourth expedition, Hudson left London on April 17, 1610, aboard the *Discovery*. The ship made rapid progress across the Atlantic, but fighting broke out among the crew, and rumors were spread about Hudson. The explorer pushed on for North America. By mid-June they sighted the coast of what is today the Canadian province of Québec, and in late June they sailed through what is now called Hudson Strait, a narrow waterway that connects the Atlantic Ocean with Hudson Bay. The strait is dangerous, with surging tides, ice floes, and thick fog. The terrified sailors pleaded with Hudson to turn back. He refused, and in early August they sailed into the bay. Hudson was sure he had found the northern route to the Pacific and the Orient. When land cut off their passage, Hudson explored the coast, looking for a way through. He did not find it.

Again crew members began fighting among themselves. This time Hudson put his first mate, Juet, on trial and demoted him along with several others. Then he promoted other sailors to take their places. Unwittingly, Hudson had divided the crew into two groups—those who supported him and those who opposed him. In the spring, when the ship broke free from the ice, Hudson headed westward, but members of the crew plotted mutiny.

On June 24, 1611, three men attacked Hudson, bound him hand and foot, and lowered him into a small boat. Crew members who were ill and those still loyal to Hudson were forced to join him. They were set adrift without food or water—and never heard of again.

The remaining crew headed for England but were inefficient sailors without Hudson. By the time they reached England, the leaders of the mutiny had all died. The other sailors were never punished for their part in the mutiny.

René Robert Cavelier, Sieur de la Salle

Explored New France, Now Known as Canada
1643–1687

Like Samuel Champlain, René Robert Cavelier, Sieur de la Salle, was one of the builders of New France, but his explorations led him far into what is now Canada. He crossed the Great Lakes, established a fort at the site of present-day St. Joseph, Michigan, went south on the Illinois River to establish another fort, then on to the mouth of the Mississippi River. He claimed the whole valley in the name of France, and finally established a fort at the site of St. Louis. For a time La Salle governed the entire territory that later became the Louisiana Purchase. But he had dreams of empire and trade that were larger than he could accomplish, and La Salle's story ended tragically.

This explorer was born in Rouen, France, in 1643 and was educated to enter the Society of Jesuits, a religious order. When he received a tract of land on the St. Lawrence River in Canada, he abandoned the religious life and in 1666 he crossed the ocean as an adventurer and trader. For three years, La Salle lived on his land grant, learning the ways of the Indians and, like many before him, puzzling out the location of a Northwest Passage to the Pacific Ocean. He dreamed of acquiring a monopoly in the fur trade and increasing the empire of New France.

In 1669, he set out on an exploratory mission but he was soon abandoned by most of his colleagues. His route is uncertain, but he may have been the first white man to find Niagara Falls and he may have explored the Allegheny Valley and the Ohio River. He did not, as some once claimed, reach the Mississippi—that distinction still belongs to Louis Joliet. Indeed Joliet's later announcement that the "Great River" flowed into the Gulf of Mexico probably spurred La Salle's ambitions.

In 1674, La Salle established Fort Frontenac at a trading post near present-day Kingston for the protection of the fur trade around Lake Ontario. Then in the fall of 1678 he set sail on the schooner *Griffin*. His party included Henri de Tonti, an Italian explorer who became his lieutenant in later adventures. The party crossed Lakes Erie and Huron and entered Lake Michigan, pushing on to Illinois where Fort Crevecouer was built. The *Griffin*, sent back with furs, was never heard of again, and finally La Salle resolved to return to Fort Frontenac on foot, a journey of 1,000 miles (1,609 km). He left Tonti behind in charge of Fort Crevecouer. Surviving the hardships of his retreat, La Salle was determined to return to Tonti with supplies, but he learned that the garrison at Fort Crevecoeur had mutinied, driving Tonti into the wilderness. The soldiers were even then cruising about Lake Ontario in hopes of murdering La Salle.

La Salle set out to find Tonti and in 1681 organized a Native American federation of tribes—the Illinois and the Miami—to fight the Iroquois, who had also been Champlain's great enemies. On Lake Ontario, La Salle captured the mutineers and sent them to the governor in irons. He was reunited with Tonti on Mackinac Island in northern Lake Michigan. His party then sailed down the Mississippi to its mouth in what we now call the Mississippi Delta. On April 9, 1682, La Salle planted France's *fleur-de-lys* flag on the banks of the Mississippi River, claiming all the territory drained by that river for France. He named the territory Louisiana in honor of King Louis XIV.

After returning to France, La Salle was given the power to colonize and govern the region between Lake Michigan and the Gulf of Mexico, an area that made up much of the Louisiana Purchase. With a party of four ships, La Salle headed for the mouth of the Mississippi. His attempt to found a colony at the site of present-day New Orleans failed. Because of the sandy shore of the coast in that area and the many tributaries in the delta, he could not identify the actual mouth of the Mississippi or find suitable land for the fort he hoped to establish. Eventually, he landed on the coast of Texas. He and his men made several unsuccessful attempts to reach the Mississippi overland and finally the men grew mutinous.

René Robert Cavelier, Sieur de la Salle, was murdered by his own men in March 1687. In some ways he was a victim of the dreams and schemes that led him so relentlessly in pursuit of power and profit.

Jacques Marquette and Louis Joliet

Explorers who Led the French Expedition to Secure France's Rights to Land in America
Marquette (1637–1675); Joliet (1645–1700)

In the 1670s, King Louis XIV of France was anxious to establish his nation's claim to the interior of North America by securing French rights to what later would be known as the Louisiana Purchase. Talon appointed twenty-seven-year-old Louis Joliet, a Canadian-born explorer and adventurer, to lead an expedition to find the Mississippi River and follow it to where it entered the sea. His party included five woodsmen and Jacques Marquette (above), a Jesuit missionary.

The seven men set off from the mission of St. Ignace, founded by Marquette at the Strait of Mackinac, near the northeastern end of Lake Michigan. They traveled in two birchbark canoes with scant provisions— smoked meat and corn, trading trinkets, ammunition, paper, and ink.

Marquette also took a storage box holding his vestments, altar wine, breviary, and Communion hosts. He planned to convert the Native Americans to Catholicism.

They paddled around the rim of the lake to Green Bay, where the mission of Saint Francis Xavier was already established. Then they went up the Fox River to a village of friendly

Miami Indian guides brought Joliet and Marquette to the Mississippi River.

Mascoutin and Miami Indians—the farthest point in the interior ever explored by the French up to that date. Joliet wanted the Native Americans to lead them south, but they were afraid of hostile Sioux—the Iroquois of the West, as the French called them—and they said the *Big Water* (Lake Michigan) held monsters. Joliet and his party amazed them by starting off anyway. Two Miamis accompanied them for a short distance and then turned back.

The Miami led them to the "Chicago portage" of the Wisconsin River. They followed that broad river to the Mississippi and sailed 200 miles (322 km) down that river before seeing any human life. Finally they came to an Illinois village where they were cordially received when they approached unarmed. They were not so well received farther downriver by the Arkansas who were poised to attack the canoes until Marquette held aloft a *calumet* (peace pipe). In the Arkansas village, they were given a feast, but a group of warriors plotted to kill the Frenchmen for their guns. The chief stopped the plot, but the men spent a nervous and wakeful night. The Arkansas dissuaded them from going farther south with tales of hostile natives who had Spanish guns. France was then at war with Spain, and Joliet decided his explorations to date were too important to risk his life by seeking the river's juncture with the ocean. He turned north.

Now the small group had to fight against the strong current of the river. The heat was excessive, and they were besieged by mosquitoes. At the mouth of the Illinois River, a Native American boy traveling with them told them to follow that river and it would take them more quickly to Lake Michigan. Joliet and Marquette marveled at the scenery and recorded the river's "fertility of soil, its prairie and woods; its cattle, elk, deer, wildcats, bustards [large, cranelike birds], swans, ducks, parroquets, and even beaver." Moving into what was once the Tallgrass Prairie, extending from western Indiana to eastern Oklahoma, the French gave it the name *prairie,* which means "large meadow" in French. Their Native American guide led them up the Des Plaines River (a branch of the Illinois) to the Chicago portage and then up the south branch of the Chicago River to Lake Michigan.

Both men took careful notes during this journey. Marquette thought in terms of establishing mission posts while Joliet saw the economic potential of land so fertile that it grew three crops of corn a year, and did not have to be cleared of forests. At the site of present-day Chicago, Marquette saw only a flat, marshy plain and thought it a dismal spot for settlement, pointing out that there was not even a Native American encampment nearby. Joliet, however, saw the value of the location for the development of agriculture and trade.

The small party returned to Green Bay in September. They had paddled some 2,500 miles (4,023 km) in about four months. Joliet never returned to the Illinois River Valley. He went instead to Québec to report on his findings, taking with him the detailed and careful notes he had made along the way. Unfortunately, his canoe capsized in the St. Lawrence River near Montreal, and his notes—as well as the lives of his companions—were lost. A copy he had left with the Jesuits of Sault St. Marie disappeared after Indians burned the mission house there. Joliet summarized his findings in his report to the government, and wrote wryly to the bishop of Québec, "But for this shipwreck, Your Excellency would have had a quite interesting relation, but all I saved was my life."

Marquette returned to the area in the fall of 1674, the wrong time of year to be on Lake Michigan in a canoe. Snow, wind, and masses of ice threatened the frail boats, and the "river of portage" was frozen solid. Marquette then became seriously ill. His small party wintered about 6 miles (10 km) from the mouth of the Chicago River—in what today would be the city of Chicago. Marquette expected to die, but by late March his health was better and the ice had broken on the river. The party followed the Des Plaines River to the village of the Kaskaskia people. On the previous trip, Marquette had promised the Native Americans of this village that he would return, and he felt the commitment strongly. The village welcomed him "as an angel from Heaven."

By the week before Easter, Marquette's health was again failing. He said Mass in a prairie clearing to a congregation of several thousand Native Americans. On Easter morning he preached again, telling them his work would have to be done by other "black robes" because illness forced him to return to St. Ignace. His health failed rapidly, and he died on May 18, 1675, and was buried on the shores of the river that now bears his name. Two years later a party of Christian Native Americans carried his bones to St. Ignace where they were buried in a vault beneath the church. In the late 1800s, a few of his bones were found at the site of the long-gone mission and taken to Marquette University.

Jacques Marquette is considered the father of Chicago and was surely the first European resident of the area. Had Joliet's notes survived, he would surely have held a more important place in Chicago history.

Later French explorers gave the area the name *Checagov,* a Native American word meaning "place of the wild onion," for the wild onion plants that lined the banks of the Chicago River.

Vitus Jonassen Bering

Explorer who Proved that Asia and America were
Not One Continuous Landmass
1680–1741

Columbus sailed east to west to explore the North American continent. About 125 years later, Vitus Bering sailed west to east to prove that Asia and America were not one continuous landmass but instead were separated by a narrow waterway. Today, that waterway is called the Bering Strait. The Bering Sea is in the Northern Pacific and Bering Island lies off the coast of Siberia.

Vitus Bering was born in 1680 in Horsens, Denmark. Today, he is honored in a museum in that city although he did not spend much of his life in Denmark. He went to sea as a young man and in 1703 enlisted in the Russian navy. He moved to Russia, married, and raised a family there, making only one trip back to Copenhagen, Denmark, in 1715.

Bering made two major voyages, now called the first and second Kamchatka Expeditions. In 1725, when he first set out, no one knew whether or not America was connected to Asia by land. Peter the Great, czar of Russia, put Bering at the head of an expedition to answer this question.

The party traveled overland from St. Petersburg through Siberia to Kamchatka, a peninsula on the eastern edge of Siberia. There they set up camp and built ships for their exploration. It was 1728 before they sailed around the northeast corner of Asia, proving that there was water between America and Asia. Unfortunately, the Alaskan coast was shrouded in fog, and Bering did not actually see the coastline. For this he was criticized. Some said he did not recognize the importance of the stretch of water he had found. But today that water is named the Bering Strait.

Bering returned to St. Petersburg in 1730 to head a second Kamchatka Expedition, sometimes called the Great Nordic Expedition. With 10,000 men, it was the largest recorded expedition in the world up to that date. Its purpose was to find and map the west coast of America. The two ships in the expedition—the *St. Peter* and the *St. Paul*—sailed around Kamchatka and founded the city of Petropavlovsk on the east coast of Russia before sailing farther east. The vessels, however, became separated. In 1741, Bering, in command of the *St. Peter,* sailed into the Gulf of Alaska, sighting Mount St. Elias in July and sending ashore a landing party headed by a scientist.

On the return voyage, the *St. Peter* sailed past the Aleutian Islands, which are southwest of Alaska and form the southern border of the Bering Sea. They were shipwrecked on a small, barren island which they at first mistook for Kamchatka. The men tried to survive the winter in driftwood huts dug into the sand, but Bering and several others died on that island, now known as Bering Island. A few survivors reached Kamchatka in the summer of 1742.

Almost no portraits existed of Bering, and the authenticity of those that have been found is doubtful. No one knows for sure what the famous explorer looked like. In 1991 a research team of Soviet archaeologists and forensic physicians, along with an archaeologist from Horsens Museum, excavated

Bering's grave on Bering Island, along with the graves of five other seamen, intending to re-create his face by studying his skull. The remains of the six men were taken to Moscow where forensic physicians did re-create Bering's appearance. An exhibition in Horsens Museum traces the second Kamchatka Expedition and displays the re-created bust of Bering, a cast of his skull, and a reconstruction from the grave. The bodies of Bering and his five seamen were returned to Bering Island for burial in 1992.

Captain James Cook

Pacific Explorer; First European to Visit Hawaiian Islands
1728–1778

Captain James Cook has been hailed as the greatest explorer of the mid-1700s and the greatest Pacific explorer ever. He was the first European to visit the Hawaiian Islands. His three major voyages brought land and great wealth to King George III of England and he made the first comprehensive map of the Pacific Ocean. Today he is often remembered as the "discoverer" of Australia.

James Cook was born on October 27, 1728, in Marton, England, near York. As a young boy, he was apprenticed to the owner of a general store in a nearby town. He worked in haberdashery—men's clothing—and groceries, and spent his spare time listening to the tales of the sailors in the harbor or outside the local pub. After a year and a half, he either ran away—the story usually told—or was dismissed by his employer. In any case, he went to sea as an assistant to the mate of a collier, or coal-carrying ship.

Cook joined the Royal Navy in 1755. When the Seven Years' War broke out in 1756, with England and Prussia fighting France, Sweden, Russia and Austria, he was sent to Canada as master of a naval vessel, the *Mercury*, to take part in the assault on Québec. Over the years, Cook had taught himself to be an expert surveyor and cartographer and had studied mathematics and astronomy. He used these skills to chart the channel of the St. Lawrence River up to the point of the French lines with an accuracy and care that drew the attention of his superiors.

In 1766, the planet Venus was expected to pass between the Earth and the sun. The government of England planned to send a ship to the Pacific to observe this celestial event. They chose Cook to captain the ship, the *Endeavour*—a collier refitted for its new duty. The government chose a workboat because it would hold all the supplies and scientific equipment needed on the voyage. A group of eighty-five naval officers and scientists would record their astrological observations and continue the search for the land known as *Terra Australis Incognita*. The *Endeavour* left England in August 1768. It was the first of Cook's three great voyages.

The expedition sailed around Cape Horn and landed at Otaheite—now known as Tahiti—the largest of the Hawaiian "Society Islands." There they observed the transit of Venus and spent three months as welcome guests of the natives. They charted and explored other islands in the group and then sailed on to New Zealand, which Cook found perfectly suited to settlement—the land was fertile and there were splendid trees. The drawbacks were the absence of domestic animals and the cannibalistic tendency of the natives. Cook covered thousands of miles of coastline on this voyage.

In 1770, Cook discovered the east coast of Australia, which he called New South Wales, for the king of England. Cook named an especially beautiful bay *Port Jackson*—today we know it as the famed Sydney Harbour, one of the world's most beautiful harbors. In May 1770, sailing at night, the

Endeavour ran aground on the Great Barrier Reef. Cook and his men stuffed the holes in the boat with clothes and manure, threw things overboard, and managed to keep the ship afloat. The ship then sailed between Australia and New Guinea, gathering the first proof that the two were separate countries before sailing for England. By the time they arrived, Cook had lost one-third of his men to malaria and dysentery.

Cook was next commissioned to "complete the discovery of the Southern Hemisphere." This time he commanded two ships—the *Resolution* and the *Adventure*. He took enough provisions to last two years including limes and lemons to fight off scurvy. He was the first captain to prevent scurvy by serving his sailors fruits and vegetables. The ships sailed from England in July 1772, sailing around Cape Horn into the Antarctic Ocean and to New Zealand, discovering many islands along the way. They introduced domestic animals in New Zealand and planted British vegetables. They sailed south until their way was blocked by ice fields. Cook sailed around the South Pole, finding that the great southern continent shown on old maps did not exist. When he returned to England, he had crossed a greater space of open sea than any ship before. On this trip, he lost only one man to disease.

Cook's third voyage came when he was again put in charge of the *Resolution*. By then he had been named post-captain and had received the gold medal of the Royal Society. This voyage was intended to determine if there was a west-to-east passage from the Pacific to the Atlantic (after all the voyages that had sought a passage going in the opposite direction!). In March 1778, he sighted the mainland of America. The *Resolution* spent a difficult and stormy summer exploring the coast from Oregon northward.

Cook decided to return to Hawaii, where the natives had always welcomed him and his crew. He was welcomed as a god but the goodwill of the natives soon disappeared, replaced by quarrels in which sticks and stones flew. Cook sailed away. But when the *Resolution* sprang her foremast he was forced to return to the island. While he was anchored offshore, one of the ship's cutters, or small boats, was stolen. Cook went ashore to demand that it be returned. In the resulting fight, he was stabbed in the back and fell dead in the water. He was fifty-one years old.

Cook was buried at sea. The British Royal Navy still maintains a memorial to Cook erected near Kona on the island of Hawaii. In England, a

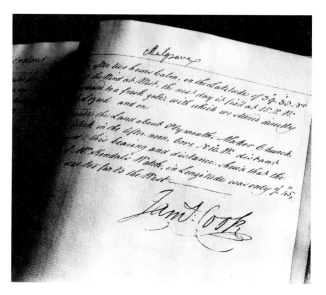

This page from Captain Cook's log features his neat penmanship and bold signature.

small obelisk marks the place where his family's cottage stood. The cottage was taken down, transported to Australia, and rebuilt in the Melbourne Public Gardens, where it is regarded as a national treasure. In further tribute to Cook, a small piece of the *Endeavour* went into orbit aboard the space shuttle that was also named the *Endeavour*.

Captain Cook kept a daily log during each of his expeditions, so we have a full record of his travels. His log is kept in the National Maritime Museum in England.

Daniel Boone

Explored Area Known as Kentucky
1734–1820

For Daniel Boone, hunting and exploring were passions. He explored the land we know as Kentucky, often called that "dark and bloody ground" because of the violent clashes that took place there between settlers and Native Americans.

Boone was born in 1734 near what is now Reading, Pennsylvania. He was the sixth of eleven children born to Squire and Sarah Boone, a Quaker couple. Growing up in Pennsylvania, young Boone no doubt helped his father as a farmer, weaver, and blacksmith. He had no formal schooling. In 1750, the family moved to what is now North Carolina, following many other Pennsylvanians who were moving south. Squire Boone moved after being "read out" of the Quaker meeting because he was unrepentant when his son Israel married outside the faith.

Daniel married Rebecca Bryan in 1756 and they had ten children, although he was an absent father for most of his children's early lives. By

1760 he was hunting in Kentucky; a beech tree was found in the Boone's Creek Valley with the inscription "D. Boone cilled a bar (killed a bear) on (this) tree in the year 1760." Daniel had gone to the frontier to hunt for himself and to look for land for a prominent citizen of North Carolina named Richard Henderson. Henderson was in financial difficulty and, to save himself, wanted to establish a colony beyond the mountains which had, so far, kept the eastern colonies close to the coast.

According to President Theodore Roosevelt, a great historian, Daniel Boone left his North Carolina home for Kentucky in May 1769, along with five other men. He wanted to find the great hunting grounds he had heard lay beyond the mountains. For five weeks the men chopped through dense forest and dark wilderness. In early June, they reached the bluegrass region of present-day Kentucky, which Roosevelt described as a land "of running waters, of groves and glades, of prairies, canebrakes, and stretches of lofty forest." The wildlife included buffalo, elk, deer, bear, wolves, and panthers. For months, Boone and his companions did little but hunt in a paradise beyond their wildest imaginings.

In December they were attacked by Native Americans; Boone and another man were captured but managed to escape. The other man was later captured again and died at the hands of the Native Americans—the first white man to die in the battle to win Kentucky. This region belonged to no single tribe but was hunted by several, and all of them killed strangers who invaded their hunting grounds. It should be noted that in this ongoing warfare between Native Americans and settlers, neither side was more violent or aggressive than the other. Daniel Boone—a fierce fighter when he needed to defend and protect himself and other settlers—was also known for his compassion for his opponents in the war over land. He lost two sons and a brother in the bloody fighting.

Boone was joined by a brother, and they spent the winter living in a small cabin on their hunting grounds. In the spring, Boone's brother set off to the settlements for horses and ammunition, leaving Boone alone for three months. He had no salt, sugar, or flour, and no companionship, not even a horse or a dog. Boone spent the days exploring the countryside and slept in the canebrake and thickets at night, without even a fire, to avoid capture by Native Americans. His brother returned in midsummer.

Other hunters came into this wilderness. Boone joined a party of five men camped on the Red River for a while and reported on the boredom of their lives, particularly in the evenings. One way they passed the time was by reading, and this group had a copy of *Gulliver's Travels* which they practically memorized. Boone recorded that Gulliver "gave an account of his young master, Glumdelick, careing him on a market day for a show to a town called Lulbegrud." One night, another of the party, Alexander Neely, came into camp carrying two Shawnee scalps and announced that "he had been that day to Lulbegrud and had killed two Brobdignags." To this day, the creek near the spot where the two Shawnee lost their lives is known as Lulbegrud Creek. In the spring of 1771, the danger from Native Americans drove Boone back to North Carolina.

In 1773, Daniel Boone attempted to establish a colony in Kentucky but failed. In 1775 he succeeded in establishing Boonesborough. After that he was a leader in opening parts of Kentucky and in fighting Indian raids. Boone was a legend in his own time by then and when he visited the family homestead in Pennsylvania, he was greeted as a hero. Unfortunately, his finances did not keep up with his fame. Deeply in debt and hounded by creditors, he left Kentucky for Missouri in 1799 and died near St. Louis in 1820 at the home of one of his sons. He is buried near Frankfort, Kentucky.

Sir Alexander Mackenzie

Led First Expedition to Cross America North of Mexico,
Opening the Canadian West to Trade and Settlement
Died 1820

In the 1790s, Alexander Mackenzie led the first expedition to cross America north of Mexico, thus beating Lewis and Clark to the Pacific Ocean. His two expeditions opened the Canadian West to trade and settlement, and for this the king of England knighted him in 1802, making him Sir Alexander Mackenzie.

Scottish-born Mackenzie was a fur trader in Canada. He and several other men had formed the North West Company, which came to be called the Nor'Westers. But in the eighteenth century, the Hudson's Bay Company dominated the fur trade. The company sent boatmen, called *coureurs des bois* (runners of the woods) in canoes loaded with goods to trade with the Native Americans—arms, tobacco, kettles, and clothing—in exchange for furs. The furs were then shipped to Europe, the United States, and China.

The Nor'Westers had two challenges: finding Native Americans willing to trade with the new company and finding shipping lanes not already controlled by the Hudson's Bay Company. Mackenzie traveled into previously unexplored parts of Canada to find hunters outside the territory of the bigger company. Because he treated the Native Americans fairly and as friends, when many traders did not, Mackenzie was successful in finding furs.

The Nor'Westers shipped their goods via the St. Lawrence River, but its winding channels made the route both slow and expensive. They talked of finding a new route. If they could get their goods to the Pacific, they could trade at the ports established there by Spain and England. In 1789 Mackenzie set out on his first exploration. From headquarters he had previously established at Lake Athabasca in Alberta, Canada, he followed a large river—now called the Mackenzie River—which would, he hoped, take him to the Pacific. Instead it took him to the cold waters of the Arctic Ocean.

In June 1793 he again left Lake Athabasca, resigned to the necessity of crossing the Rocky Mountains on foot. He chose a north-flowing river called the Peace, but he and his companions had to make many portages and *décharges.* (In *décharges,* the boats were left in the water but the goods they carried were removed to let the boats ride higher.) In November they reached Fort Forks, the westernmost outpost in Canada. They camped there until spring, living in log cabins and eating the plentiful game around them and the pemmican that Mackenzie had brought. (Pemmican was an Indian food made of meat pounded fine and soaked in its own fat.)

In May, accompanied by four boatmen, two women, and two Native Americans who acted as guides and interpreters, Mackenzie headed west. Within weeks, he sighted the Rockies. The closer the party got to the mountains, the more difficult it was to travel. They went sometimes by land, sometimes on narrow streams interrupted by rapids and waterfalls. The canoes were smashed on the rocks and had to be repaired. The Indians they met were friendly but not particularly helpful. They could not tell Mackenzie how far away the sea was o if there was a river that could carry them to it.

On June 16, the party reached the Fraser River, which Native Americans said emptied into the ocean. However, it was a winding and difficult river, and on June 1 Mackenzie decided to go west on foot. In late July they came to a small stream called the Bella Coola that carried them to the Pacific near Vancouver Island. Mackenzie thus became the first explorer to lead an expedition to the Pacific.

The Nor'Westers prospered, and Mackenzie held government posts in Canada. He published his journals in 1801 and was given a title in 1802. In 1812, Mackenzie moved back to Scotland, where he married and had children. A sudden illness took his life in 1820. The North West Company and the Hudson's Bay Company merged in 1821.

The Franciscan Friars

Roman Catholic Priests from Spain who
Established the Mission System in California
c. 1769

The Roman Catholic priests who had the courage to face an unknown land and establish the mission system in California did much to colonize that state. They developed a profitable agricultural land from what appeared to be barren wasteland. Generally, the mission period is considered to have begun in 1769, with the settlement of the first Franciscan mission, but actually missions and priests were in California territory before that date.

By 1600, the conquest of the Philippines had brought great riches to Spain, and Spanish galleons brought the treasures of those lands to Mexico by way of the California coast. King Philip II of Spain needed a safe harbor on that coast where his galleons loaded with treasure could hide from the English raiders. However, attempts to take California by sea failed. Philip then sent a military expedition into the area, but it too was unsuccessful. The land was finally settled by a group of Jesuit priests who made their own terms for establishing missions. They would have control over the military commanders and they would enforce respect for the rights of the Indians. They followed the will of Queen Isabella who had decreed much earlier that the rights and liberties of the Indians were to be respected. Their land was not to be seized,

Father Junípero Serra

and they were not to be made slaves, as had been the practice of explorers and colonists throughout much of the New World.

The Spanish military were displeased with this arrangement. They saw only ignorant savages and a barren land that offered no reward for their conquest. But under the Jesuits, the land began to prosper. By 1767, the Jesuit order in California had become strong enough to be envied for its wealth and position. The Jesuits were then removed and replaced by Franciscan friars who had no control over the military. Chaos resulted—the soldiers were mainly interested in finding the buried treasure they thought the Jesuits had left behind—so control of the military was restored to the friars.

The Franciscans founded the California mission system as we generally think of it today. In 1769, Father Junípero Serra founded Mission San Diego de Alcala, the first of twenty-one missions built about a day's ride apart to keep other countries from trying to settle the territory. The missions stretched from southern California to just north of present-day San Francisco. The friars were to teach the natives Christianity, teach them to read, grow crops and raise animals, and make them loyal Spanish subjects. In other words, they were to settle the land peacefully.

Establishment of the mission system was not easy. Of three ships sent north, one was lost at sea, another lost eight men to scurvy, and on the third, all but two members of its crew were sick with the same disease. Many were near death. Land expeditions were similarly difficult. The land seemed all shrubs and sand, with no good land for agriculture and nothing else to attract settlers. Colonists never arrived, soldiers deserted, and some of the priests wrote to Mexico City asking permission to return. But Father Serra and his closest allies—Fathers Francisco Palou, Juan Crespi, and Fermín Lasuén—slowly built the mission system until it began to prosper.

With Indian labor, the fathers supervised the building of missions. Usually, each was a large, four-sided building with a patio in the center and a church at one corner of the square. There were rooms for the priests, quarters for unmarried women, storage rooms, workshops, and a mission office. The number of courtyards and arches often indicated the wealth of a particular mission.

Because of the Franciscans' determination, the land supported a rich agriculture by 1800. Crops included oranges and grapes introduced by the friars and each mission had large herds of cattle and sheep. Colonists swarmed to the land hoping to make their fortune, only to find that the missions controlled the wealth and insisted that the land belonged to the Indians. The fathers were charged with injustice to the natives, which was probably true in some cases but not all. The legend of Fransciscan mistreatment of the Indians persists to this day.

In 1833 an order was issued that took control of the missions away from the religious orders and transferred it to the Indians. The natives, however, were not capable of taking charge of the wealth. Control soon fell into the hands of greedy politicians who divided the wealth among themselves, ignoring the needs of the Indians.

In the political upheaval of the nineteenth century, which brought Mexico's independence from Spain and the United States annexation of Califiornia, the mission system collapsed. Today, many missions that had fallen into disrepair have been restored, and many people are working to preserve both the history of the mission system and the actual missions. The most famous is San Juan Capistrano, known for the legend and the song of the swallows that return to Capistrano every March.

William Clark and Meriwether Lewis

Explored the American Continent in a Journey that Came to be Known as the Lewis & Clark Expedition, 1803
Clark (1770–1838); Lewis (1774–1809)

In 1800, the Mississippi River was the western boundary of the United States. The West was a blank space on maps, and no one knew how high the Rocky Mountains were or where the rivers went. Most people believed the rivers all ran into one another until they reached the Pacific Ocean. There were wild stories of superhuman beings and unusual natural features, such as a mountain of salt. The best maps at the time were no more than guesses compiled from bits and pieces of information collected over two hundred years.

In 1802, President Thomas Jefferson decided the United States should explore the land west of the Mississippi and Missouri Rivers. He asked Congress to authorize such an expedition. The problem was that almost all the land west of these rivers was claimed by Britain, France, or Spain.

He would be sending explorers into territory not owned by the United States.

But in 1802, Napoléon of France had two large military campaigns to finance: one to regain control of the Caribbean and the other to control Louisiana. Instead of fighting, Napoléon decided to sell Louisiana to the United States. The 1803 Louisiana Purchase instantly doubled the size of the United States. The land involved stretched from the Mississippi River as far north as Canada and as far west as the Rocky Mountains. The French had called it *pays inconnu* (unknown land). In April 1803, the two countries agreed on the terms that gave the United States control of all this land. Now Jefferson had a legitimate reason and a legal right to send explorers into the region. Congress authorized funds for the expedition in February 1803.

President Jefferson had previously asked Captain Meriwether Lewis, his private secretary, to lead an exploratory expedition from the Mississippi River to the West Coast. Lewis was twenty-nine years old and knew how to live in the wilderness. Born in August 1774 near Charlottesville, Virginia, he had been a boyhood neighbor of Jefferson's. Lewis had served in the militia during the Northwest Campaign against the British and the Indians. Jefferson had taken him on as secretary in part because of his knowledge of the west and of the army.

Lewis chose William Clark as his second in command. Born in Virginia in August 1770, Clark had been Lewis's commanding officer at one point. Like Lewis, he was adventurous, resourceful, and a born woodsman-frontiersman. Clark, then living in the Indiana Territory with his brother, accepted the appointment, saying it was an enterprise he had long anticipated. Although the two men were similar in background and experience, they were very different in personality. Lewis was moody and often kept to himself while Clark was outgoing and even-tempered. Clark was a practical man who dealt with action and realities; Lewis was a dreamer and a romantic.

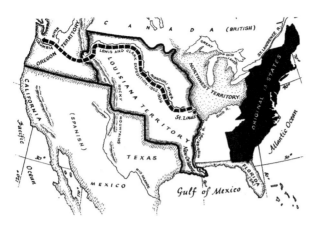

The broken line traces the Lewis and Clark Expedition along the Missouri River through the Rockies to the Pacific Ocean.

The expedition would sail up the Missouri River to its source, cross the Continental Divide and follow the Columbia River to its mouth. The expedition expected to find a water route to the Pacific Ocean: Lewis and Clark were also expected to bring back detailed reports on the region's geography, the Indians they met, and the plants and animals they observed.

The Lewis and Clark Expedition is sometimes called the Corps of Discovery. At that time, it was the most important exploration ever undertaken and it remains probably the most significant exploratory expedition in American history. To prepare himself, Lewis studied botany, zoology, Indian history, and fossils, and he read Alexander Mackenzie's 1801 book, *Voyages from Montreal*. Lewis packed clothing, tools, scientific books, medicine, rifles, and trade goods. The expedition took a large supply of trinkets and gifts—colored beads, calico shirts, handkerchiefs, mirrors, bells, needles, thimbles, ribbons, kettles, and brass rings that the Native Americans liked to wear on their fingers.

Clark was the mapmaker of the group. During the long journey, he tried to follow the primitive charts and maps given to him. He measured and described what he saw and drew his own versions of the land and water. He added greatly to knowledge of the land and people and the nature of the American West. The notes on his geographical sketches and the dozens of notebooks he filled were the basis for the first detailed maps of the American West and Pacific Northwest.

The expedition, which included fourteen soldiers, nine frontiersmen, two boatmen, and Clark's slave—an African-American called York—in addition to the two leaders, started up the Missouri River in May 1804 in a specially built 55-foot (17-meter) covered keelboat, or shallow freight boat, and two smaller crafts. They soon began to see new animals—antelope, prairie dogs, jackrabbits, and coyotes. "This scenery already rich pleasing and beautiful was still farther heightened by immense herds of Buffaloe, deer Elk and Antelopes," wrote Lewis. They also met mosquitoes, gnats, and ticks. And they met Native Americans—the Hidatsa and Mandan, the threatening Teton Sioux and the friendly Yankton Sioux.

Lewis and Clark made a winter camp in what is now North Dakota among the Mandan people. They built Fort Mandan. Chief Big White drew rough maps in sand of the Upper Missouri River and its tributaries. Big White told Lewis and Clark of a large river a half-day's march away. Clark translated the maps in the sand into a chart that the expedition could follow. In the Mandan camp, the expedition found a French trapper named Toussaint Charbonneau and his wife, fifteen-year-old Sacagawea, a Shoshone. The two agreed to go with them as guides and interpreters. Charbonneau proved to be difficult, but his wife was the savior of the expedition. She had been captured at an early age by Minnetaree warriors and sold to Charbonneau. By the time Lewis and Clark found her, she was expecting Charbonneau's child. She gave birth at Fort Mandan and carried the child on her back for the rest of the trip. Lewis and Clark hired her because they thought she would be a help when they met the Shoshone Indians to the west. She proved to be invaluable in many ways.

In April 1805, the expedition left the Mandans. Messsengers were sent back to St. Louis, with dispatches for President Jefferson and natural-history specimens. In May they sighted the Rocky Mountains. In June, when they came to the Great Falls of the Missouri, they were astounded—the falls were 900 feet (274 m) wide and 80 feet (24 m) high. The party had to carry their boats and goods 18 miles (29 kilometers) around the falls to enter the water. They built crude wagons for this portage. On July 25 they reached Three Forks where three rivers join to form the Missouri. They named the rivers the Madison, the Jefferson, and the Gallatin, and followed the Jefferson River.

In the high country of the Shoshone, Sacagawea recognized landmarks and guided the expedition into the mountains and to the Continental Divide. The Shoshone also recognized Sacagawea—the chief was her brother. Because of her presence, the Shoshone sold the expedition the horses they needed to cross the difficult Bitterroot Mountains. At the Divide, they followed the Missouri River and its headwaters for 2400 miles (3,860 km). From there, the party descended 2 miles (3 km) through what is now Lemhi Pass and arrived at the Columbia River. From this point, they could proceed by water. Lewis wrote, "Here I first tasted the water of the great Columbia River." Actually, the river was only a tributary of the Columbia.

On the other side of the mountains, they reached the Clearwater River and the friendly *Nez Perce* (Pierced Nose) Indians. They followed the Clearwater to the Snake and then the Columbia River. In November 1805, coming down the spectacularly beautiful Columbia River Gorge, they sighted the Pacific Ocean. "Great joy in camp we are in view of the Ocian, this great Pacific Ocean which we been so long anxious to See, and the roreing or noise made by the waves brakeing on the rockey Shores (as I suppose) may be heard distinctly."

The expedition built a stockade and winter quarters, which they named Fort Clatsop. They stayed there until March 23, 1806, when they headed back east toward home. For a time, Lewis and Clark separated. Clark followed the Yellowstone River to the Missouri while Lewis took nine men and explored a branch of the Missouri he called the Marias. They were reunited in August at the mouth of the Yellowstone River. In September they passed a French settlement—the first sign of European civilization they had seen in nearly two years. At Fort Mandan, they left Sacagawea and her family. Lewis and Clark arrived in St. Louis in September 1806. They had traveled about 8,000 miles (12,800 km) in two years, four months, and nine days—and opened the way to half a continent. The first official map of the country they traveled through was compiled from Clark's notes and drawings and published, with his notations, in 1814.

After the expedition, Lewis was appointed governor of the Louisiana Territory and Clark was promoted to brigadier general and appointed super-intendent of Indian Affairs. Lewis died just three years after the expedition at the age of thirty-five; Clark lived to the age of sixty-eight, spending most of his life in St. Louis. Together they are recognized for having conducted the most important expedition in the early history of the United States. They opened the Northwest to exploration and settlement, and they brought back a rich store of knowledge about the land they had traveled over.

Sacagawea

Shoshone Indian who Aided Lewis and Clark on Their Journey
c. 1787–c. 1812

The 1804–1805 expedition of Meriwether Lewis and William Clark across the northwest range of the Rockies and the Pacific Northwest would not have been successful without the help of a fifteen-year-old Shoshone Indian named Sacagawea. At Fort Mandan in the Dakota Territory, Lewis and Clark had hired Toussaint Charbonneau, a French-Canadian trapper known for his ability to communicate with the river tribes. He brought two Indian women with him to the expedition's winter camp on the Missouri—"squars" as Clark's journal described them. Sacagawea was Charbonneau's wife and so, probably, was the other woman. Sacagawea was expecting a child, which she delivered well before spring, allowing the expedition to move westward. The baby, a boy, was christened Jean Baptiste but nicknamed *Pomp*, a Shoshone word meaning first-born.

Sacagawea had been kidnapped five years earlier by a party of raiders and later traded or sold to Charbonneau. She knew both the language and the land of the Shoshone—or Snakes as they were often called—and she would be much more important to the expedition than her husband.

The expedition left Fort Mandan on the Missouri in April 1805. One of Sacagawea's earliest contributions was to help the company find roots and berries, an important addition to their diet. When one of the pirogues almost overturned, it was Sacagawea who calmly saved many irreplaceable supplies and records. (A pirogue is a native canoe, usually hollowed from the trunk of a tree.)

When the expedition was on land, Sacagawea walked with her baby strapped on her back. By mid-July, she recognized the country they were crossing and assured Lewis and Clark that they would soon be in the land of the Shoshone. Lewis pressed ahead, leaving Clark and Sacagawea and the others to follow with the equipment. Thus, Lewis and a few companions were the first to meet Sacagawea's people and their chief, Cameahwait. Though they could not communicate, Lewis persuaded the chief and a group of his people to backtrack and meet the rest of the expedition party.

The reunion between Sacagawea and her people was apparently touching and certainly reassuring to the Shoshone. When Sacagawea was called to translate at a powwow with the chief, she recognized Cameahwait as her brother. The Shoshone eventually supplied the expedition with the horses they needed to take them across the Rockies, in exchange for gifts.

Although she was overjoyed to have found her people again, Sacagawea chose to continue with Lewis, Clark, and Charbonneau. Whenever the company encountered hostile Nez Perce, Flathead, or others, the presence of a woman was reassuring to them—a sign of peace.

When the company returned to the Mandan village in August 1806, Lewis and Clark paid Charbonneau for his services—a little over $500 for sixteen months—and said goodbye to the family. Clark had become particularly fond of Sacagawea—he sometimes called her Janey—and Pomp, and he later wrote to Charbonneau, "Your woman . . . deserved a greater reward for her attention and service than we had in our power to give her at the Mandans." He also offered to raise and educate Pomp, and the child was brought to St. Louis some five years later. He was schooled in St. Louis and later in Europe, but in 1829 he returned to the frontier.

The U.S. Golden Dollar coin with the likeness of Sacagawea and her infant son Pomp

According to Shoshone tradition, Sacagawea lived to be 100 years old and was much honored in Shoshone villages. But a fur trader at Fort Manuel on the upper Missouri River recorded on December 20, 1812, that the wife of Charbonneau, "a Snake squaw, died . . . she was the best woman of the fort, aged about 25 years."

Sacagawea is honored in many ways, even having novel written about her life. An important monument is the statue dedicated to her memory at Portland, Oregon, at the Lewis and Clark Exposition in 1905—a century after her great trip. The statue shows Sacagawea in fringed buckskins, her baby on her back, her arm stretched out, forever pointing the way. In 2000, the U.S. Mint released the new Golden Dollar coin bearing an image of Sacagawea with her baby on her back.

Davy Crockett

Mountain Man and Explorer; Died a Martyr at the Alamo
1786–1836

Any child raised in front of the television in the 1970s can sing the song, "Davy, Davy Crockett, King of the Wild Frontier." That song—and the Disney movie from which it came—represent the most recent and perhaps most obvious fictionalization of Crockett's life. Today we remember him as a Tennessee mountain man and explorer who went to Texas for adventure and died a martyr fighting Santa Anna at the Alamo. That familiar story overlooks Crockett's service in the Tennessee state legislature and the U.S. Congress, and it also overlooks the controversy over exactly how Crockett died.

Davy Crockett was born in 1786 in Greene County, Tennessee. As a young boy, he was more interested in herding cattle than attending school, and at one time signed himself up to drive cattle in order to escape punishment for playing hooky. At the age of thirteen, he left his family for two years to work at odd jobs in Virginia. He returned to his family in 1802 and attended school sporadically, but his entire education probably consisted of less than 100 days of study.

By 1813, Crockett was fighting with the Tennessee Volunteer Militia under General Andrew Jackson in the war against the Creek, a war that raged across the entire southern United States. Crockett was at the 1814 Battle of Tallussahatchee and was later part of an attempted walkout of volunteers whose enlistment time had expired. General Jackson stopped the walkout, an incident that was probably the beginning of Crockett's lifelong enmity with Jackson.

Crockett first entered politics in 1818. He was urged to run as a candidate for the elected militia by a man who wanted a "weak" candidate to oppose his son, who was also running. Crockett found out about the scheme, ran against the father instead of the son, and soundly defeated him, earning the rank of colonel. In 1821, at the age of thirty-five, he was elected to the Tennessee state legislature where he soon developed a reputation as an effective campaigner. He traded upon, rather than hid, his backwoods roots. Defiantly, he wore the coonskin cap that became the trademark of the fictional Davy Crockett in the twentieth century. In the state House of Representatives, he favored homesteaders, insisting they should buy the land they had settled at a reduced price, rather than letting the state profit from the sale of that land. In 1825, he was defeated in his first bid for the U.S. Congress and moved his family westward, making a living by killing bears—105 in six months.

During his entire lifetime, Crockett lived in or near poverty, and was never successful as a businessman. Many of his failures seem accidents rather than failures caused by lack of business sense. For instance, one business was destroyed by a powder explosion; on another occasion, he lost all the barrel staves he was marketing when the ship carrying them sank in the Mississippi

River. Crockett himself was trapped below deck and rescued only minutes before the ship went down. That was only one of several narrow escapes he had. In another, he nearly died of malaria. And once he came close to death crossing a flooded river in the dead of winter to get gunpowder for hunting.

Crockett ran successfully for Congress in 1827, and showed the sense of humor he had earlier used against eastern legislators who had called him "a gentleman from the cane" (canebrakes—the underbrush of the backwoods). This time, when guinea hens interrupted his opponent with their peculiar cry, Crockett claimed they were calling, "Crockett! Crockett!!" Once in Congress, Crockett found himself the only one in the Tennessee delegation who opposed President Andrew Jackson, a fellow-Tennessean, over the land bill. By 1834, Crockett's opposition to Jackson was so intense that he made an "anti-Jackson" speaking tour of the eastern states and began to think about running for the presidency. He was defeated for Congress, however, by a Jackson supporter.

Wearing his coonskin cap, Crockett took off for Texas, where he planned to become a political leader in the new government. Instead, he died at the Alamo, joining other Texans who defied Sam Houston's orders to abandon the mission and retreat. A famous story about the Alamo has William Barrett Travis drawing a line in the dirt and urging all those who would fight to the death to step across the line and join him. Crockett presumably did so, and fiction portrays him going to his death still swinging his muzzle-loading rifle. However, the recently publicized diary of a Mexican general claims that Crockett was captured and later executed.

Whatever the truth about Davy Crockett's death, he went down in history as a hero. When Disney Studios made a movie of his life, starring Fess Parker, millions of children begged for coonskin caps and sang, "The Ballad of Davy Crockett." The video is still available and it's a good story, but it shouldn't be taken as the real life of Davy Crockett.

Sir John Franklin

Explorer of the Arctic Region
1786–1847

British explorer Sir John Franklin became much better known after his death than he was in life. In the late 1840s Franklin disappeared in the Arctic, along with two ships and about 129 officers and men. His disappearance was one of the great mysteries of the nineteenth century. In the 1990s, it still aroused curiosity and sparked investigations.

Born in a small village in eastern England in 1786, Franklin apparently always knew he wanted to go to sea. When he was quite young, his father sent him on a merchant ship, hoping to discourage him. It didn't work, and Franklin signed on as a midshipman at the age of fourteen. In the years that followed, he had several harrowing shipboard experiences, both in battle and in such maritime disasters as being stranded on a coral reef.

Franklin sailed to the Arctic in 1818, his first experience in command. Even this expedition nearly met disaster when a distant musket shot caused a huge chunk of ice to break loose from an ice cliff. The ice fell into the water, creating a huge wave that threatened both ships. Storms and crashing ice floes badly damaged the ships, which had to be repaired at Spitsbergen before Franklin could lead his expedition back to England.

After exploring the northern coast of Canada from 1819 to 1822, his next Arctic exploration was on land, from 1825 to 1827. This time, Franklin and several members of his party nearly died of starvation; they ate lichens, decayed deerskins, and even their own shoes. They traveled from the Mackenzie River to northeastern Alaska. In spite of the disastrous aspects of his expedition, Franklin was given a title. He became Sir John Franklin on his return to England in 1829 and was appointed governor of a British penal colony in what is now Tasmania from 1836 to 1843.

He continued to explore, however, and surveyed much of the northern coast of North America, from Prudhoe Bay to the Simpson Straits. In 1845, the British planned an expedition to follow up on the twenty-year-old expedition of Captain William Edward Parry, which had traveled farther west by water in the inland Arctic than anyone before or since. The new expedition would continue the search for passage to the Pacific. Although he was then nearing sixty and not as active as he had been as a young man, Franklin was chosen to lead the expedition. He left England in May 1845 in command of two ships: the *Erebus* and the *Terror*. The ships were packed with supplies such as pickled potatoes, pemmican, and that new invention— canned meat. Franklin's party reached Lancaster Sound in August and was never seen again by Europeans.

More than a dozen expeditions, official and unofficial, British and American, searched unsuccessfully for the ships and their crew. They found only the site of Franklin's first winter camp, which was marked by three graves and a pile of empty meat cans. In 1854, a surveyor for Hudson's Bay Company came upon an Inuit hunter who had an unusual cap. It had a gold cloth band and looked like a naval officer's cap. The hunter, In-nook-poo-zhe-jook, reported that a large party of white men had died of starvation "a long distance west . . . beyond a large river."

In-nook-poo-zhe-jook said that several Inuit families, hunting seals near King William's Island, saw forty white men dragging a boat and sled over the ice. In sign language, the men told the Inuit that their ships had been crushed by ice and they were going to a place where they might find deer to shoot for food. Sometime later, according to the hunter, thirty corpses and some graves were discovered. It appeared that the last to die had turned to cannibalism in a desperate effort to survive. To corroborate his story, the hunter gave the surveyor numerous artifacts from Franklin's ships, including one of the captain's medals.

When the story reached England, there was an uproar. Newspapers headlined the cannibalism, and Franklin's widow, Lady Jane Franklin, was outraged enough to send a private expedition to question the Inuit. The leader of this expedition, Captain Leopold McClintock, learned that Franklin had died much earlier, on June 11, 1847, and nine officers and fifteen crew members had died before him. This news raised several questions: why—proportionately—did more officers than crew die? How did 105 survivors become reduced to the 40 men reported by the Inuit—where were the others? Why were the 40 men headed to Hudson's Bay by way of a river that presented impossible obstacles in waterfalls and rapids? To pull a boat and sled along that route would be impossible for healthy, vigorous men, let alone a crew almost certainly weakened by scurvy and perhaps also by lead poisoning. (The tins that held the canned meat had been improperly soldered.) In spite of these questions, it seemed the mystery was solved.

But other explorers over the years uncovered evidence that raised more questions. A newspaperman named Hall, intrigued that similar exploring parties had survived when Franklin's did not, learned that several survivors from the party had wintered with the Inuit Indians and then headed south—never to be heard from again.

Until recently it was generally accepted that the party abandoned its ships and headed for Fish River—that impossible river route to Hudson's Bay—and that many men died along the way. Then in 1989, David C. Woodman published *Unraveling the Franklin Mystery: Inuit Testimony*. Woodman had studied the stories told by the Inuit and realized that the witnesses were almost all blood relations who told and retold the stories among themselves. In general, he concluded that the witness accounts were accurate.

Interviewing descendants of the witnesses, Woodman learned that Franklin had invited some Inuit aboard the ships. The Inuit had seen one ship sink, with great loss of life, and they presumed the surviving crew of both ships came ashore at that point. When they found the second ship abandoned, the Inuit went onboard and discovered many corpses. They left the bodies undisturbed but took knives, utensils, wood, and gun barrels. Woodman argued that the ships were abandoned and then reclaimed more than once and that the party had remained on King William Island until 1850, possibly 1851. This conclusion gave credibility to In-nook-poo-zhe-jook's story of sighting forty men in 1850.

Searching King William's Island himself, Woodman found the previously known sites, cairns (graves covered with stones), and artifacts. Finally he was able to trace every move of the expedition and to demonstrate that only six or seven men, rather than forty, reached "Starvation Cove" on the island. He also found definite evidence that some survivors lived as guests of the Inuit for a time. His second book, *Strangers Among Us*, hypothesizes the history of the survivors.

We will never have a final answer to the Franklin mystery. No papers from the expedition survive, probably because the Inuit regarded paper as useless and did not preserve any records they found. Nevertheless, more than 150 years later, investigators still hope to find a box of documents hidden under a stone cairn. Searches are still being made using the latest technology, such as ground-penetrating radar. The permafrost, investigators argue, preserves things almost perfectly—one crew member was so well preserved that he looked as if he could be alive. Tests revealed that this man did indeed suffer from lead poisoning, but no one knows if that—or scurvy or starvation—killed him and the others. The English, of course, have a ballad about it:

> In Baffin's Bay where the whale-fish blow
> The fate of Franklin no man can know
> The fate of Franklin no tongue can tell
> Lord Franklin with his seamen does dwell.

Hamilton Hume

Settler and Explorer of Southern Australia
1797–1873

Hamilton Hume was an early settler and explorer of southern Australia. His father was given land south of Sydney for his work in convict supervision, and Hamilton grew up there. Born Andrew Hamilton Hume near Sydney in 1797, he was educated at home and by his late teens he had a good knowledge of the Australian bush. He first explored the region between Sydney and Canberra and then accompanied a surveyor on an expedition that discovered the Yass Plains. Hume continued to join exploring parties and was given several land grants for his work.

In 1824, Governor Thomas Brisbane asked Hume and William Hovell, a British sea captain, to go from Lake George (near present-day Canberra) to the Spencer Gulf in south Australia. Hovell did not have Hume's bush knowledge but he was a capable navigator, and the two men's skills complemented each other. They paid most of the expenses of their trip themselves, with some equipment provided by the government.

Hovell and Hume set out from Lake George in October 1824 with six servants and sixteen weeks' supplies on a couple of ox-drawn carts. They had three horses, an extra ox, and a pack of dogs, which proved useful in hunting kangaroos.

After they crossed the flooded Murrimbidgee River, they were in country so mountainous that they left the carts behind and loaded their supplies onto the oxen. By mid-November they reached a river now named the Murray and crossed it in a boat they built out of poles and a tarpaulin. They used ropes to pull the horses and oxen across the high river. Heading south-west, they came to the Ovens and Goulburn Rivers (the latter is now known as the Hume River). In Australia the December weather is warm, and the two adventurers were plagued by flies, mosquitoes, ticks, and leeches.

They skirted Mount Disappointment and Mount Macedon and crossed the Werribee River by mid-December, camping at the site of what is now the city of Geelong. Unfriendly aborigines soon convinced them to begin their homeward journey. Their return was easier than the trip out because the rivers that had been flooded with spring thaws were now little more than puddles in the heat of the Australian summer. At a place near Lake George where the ground was rough with sharp stones, they were forced to abandon the oxen.

Hume and Hovell miscalculated their position by about 40 miles (64 km). They had reached Port Phillip, not Westernport. In the late 1820s, Hume was still reporting on his expedition to Westernport, but later he claimed he knew all along that he had actually been at Port Phillip. In 1831, William Bland edited the journals both men kept on the expedition and published them. Bland blamed the error on hurried observation and damaged instruments.

Hamilton Hume went on one more expedition, accompanying Charles Sturt in 1828 when he discovered the River Darling. He did no exploring after that because of ill health but he lived on his land grants in the Yass Plains for almost fifty more years, dying in 1873.

Because Hume's journey with Hovell proved that South Australia had much open land suitable for farming and grazing, it opened vast new terri-tories for settlement. Sir Thomas Brisbane was well pleased with the results of the expedition he had requested and spoke of the "new and valuable country" that was Hume's contribution to Australian history.

Charles Wilkes

Explorer who Confirmed the Existence of an Antarctic Continent 1798–1877

As part of the United States Exploring Expedition of 1839–1842, Charles Wilkes was the first to sight land as he sailed along the ice pack south of Australia and thereby confirmed the existence of an Antarctic continent. The Wilkes expedition brought back valuable geological, botanical, zoological, and anthropological information which provided a base for modern scientific investigations of the Antarctic and southern Pacific areas. Although his discovery laid the groundwork for future explorations into Antarctica, Wilkes's naval career was fraught with controversy—and two courts-martial.

In the early 1800s, America's sealing and whaling ships were a source of wealth because there was a great demand for furs, whalebone, oil for lamps, and ambergris—a substance secreted by the intestine of the sperm whale that was used in perfume. But the hunting grounds off Chile and Peru were soon exhausted, and sailors were forced to move south, toward Antarctica, in search of whales. Whaling ships soon found themselves trapped and wrecked by weather, uncharted islands, and submerged reefs. Shipowners and captains petitioned the government to explore and map the area, in the hope of finding better hunting grounds.

In May 1836, Congress authorized a surveying expedition to the Pacific Ocean and South Seas that included exploration of the oceans south of Australia. The expedition was primarily designed to help business and navigation, but it was also supposed to increase scientific knowledge.

Charles Wilkes was the fifth man approached to head the expedition. Others declined for several reasons, including doubt about the appropriateness of the expedition. Wilkes had little sea experience but he was a determined man with strong national pride. Unfortunately, he also proved to be such a strict disciplinarian that his crew disliked him intensely. Wilkes sailed in August 1838 with four ships—the *Peacock, Porpoise, Vincennes, Relief*—and two pilot boats, the *Sea Gull* and the *Flying Fish*. He took 82 officers, 9 naturalists and scientists, and 342 sailors. Only 223 of the sailors returned from the expedition—some were fired as unsuitable, a few deserted, and 15 died of disease, drowning, or injury.

Near Tierra del Fuego, Wilkes split the expedition into three teams. At this point, the routes of the various vessels are confusing and hard to follow, but they all ran into dangerous weather conditions such as blinding fog, fierce storms, and ice floes. The ships would be separated only to meet again and then lose one another. One—the *Sea Gull*—apparently went down with all hands somewhere along the Chilean coast.

During the Antarctic winter, the expedition studied the waters and coastlines of the Paumoto islands, Tahiti, Samoa, the Marshalls, and Hawaii, collecting botanical and geological specimens. They sailed south again from Australia in December 1839. Wilkes, on the *Vincennes*, sailed into what he called "the icy barrier." Having sailed as far south as possible, he turned the ship west to seek a passage through the ice pack. Sighting land, he sketched what seemed to be a range of mountains; he named one peak Ringgold's Knoll, after the captain of the *Porpoise*. Within days, an officer on the *Peacock* captured an emperor penguin and found that the bird had pebbles in its stomach—further evidence of the existence of land. On February 12, Wilkes again sighted land, and on February 21, the *Vincennes* once again faced a seemingly endless wall of ice. Wilkes named it Termination Land. Later it was renamed Shackleton Ice Shelf and found to extend 180 miles (290 km) from the shoreline.

Having logged several sightings of land and a list of mountains and headlands, Wilkes sailed for Australia. He dated the discovery of the Antarctic continent as January 19, 1840.

Over the next two years, Wilkes surveyed the North American coast, then sailed to the Philippines and around the Cape of Good Hope. By the time he returned to the United States, he found that an English explorer, Sir James Clark Ross, claimed an earlier sighting of Antarctic land and a French explorer, Dumont d'Urville, claimed a sighting on the same day as Wilkes. It is possible that these men might have experienced a phenomenon known as "looming," or polar refraction, in which a mirage projects a perfect image, relayed by the upper atmosphere. An observer is convinced that what is sighted is closer than it is in reality. Unfortunately, Wilkes tried to change the date of his discovery, which aroused suspicion.

On his return to the United States, Wilkes also found that officers under his command had brought charges against him. Angry, Wilkes turned his efforts to writing a five-volume narrative of his voyage. His Antarctic accomplishments were not recognized until many years later.

Jim Beckwourth

Mountain Man and Trapper
c. 1798–1866

I f Jim Bridger is an example of a mountain man being misunderstood, Jim Beckwourth's story—or what is believed to be his story—illustrates the difficulty of knowing the truth in a time when people's lives were undocumented. Beckwourth dictated his memoirs to Thomas D. Bonner, recounting fifty years as a trapper and comrade, a partner or an employee of almost every mountain man of importance. It is hard, however, to reconcile Beckwourth's account in *Life and Adventures*, published in 1856, with historical fact. Most say he was friendly, outgoing, and eager for fun. But explorer and historian Francis Parkman called him cruel, treacherous, and inhumane. One "authority" placed Beckwourth at the Alamo as a sixteen-year-old valet, even though he never was near the Texas mission and would have been in his early thirties at the time of the battle fought there. The most foolish charge ever leveled against Beckwourth though was the accusation that he brought smallpox to the Indians, a deed for which no single Anglo (white American) is responsible.

Beckwourth wrote that he was born in Fredericksburg, Virginia, in 1798; most historians agree he was not born before 1800. Without dispute, he was the son of Sir Jennings Beckwith, a Virginia planter. Many thought that Beckwourth's mother was a slave or a mulatto, a charge he vehemently denied. Yet throughout his life, he was known on the frontier as "the Negro"or "the Mulatto." Details about his young life are equally uncertain, although his family moved to Missouri when he was still quite young. When he was nineteen he was apprenticed to a blacksmith and in a hurry to be shed of such obligations. Beckwourth didn't submit well to authority and he had fallen, inappropriately, in love. With his father's blessing, he left for an eighteen-month adventure in the Louisiana wilderness.

In 1824, he joined General Ashley's expedition—Jim Bridger would have been his companion. We know little about Beckwourth's activities on this trip except that he was introduced to starvation and storms. The trip earned him the title of a gaudy liar because of his tales of countless buffalo—no doubt they were true—his rescue of Ashley from the Green River—also later proven true—and the taking of a Blackfeet fort. There were also tales of his many wives among the Blackfeet.

After the 1828 rendezvous of mountain men and trappers, Beckwourth went to live with the Crow and took a Crow wife—or several—and became known as a warrior chief of the Crow. He was given the warrior name of "The Antelope." During these years he trapped for the American Fur Company, but in 1834, he and the company parted, apparently because of mutual dissatisfaction.

Beckwourth retreated to St. Louis where, on one memorable occasion, he was involved in a massive brawl in a theater. In 1837 he went with the army as a high-ranking officer to the Florida Everglades to fight in the Seminole

Wars. Again there is a striking lack of documentation of his activities, but we know he was caught in a disagreement between volunteers and regular army. When the volunteers pulled out, so did Beckwourth, making his way alone through dangerous, swampy country filled with hostile Indians. He was apparently bored with the war.

Beckwourth next went to the Santa Fe Trail with a small trading party. There he was introduced to thirst and heat and reintroduced to threats from the Indians. From this period, he used to tell many stories, mostly centering around his friendship with the Cheyenne. Too ill to travel for a long time, he regained his health and was once again restless. He went to Taos (now in New Mexico) and married a Hispanic woman. (There is apparently no record of how he separated himself from his earlier wives, and he married several others—Hispanic and Native American—before his death.)

Beckwourth was in California for the Battle of Cahuenga when Californians revolted against Mexico, but he lived mainly in and around New Mexico during the next years. During the Civil War he was in Santa Fe and among those who punished the Indians after Santa Fe Trail trader Charles Bent was murdered by the Pueblo in Taos. By then, he was in his late forties and referred to as "the old mountain man." He carried dispatches from Santa Fe to California for the U.S. Department of War; contemporary journals confirm the accuracy of Beckwourth's account of these adventures. Beckwourth was briefly in the gold fields as a trader and then, footloose again and wandering the Sierra Nevada Range, he discovered the landmarks now known as Beckwourth Peak, Beckwourth Valley, and the Beckwourth Trail. In the early 1850s, he ran a hotel in "his" valley.

Beckwourth left California in 1854, "just ahead of the vigilantes," according to one report. He was suspected of horse thefts in the area, though nothing was proved. Once again, his reputation did him more harm than good. He landed in Kansas City where he was hired to take a wagon train to Denver as trader and agent. Beckwourth was by then about sixty, an old man in those days.

The *Rocky Mountain News* reported that where a "rough, illiterate back-woodsman" had been expected, instead they found a "polished gentleman with a fund of general information." Indeed, among his talents, Beckwourth had a perfect command of the English language, a knowledge of foreign phrases, and familiarity with most Native American dialects. In Colorado, he became an acting Indian agent and undertook a campaign to secure justice for those he represented and to fight atrocities against them. But trouble followed him. In Denver, once again newly married (to a "paleface," supposedly), he was accused of theft from the army and then manslaughter in the death of a man who invaded his home. Both cases went to trial, and Beckwourth was acquitted, but he saw the events as evidence of changing times. In his heyday, the problems would have been solved outside the law.

Beckwourth's last adventure was his participation as guide and interpreter in the U.S. Army action against Black Kettle's band of Cheyenne, now known as the Sand Creek Massacre. It was a strange mission for a man who sought justice for the Native Americans. Cheyenne people of all ages and both sexes were slaughtered in this battle, and Beckwourth testified about the atrocities at a later army inquiry. When the Cheyenne asked why he had turned against them, he said the white men would have hung him if he had not. The Indians, unimpressed, told him to go and live with his white brothers, which probably stung "the old war horse."

In 1866, Beckwourth spent the final months of his life among the Crow. He became ill and died suddenly, and the moment his death was announced, storytellers tried to make the most of that story. Some said he had been trampled in a buffalo stampede, others that the Indians had fed him poisoned dog meat. Reliable accounts say he felt unwell, developed a severe nosebleed, and died quickly. He was buried by the Crow on their land.

Joe Walker

*Mountain Man and Explorer of the Trans-Mississippi Region
from the Rockies to Mexico*
1799–1876

Joe Walker is perhaps the least known of the major mountain men but he was the most skilled at exploration and survival and also the most reliable. Walker spent more than fifty years exploring the trans-Mississippi region from the Rockies to Mexico. He led his own expeditions but was glad to help others, such as famed explorer John Charles Frémont. Walker once found Frémont's party in perilous trouble and guided them away from hostile Indians and across the Rockies. Walker had an inborn sense about the land he was crossing. A fellow trapper said of him, "He could find water quicker than any man I knew."

Walker was thirty-four when he went to California, 6 foot (183 centimeters) tall and over 200 pounds (90 kg). He had long hair and a beard, and wore beautifully beaded shirts made by various Indian women. At rendezvous—the annual get-together that broke the monotony of a mountain man's life—Walker stood out as a colorful and attractive figure.

Walker was born in Tennessee, the son of an explorer who was among the first to settle in the Appalachians. One of his brothers led wagon trains; another died at the Alamo, having followed Davy Crockett there. Joe Walker first went west in 1818; in 1820 he joined an illegal party taking goods into

Spanish territory near Santa Fe. Imprisoned, he won release for himself and the others by offering to help the Spanish fight the Pawnee. Later he helped map what became the Santa Fe Trail. Then he went to Missouri where he was elected sheriff of Jackson County, a post he held for two terms. Used to roaming, Walker found the work confining. In 1831 he was off to the Cherokee Nation on a horse- and cattle-buying trip. In 1832 he joined a party of 110 led by Benjamin Bonneville and spent two seasons trapping on the Salmon and Snake Rivers. The party fought off Native Americans and hunted for beaver, but the hunting was poor.

By 1833 the mountains were full of trappers—so many that one man could no longer make a good living. California offered new opportunities. At the trappers' annual rendezvous in 1833, Walker called for men to track the land to the west with him. At that time present-day western Utah, northern Arizona, all of Nevada, and eastern California were unexplored and the size and difficulty of the Sierras were not yet known. Expeditions in the region had been tried before without success. For example, Jedediah Smith in 1826 and again in 1827 followed the southern route into the barren desert where he met hostile Indians. Eventually he reached California but his expedition was neither well planned nor well carried out. Peter Ogden of the Hudson's Bay Company tried in 1829. In spite of these earlier failures, however, many men volunteered to go with Walker, partly because of the warm California climate and partly because they respected and trusted Walker. He chose forty men.

Walker planned to head west into the Great Basin from the Great Salt Lake and make a trail into California. Each man in his party was mounted and led three extra horses packed with everything they could possibly need. Walker was known for being more knowledgeable about horses than most mountain men and for using them wisely. Early in the trip Walker sent the men out hunting so they gathered another 60 pounds (27 kg) of dried and preserved meat. Most mountain men ate too much when they had food and starved when they had none but Walker paced out the supply. When they came to the Great Basin, Walker did what Lewis and Clark had done—he asked the Bannock Indians the best route. As a result, he headed due west across northern Nevada—it was hard going but not as bad as the desert.

In western Nevada in early September, they encountered the Diggers, a poor tribe who wanted the white men's goods and stole them when they could. When some of the party killed three Diggers caught stealing, Walker was furious. Soon the forty men were surrounded by hundreds of Indians. Walker had the men quickly build a fortification, and when the Diggers asked to approach as friends, he denied their request. The natives advanced; they were not intimidated by guns, probably because they had no idea what guns could do. Walker had his men demonstrate by target-shooting at a beaver skin but the Diggers persisted. Eventually the mountain men charged their enemies, killing nearly forty of them. The rest fled.

The party now faced the Sierras, already covered in snow so deep the men traveled no more than 8 to 10 miles (12 to 16 km) a day. After three weeks of cold and hunger they reached the crest of the mountains. Yosemite Valley lay below them in all its beauty—but there appeared no way to make the descent. At last they lowered the horses down one at a time by fastening rope slings around them. The baggage followed. Once on the valley floor, the men faced a scene so spectacular that many called it the most memorable moment of their lives in the West.

Suddenly, they were in California, with its warm weather and plentiful game, enough deer and elk for everyone. They were the first white Americans to see the giant redwood trees, and they witnessed their first meteor shower. Late in November they reached the Pacific Ocean south of present-day San Francisco. Instead of rushing in, Walker stopped the party long enough to determine what kind of reception they would receive from the Spanish. Unlike Jedediah Smith, they were warmly welcomed. The party stayed three months and when they left, six men stayed behind. The Mexicans offered Walker land that would have made him wealthy and important in California but he was an explorer and not ready to settle down in one place.

In February 1834 he collected horses, cattle, and dogs (the latter two as food supply) and headed east. At the Sierras he turned south, looking for an easier crossing. The pass he used is now known as Walker Pass and became a major entryway into California. The way home was as difficult as the way out—stock died in the Nevada badlands and the thirsty men drank the blood of the fallen animals. The Diggers, apparently not remembering their previous meeting, harassed them again until the men attacked and killed fourteen of them.

Walker's party returned to rendezvous one year after they left. They brought back some knowledge of the Great Basin and the Sierras, and they could now guide others over that route. Moreover, they'd had a good time in California.

Joe Walker continued to explore the West. He traded horses, driving them eastward from California to sell to the army. He also explored the Colorado River and Zuni villages and he recommended Walker Pass to the California legislature as a railway passage through the Sierras. And he scouted for the army with Kit Carson.

In 1862, Walker agreed to lead a party of gold prospectors into southern Colorado. He was then sixty-four years old and in good health except for failing eyesight. They entered New Mexico through Raton Pass in October. Near Deming, the party became anxious about their water supply, but Walker knew where to find springs. So in spite of their doubts about the now-aging mountain man, the men drank their fill. He warned them about the Apache—and they soon found three white men who had been gruesomely killed by the Indians. But Walker led the men to gold, just as he had led them to water. They found it north of present Wickenburg, Arizona.

The miners declared Walker president of their quickly thrown-up Lynx Creek settlement. He declined. But in 1867 when the settlement ran out of food, Walker, now nearly blind, set off for a trading post. When his companion was jumped by outlaws, Walker drew and fired, driving the outlaws off. That was his last adventure. Soon after, he left to spend the remainder of his life on a nephew's ranch in California. He died at seventy-seven in 1876. His epitaph includes, "Camped at Yosemite, Nov. 13, 1833." Joe Walker's name lives on in Walker Pass, Walker Lake, Walker River, Walker Trail, and the Walker Mining District.

Jedediah Strong Smith

Trapper and Trader in the American West
1800–1832

Trappers and tra-ders were the first to explore the unknown regions of the American West at the start of the nineteenth century. One of the earliest was Jedediah Smith, the first Anglo to reach California by cros-sing the Mojave Desert and the first white American to cross the Sierra Nevada and the Great Salt Lake Desert. Unfortunately, Smith's story is not a tale of great triumph.

In 1823, this native of New York was twenty-three and in St. Louis when he answered William Ashley's advertisement for young men to go west as trappers. Ashley led a group of more than sixty men from St. Louis, headed toward the Yellowstone country to trap beaver. But near the border of present-day North and South Dakota the Arikara Indians attacked them. Twelve men were killed, and the remaining trappers beat a hasty retreat. Reinforcements arrived, but when the trappers went to retaliate, the Arikara slipped away by night, leaving the Missouri Legion—as the group was known—to attack a deserted village. During this battle, however, Ashley took note of Smith's coolness and bravery and appointed the young man a squad leader.

Contemporaries of Smith said he was a devout Christian—unusual for a trapper. He, his Bible, and his rifle were inseparable, and Smith was apparently a more civilized and high-minded man than many of his fellow trappers. Smith worked for Ashley for four seasons; in the 1824–25 season he took 668 beaver pelts, which may be a record for any mountain man. In 1826, he joined two other trappers—Billy Sublette and David Jackson—to buy Ashley out. The other two would work the Central Rockies; Smith would explore the Southwest.

In 1826, Smith headed southwest with a party of seventeen men. They passed the Great Salt Lake and Utah Valley, encountering Ute Indians to whom they gave typical gifts—razors, tobacco, knives, and ribbon. Having gained little geographical knowledge from the Ute, they continued south, wandering through the Wasatch Mountains into what Smith called a "Land of Starvation." It was clearly not land where they would find beaver.

By the time the party reached northwestern Arizona, they had lost so many horses that all were on foot. After crossing the Black Mountains, they stumbled into what seemed a fertile valley. The Mojave people there received them with hospitality, and though Smith knew he would not find beaver, he decided it was best to move ahead rather than turn back. The Mojave told him it was not far to the missions of California. But they neglected to mention that the Mojave Desert lay between Smith and the missions.

For fifteen thirsty and hungry days the party trudged across the salt-crusted desert. They followed the Mojave River, but that water source kept disappearing underground. Exhausted, they arrived in the Los Angeles area in mid-November. The Californios were not sure what to do with Smith and his men. Because they did not know about beaver trapping, they called him a fisherman, but clearly he had entered California illegally. (California was then Spanish territory.) Smith was kept under house arrest by the Spanish governor for several months and released on condition that he leave California by the same route he took to get there. He agreed—but then he took his men north and spent the winter in the San Joaquin Valley.

In May, Smith and his group tried to cross the Sierra Nevada, but snow killed several horses and drove the party back. Smith and two companions tried the crossing a second time, leaving eleven men behind. The party of three once again found themselves in the desert. When one of the men collapsed, Smith pressed on, found water, and brought it back to save the man. The three reached the 1827 rendezvous in early July.

Smith stayed only ten days, however. Then, with a party of eighteen, he returned for the eleven men he had left in California. This time the Mojave were hostile and attacked them, killing ten men and taking two women as prisoners. The remaining small band survived yet another crossing of the Mojave Desert and reached California in August.

Once again, Smith was arrested—not only for entering illegally but also for violating his parole of the previous year. This time he was jailed, but he was finally released on the condition that he leave California and never return. Instead, he picked up his stranded men, and they spent the winter in the Sacramento Valley. The next summer he made his way north to the Columbia River. Once again, Native Americans attacked, wiping out all but four of the party. The four survivors eventually made their way back to the United States.

In three years, Smith had taken thirty-three men on expeditions to California. Twenty-six of them had been killed, and two had deserted.

Smith's next expedition was to Santa Fe. With eighty-three men, he traveled into the Cimarron River country. But the party, overconfident of their mountain-man skills, had not taken enough water. Soon they had to break into smaller groups to look for water. A Comanche hunting party found Smith, alone and weakened, and killed him. He was thirty-two years old.

Jedediah Smith was known for his courage. At an extremely early age, he had a receding hairline as a result of a mauling by a grizzly bear. The bear had torn his scalp from just above one eye well past his hairline. When the Comanche killed him, he had one chance to get off a shot—and he killed the chief of the band that attacked him. Mountain men have been accused of muddling through rather than proceeding according to a plan—and Smith may have done that. But he left a legacy of courage and endurance that few can match.

Jim Bridger

Mountain Man and Explorer of the Rocky Mountains
1804–1881

Jim Bridger—mountain man and explorer of the Rocky Mountains—has not been treated well by history. Fiction and film have portrayed him as a drunken, unsophisticated man. He has been categorized as an "Injun fighter" without any regard for his friendship with and respect for most Plains Indians. His accurate accounts of what is now Yellowstone Park were considered so unbelievable that some men branded him a liar. Jim Bridger, known among mountain men as "Old Gabe," was important in opening the Rocky Mountains to trappers, railroad men, settlers, cowboys, and soldiers. In his day, he was the best guide and interpreter in the Rocky Mountain West.

Born in Virginia in 1804—the very year of the Lewis and Clark expedition—Bridger was raised near and in St. Louis, Missouri. When he was in his early teens, his family died, leaving him the sole guardian of a younger sister. To support his sister and the maiden aunt who cared for her, young Bridger ran a flatboat on the Missouri, then apprenticed himself to a blacksmith. In 1823 at the age of eighteen he headed for the upper Missouri River with an exploration party headed by Colonel William H. Ashley of the Rocky Mountain Fur Company. Bridger and the other "enterprising young men" who had responded to an advertisement were expected to trap animals for their fur and to fight the Blackfoot, Sioux, Shoshone, and Assiniboine. Bridger's colleagues on this trip would become, like him, famous mountain men—Jedediah Smith, the Sublette brothers, and others.

From 1823 until 1839, Bridger was a hunter and trapper—and during these years he earned his reputation as an Indian fighter. The party built a small fort at the mouth of the Yellowstone River and wintered there. Of necessity, Bridger learned from native women how to make his own buckskin clothing and moccasins—he never wore shoes again. By spring, Bridger was a true mountain man.

Bridger stayed with Ashley's party until his contract was up and then organized his own brigade to trap beaver. He sold the plews (pelts) to Ashley's Rocky Mountain Fur Company and in time became one of the owners of the company. He brought in enough beaver plews to pay for his equipment, support his sister, save a little, and buy goods for trade.

Bridger soon found he was a born explorer, able to hold in his mind the details of lands and rivers and to lead his men to beaver. He learned the mountain passes and when they could be crossed, the streams and where they could be forded, the valleys that were free of snow in winter, and the Native American and game trails. Bridger was the first to discover South Pass and open that Indian trail over the Continental Divide to emigrants headed for Oregon and California. He was also the first to discover the Great Salt Lake, even though his comrades told him he had reached the Pacific because he had tasted salt.

Several brigades, similar to the one led by Bridger, brought furs to Ashley and his fur company. To keep in touch with them, Ashley told his brigade leaders he would meet them in July 1825 at Henry's Fork on the Green River. There he would pay them for their work, pick up their furs, and give them supplies for the coming season. Since it was not trapping season, the men could linger, drinking whiskey, pursuing native women, and gambling. The invitation was open to trappers who did not work for Ashley too. Thus began rendezvous—the best-known tradition of American mountain men. After the first year, rendezvous sites changed annually. Bridger attended every rendezvous until the last one in 1839.

Life as a trapper was a constant battle with hostile Indians, and Bridger had too many encounters and close escapes to list here. Fairly early in his hunting days, he got two arrow wounds in his back. He carried one of the arrowheads until the 1835 rendezvous when Dr. Marcus Whitman, the physician-missionary later killed by Indians in Oregon, dug it out of Bridger's back. In another battle, he was shot in the shoulder, leaving his right arm temporarily useless. Another time he rescued his friend Joe Meek, who had been captured and marched several days by the Crow. Bridger tricked a Crow chief into meeting him to talk, then held the chief captive until Meek was released and an even trade was made. Bridger did not dislike the Native Americans and never set out after them deliberately, but he defended himself and his companions when necessary. During his years in the mountains, he was married to at least two native women: one was a Snake and one was a Ute.

Bridger returned to St. Louis in 1839, but he disliked city life after having been so long in the mountains. He returned to rendezvous, held that year on Green River. Most of the men knew this would be the last rendezvous—beaver prices continued to fall now that silk was being used for hats back east instead of beaver, and the supply of beaver was dwindling. Mountain prices were high—a plug of chewing tobacco cost $2, a pint of sugar cost $3. At that time you could buy a good dinner for 50 cents almost anywhere in the civilized states. But Bridger feared having to return to the settlements.

At Fort Laramie, Bridger saw his first emigrant train—and he knew what he would do next. He would build a fort to serve pioneers on the Oregon Trail. As a blacksmith, he could repair wagons and guns, and shoe horses and oxen. And as a skilled ferryman, he could help the settlers cross a river. In fall and winter, when there were no travelers, he would hunt and trap. Fort Bridger was built in 1843 in southwestern Wyoming at the point where the Oregon Trail crossed the Black Fork of the Green River. Bridger settled there with his wife. When his wife died in childbirth, Bridger raised his infant daughter alone.

Bridger, known as the Blanket Chief and trusted by many Native Americans, was a peacemaker. He was an active participant in the treaty of Fort Laramie, where many Plains Indians tribes took part in a half-successful meeting to reach terms of agreement with the U.S. government. But Bridger could not make peace with the Mormons who, under Brigham Young, had settled in the Salt River Basin not too far from Fort Bridger. Many factors caused the feud between Young and Bridger; they were two strong-willed men with differing views of the world and how to conduct oneself in it. The Mormons did not want to share their land with Bridger, nor did he want to share "his paradise" with them. But for their own economic survival, the Mormons also badly needed the ferry business and trade Bridger had established. Brigham Young used politics, force, and every power he could think of to drive Bridger out. Eventually the "Saints" stole all Bridger's goods, burned most of his fort, and nearly killed him.

With trapping no longer profitable and his fort closed—and later leased to the U. S. Army—Bridger became a guide, working primarily for the army. In 1857, he guided an army expedition against the Mormons who were suspected of plotting against the U.S. government. He led the U.S. Army Corps of Engineers on an exploration of the Yellowstone River—which may have been an exploration for them but was a revisiting of familiar territory for Bridger. After the Civil War, he was a scout and guide during the Indian Wars for many army expeditions, including one that involved him in the Battle of Fort Phil Kearny. He was also a close spectator of the Fetterman Massacre, where an entire U.S. Army command was trapped and killed.

In 1868, Bridger returned to Missouri. But he made one last trip west to warn General Phil Sheridan against the folly of an expedition he was about to undertake. Sheridan did not believe him, and Bridger returned to Missouri in disgust. In the last years of his active life, many young army officers questioned his judgment and considered him a quaint old figure rather than respecting him for his knowledge and experience. That attitude among what he called "paper-collar soldiers" angered Bridger.

The famed explorer and scout lived out the last years of his life with his daughter, Virginia, outside Kansas City. In failing health and almost blind, he had a gentle horse to ride about the farm and a faithful dog to guide him. Still, he was lonely and missed the companionship of his old mountain men friends.

Jim Bridger died on July 17, 1881, at the age of seventy-seven. The epitaph on his memorial monument reads, "Celebrated as a hunter, trapper, fur trader, and guide. Discovered Great Salt Lake 1824, the South Pass 1827. Visited Yellowstone Lake and Geysers 1830. Founded Fort Bridger 1843. Opened Overland Route by Bridger's Pass to Great Salt Lake. Was a guide for U.S. exploring expeditions, Albert Sidney Johnston's army in 1857, and G.M. Dodge in U.P. (Union Pacific) surveys and Indian campaigns 1865–66."

Christopher "Kit" Carson

Mountain Man and Trapper
1809–1868

Kit Carson is probably America's best-known mountain man and trapper. A legend in his own time, this trapper, scout, Indian guide, and soldier lives on in our history as typical of that mythical breed—the mountain men.

Carson was born in Kentucky on Christmas Eve 1809 and spent his childhood with his family at Boone's Lick, Missouri. The early death of his father meant that young Carson had to work to support his family and did not get an education. By the time he was in his mid-teens, he had shortened his name to Kit and was apprenticed to a saddle-maker. In 1826, he left home—and the saddle-maker—to join a wagon train headed for Santa Fe, New Mexico. The Santa Fe-Taos area would be his home base for the rest of his life.

Because he showed a strong talent for languages, Carson became a translator on a wagon train going to Chihuahua, Mexico. Then he turned to trapping and for several years went on fur-trapping expeditions throughout the West—north to the Rocky Mountains and as far west as California. From 1832 to 1840 he hunted for William Bent, who ran Bent's Fort outside present-day Denver.

Carson was right at home in the world of the Native American tribes. He traveled among several tribes and lived with them from time to time. His first two wives were from the Arapaho and Cheyenne people. In the rough and wild world of mountain men, where liquor, fighting, womanizing, and thievery were often the general rule, Carson was known for great courage, a moderate lifestyle, and restraint. Men knew that when he gave his word, it was good. In 1843, Carson bought a large adobe home in Taos as a wedding present for Maria Josefa Jaramillo, presumably his third wife. The two considered that house to be their home until their deaths in 1868.

On an 1842 visit to his family in Missouri, Carson met explorer John Charles Frémont, who hired him as a guide. For the next several years, Carson guided the famous explorer to Oregon and California and through much of the central Rocky Mountains. Frémont's explorations were soon nationally talked about because of the reports written by the explorer and his wife and submitted to the U.S. Congress. These reports, which often read like vivid fiction, mentioned Carson prominently, and the mountain man soon found himself a national hero. In dime novels of the day, he was presented as the stereotypical mountain man, capable of fighting off wild bears, defeating bloodthirsty Indians, surviving the challenges of the wilderness, and never, of course, getting lost on the frontier.

Just before the Mexican War (1846–1848), Frémont led the short-lived Bear Flag Rebellion, in which he tried prematurely to claim California for the United States. Carson was with him on that adventure. Soon after, Carson led the U.S. General Stephen Kearny and his troops from New

Mexico into California to put down a challenge to the American occupation of Los Angeles.

Carson returned to New Mexico and took up sheep-ranching, making a handsome profit by driving flocks to California. In 1853, he was appointed Indian agent for northern New Mexico, representing several tribes but not the Navajo. Today, his methods would not be considered politically correct or even legal. Because the Navajo refused to settle on the reservation set up for them, Carson launched an economic war against them, riding through their territory destroying crops, orchards, and livestock. Seeing the tribe weakened, the traditional enemies of the Navajo—the Ute, Pueblo, Hopi and Zuni—also took advantage of them.

In 1862, during the Civil War, Carson helped organize the New Mexico volunteer infantry, which saw action at Valverde. But his main efforts continued to be directed against the Navajo. In 1864, the Navajo surrendered to Carson, who forced nearly 8,000 men, women, and children to march 300 miles (483 km) from Arizona to Fort Sumner, New Mexico. There they were held in unsanitary and unhealthy conditions for three years. That march has come to be known as "The Long Walk."

Carson went to Colorado to expand his ranching empire but died there in 1868. His remains were returned to a small cemetery near his home in Taos. Today his house is a historic museum, open to the public for a fee, with exhibits tracing his life and story as well as the history of New Mexico during his lifetime.

John Charles Frémont

Surveyor and Builder for the Railroads
1813–1890

John Charles Frémont, sometimes called the Pathfinder, was an explorer for the U.S. Army Corps of Topographical Engineers, a surveyor for the railroads, and the builder of railroads. He was also a mine owner, the first Republican candidate for U.S. President, a Civil War general in the Union army, and a territorial governor. His early expeditions to the American West earned him fame and fortune, but he was eventually court-martialed for failure to obey orders. His other ventures—from presidential candidate to territorial governor—ended in failure, and he died penniless.

Frémont was the illegitimate son of a well-born Virginia woman who, though married to a man named Pryor, ran off with a French refugee named Fremon. The stigma of his birth haunted Frémont all his life and may be why he added the "t" and the accent over the "e" in his name. Frémont spent his youth mostly in Charleston, South Carolina, where he was a distinguished student at Charleston College. He was befriended by Joel Poinsett of that city, and when Poinsett became secretary of war in 1837, he got Frémont a commission as second lieutenant in the Army Corps of Topographical Engineers. On Frémont's first expedition—to the upper Missouri and Mississippi Rivers—he worked under Joseph Nicollet, one of America's best cartographers, or mapmakers, at the time. In 1839, Poinsett and Frémont established headquarters in Washington, D.C.

There the handsome young army officer met Jessie Benton, the daughter of Senator Thomas Hart Benton of Missouri. Jessie served as her father's assistant, secretary, and hostess because her mother was an invalid. Benton was an enthusiastic spokesman for "manifest destiny," the idea that America's land should stretch from the east coast to the west coast. He liked Frémont because the young man agreed with his views and was, Benton thought, the ideal person to carry out his expansionist dreams by charting the way west. However, Benton did not like Frémont's interest in his daughter. He thought Jessie was too young to marry and that Frémont would not provide the life her father had in mind for her. He made the young couple promise to wait a year before they considered marriage. Instead, they eloped. Benton, furious, disowned his daughter. After some months, however, he relented and the couple moved into the Benton home.

Benton helped push through Congress a $30,000 appropriation for a survey of the Oregon Trail. Because Nicolett was ill, Benton saw to it that Frémont, then only twenty-nine years old, headed the expedition. Frémont was to proceed on the Missouri River to the central Rockies, record the topography of South Pass—considered the gateway to Oregon—and then return home. Unofficially, Frémont was to make travel to the west look so good that Americans would settle there in great numbers.

Frémont departed in mid-June 1842 and returned in mid-October. His party included mountain man Kit Carson, and the two soon became fast friends. Also in the party was Charles Preuss, a mapmaker whose journal revealed that he saw Frémont as unscientific and self-centered. Frémont pushed his men unnecessarily to climb a difficult but unimportant mountain and then insisted on shooting rapids in the Platte River. As a result, their inflatable boat collapsed and valuable scientific records were lost or ruined.

A few days after Frémont returned to Jessie, she gave birth to their first child, a daughter named Lily. Frémont settled down to write his account of the expedition but found himself disabled by nosebleeds. He told the story of the expedition to Jessie, who wrote it in dramatic phrases and sentences. When it was presented to Congress in 1843, legislators ordered the printing and distribution of 10,000 copies.

Frémont was already planning his second expedition, which would go all the way into Oregon. In May 1844 he was in St. Louis, assembling his equipment which, strangely, included a small howitzer cannon. When officials got word of the cannon, they ordered Frémont to return to Washington and explain why he needed a cannon on a peaceful mission. Since Frémont had already left, Jessie intercepted the message. Instead of sending it on to him by messenger, she sent her own message which said, "Only trust me and GO." Frémont was soon beyond the recall of Washington.

The cannon was a difficulty for the men who had to drag it across more than 3,000 miles (4,800 km) of prairie, desert, and mountain. Frémont justified it as protection against hostile Indians but some people suggested he simply liked the idea of having a cannon in his equipment. The party arrived in Fort Vancouver on the Columbia River on November 8. Instead of returning for home, as his orders said, Frémont decided to take the party to California.

It was a bad decision. In the Sierra mountain range, the party was often lost, always cold, and so hungry that they had to eat some of their horses. Eventually they got out of the mountains and arrived at the fort established by pioneer trader John Sutter on the Sacramento River. After resting there, they headed east. The way home was long, beset with attacks by hostile Indians, and saved by legendary mountain man Joe Walker. Frémont returned to Washington in August 1845. Once again, Jessie wrote his report, and it was an even greater success than the first, although it contained errors of fact that any mountain man could have corrected.

On his third expedition, Frémont planned to enter California through the high passes in the Sierras. He led his men to California without great incident but when he got there, the Mexican authorities were less than welcoming. They had recently seen Texas taken by settlers and joined to the United States and they did not want the same thing to happen to California. The Mexican government ordered Frémont out of California. Instead, he withdrew to a peak in the Galiban Mountains and raised the U.S. flag, challenging the Mexicans to dislodge him. As they prepared to attack him, Frémont slipped away under cover of darkness. He rested a month in Oregon and then returned to California. At this point, war had been declared between Mexico and the United States. When Frémont and his band of sixty armed men returned to California—under directions, he thought, from the American consul in California—the Mexicans thought it was an invasion. By then, the Bear Flag revolt by American settlers in northern California had begun. Frémont organized the rebels into the California Battalion that, without fighting, raised the American flag in Sonora. Marching southward, the battalion met the Army of the West commanded by General Stephen Kearny who was ordered to conquer California. No one was sure whether the army or the navy had control, but the naval commander, Commodore Robert Stockton, appointed Frémont civil governor of California. General Kearny ordered Frémont to disband the battalion and when he refused, had him arrested. He was returned to Washington in chains and court-martialed on charges of mutiny, insubordination, and conduct prejudicial to good order and discipline. Found guilty and facing a dishonorable discharge, Frémont resigned from the army.

In 1848, Benton arranged for Frémont to command a private expedition to scout a route for a transcontinental railroad. Once again Frémont pushed on when wiser heads counseled against it. The party was stranded by snow in the high mountain passes. Ten men died, and others survived by eating their shoes, gun cases, pack straps—and, possibly, the dead. Others disappeared, presumably lost to Native Americans. Frémont made it to Taos, New Mexico, where he recuperated and then rode off to California. There he purchased land in the Sierras where gold was discovered almost the next day. Suddenly, Frémont was rich.

In December 1850, Frémont was elected by the territorial legislature to represent California in the U.S. Senate when the territory became a state. That happened in late summer 1850, but Frémont served only briefly. Another election was held and he lost his seat because he voiced his opposition to slavery. Jessie and the children joined him in California for several peaceful years, Frémont working as a miner and being more of a family man than at any other time in his life.

In 1856, the new Republican Party drafted him as a presidential candidate, but he was defeated by James Buchanan. Next came the Civil War (1861–1865), where he was so bold as to declare emancipation of all slaves in Missouri before President Abraham Lincoln could declare national emancipation. Lincoln stripped him of command, even though Jessie personally went to the president to plead for her husband. Lincoln dismissed her curtly, accusing her of meddling in men's business.

Frémont's California property lost its value, and he was soon out of money again. Toward the end of his life, Jessie supported the family by writing articles and books. Though they lived in California, Frémont died broke in New York in 1890.

Dr. David Livingstone

Explorer and Missionary in Africa
1813–1873

Most people who remember Dr. David Livingstone today know only the famous line uttered by Henry Morton Stanley when he found Livingstone in the jungles of Africa: "Dr. Livingstone, I presume." But there are much more important reasons to remember this nineteenth-century explorer and missionary. He opened Africa to civilization and Christianity; he discovered many famous lakes as well as the Zambezi River and other rivers; he was the first white man to see—and name—Victoria Falls in Africa; he was probably the first to travel the entire length of Africa's Lake Tanganyika; and he traveled 29,000 miles (46,600 km) in Africa. Livingstone devoted his life to helping the people of Africa and converting them to Christianity.

He was born in Blantyre, Scotland, in March 1813, the son of poor but devoutly religious parents. At the age of ten he went to work in the local cotton-weaving mill and attended classes at night, often studying until mid-night, even though he had to be at work at 6 a.m. In 1836 he entered Anderson's College, Glasgow, and four years later he earned a medical degree from the Glasgow University. He studied Greek, theology, and medicine. At the age of twenty, he became extremely devoted to Christianity.

The path of Livingstone's life was determined when in 1838 he was accepted as a candidate by the London Missionary Society. In 1839 he met missionary Robert Moffat, home from Africa on leave. Moffat preached about the missionary needs in Africa, and Livingstone was convinced it was God's will that he go to that land. In 1841 he arrived at Kuruman, the missionary outpost in southern Africa run by Moffat. Kuruman was 700 miles (1,126 km) north of Cape Town, the point where Livingstone landed, but he showed an unusual ability to withstand the hardships of the ten-week trip north. He soon also showed a great understanding of—and sympathy for— the African people, who were won over by his medical abilities. At Kuruman, Livingstone preached, cared for the sick, and built a chapel, even while making several trips into the interior of Africa. Finally he was authorized to establish a settlement at Mabotsa, where crowds of sick people waited for him to heal them. He listened to their complaints and told them of Jesus Christ.

Mabotsa was in an area endangered by lions. Livingstone believed that if you killed one lion, the others would leave. Accordingly, he took some helpers and set out on a hunt. He shot a lion and wounded it. The animal then sprang at him, tossing him as a cat tosses a mouse. Livingston's left arm was crushed and was useless and painful to him ever after. Two other people were wounded in the attack. Livingstone went back to Kuruman to recover and there fell in love with Moffat's daughter, Mary. They were married in March 1845.

After the marriage, the Livingstones moved to several locations in Africa, always seeking the perfect place for a mission. On one trip to seek a new location, he became the first white man to see Lake Ngami. Livingstone soon realized the difficulty of finding a suitable place for his family, which now included four children. One of their settlements was destroyed by Boers, the white descendants of Dutch settlers who populated much of South Africa and resented Livingstone's efforts to help the natives. Other locations were ruled out by drought and famine. Livingstone came to realize that where living conditions were healthy, the natives were hostile. And where the natives were friendly, living conditions were hostile. When his infant daughter sickened and died, he decided reluctantly to send his family back to England. In 1852 he journeyed with them to Cape Town—the first time he had been to civilization in eleven years—and bid them a painful goodbye.

Livingstone was determined, however, to find a way to the sea that would open the interior of Africa to successful commercial trade and undercut the slave trade, which he detested. The 1840s and 1850s were the years when thousands of Africans were kidnapped and taken to America as slaves. Among the traders Livingstone fought were the Arabs and the Portuguese. On his 1850s journey into the interior—called the Zambezi expedition— Livingstone did find a way to the Atlantic Ocean. Once he arrived at the port of Luanda, he was offered safe passage to England but refused because he would not abandon the Africans who had come with him. He had to return them to their home district. During this difficult journey, Livingstone was nearly blinded by a branch in a dense forest and nearly deaf because of rheumatic fever. He considered going to England but was too ill to make the journey. Instead, he sent his maps and journals. Sadly, the boat on which he sent them sank, and those important documents were lost forever, although Livingstone tried his best to re-create them.

In 1855, with 100 Makololo tribesmen, he set out to follow the Zambezi River and within only 50 miles (80 km) came to the most magnificent waterfall any man had ever seen. Livingstone named it Victoria Falls in honor of the queen of England. Being sure the tribesmen were in good hands, Livingstone departed by boat for England. But he had received a letter of dismissal from the missionary society, who felt that his efforts were directed more toward exploration than conversion. In spite of this rebuff, other honors came his way. In England, where Livingstone was now famous, he was asked to give lectures and write, and given honorary degrees from the universities of Cambridge, Oxford, and Glasgow. The Royal Geographical Society awarded him their highest honor, a gold medal, because he had crossed the entire African continent from east to west, something no man had done before.

The second phase of Livingstone's career began in 1858 when he traveled into the Zambezi region for the British government, with a salary and excellent equipment—a first for him. His wife and youngest son went with him, but soon after their arrival in Africa, Mary Livingstone became ill and went to Kuruman to live with her family. She died of malaria in April 1862, after giving birth to a baby girl. Mary Livingstone was buried in Africa.

Livingstone, meanwhile, had been actively exploring Africa. He had taken his younger brother, Charles, with him, but Charles proved a difficult companion on an expedition. And apparently Livingstone could manage native helpers much better than he could deal with white explorers. Still, he reached the Makololo tribesmen and explored several regions—Lake Nyasa, the Shire River, Lake Shirwa, and the Rovuma River. Slave trading was still an enormous problem, and he felt the Portugese government used his name to trick natives and capture them for slavery. Then in 1863 the British government recalled him, saying his expedition was too costly. Added to his grief was the death of his son, Robert, who fought with Union soldiers in the American Civil War to abolish slavery. Robert died at the Battle of Gettysburg. David Livingstone returned to England on what would be his last trip there.

The Royal Geographical Society sponsored his last expedition to Africa. This time he was to find the sources of the Zambezi, Congo, and Nile Rivers. The trip was full of difficulties, and, ultimately, he was cared for by people he hated—the slave traders. He discovered the southern end of Lake Tanganyika as well as Lake Moreo and Bangweolo. At last he reached Ujiji, headquarters of the slave and ivory trades. But he was too ill to continue. He suffered from dysentery, loss of blood, fever, and malnourishment.

Rumors of Livingstone's disappearance or death had reached the civilized world, and the *New York Herald* sent Henry Morton Stanley, then an English reporter, to find the great explorer. When Stanley saw Livingstone approaching him, he uttered the famous words, "Dr. Livingstone, I presume?" Stanley obtained food and mail for Livingstone—previous shipments had apparently been stolen by Arab traders—and stayed with him for the winter. He nursed Livingstone and failed to convince him to return to Britain. Later, Stanley said, "I was converted by him, although he tried not to do it."

With trusted comrades, Livingstone set out on another expedition, this time to Lakes Tanganyika and Bangweolo. But he soon became too weak to travel and was carried on a stretcher by native porters. However, he kept traveling and mapping until within a day of his death. David Livingstone was carried into the village of Chitambo on a litter and died there in an attitude of prayer. His last written words were, "All I can say in my solitude is, may Heaven's rich blessing come down on every one American, English, Turk who will help heal this open sore of the world." Africa was the open sore.

Native Africans gave him the longest funeral procession in their history, having buried his heart under a tree near the place where he died. His African friends carried his preserved body from Chitambo to the coast—a nine-month journey—for shipment to England, where its identity was questioned until his withered left arm was examined. Dr. David Livingstone was buried in Westminster Abbey with kings and other great heroes of the

British Empire. He left two published works—*Missionary Travels and Researches in Africa, 1857* and *Narrative of an Expedition to the Zambesi and Its Tributaries* (with Charles Livingstone, 1865). *Last Journals of David Livingstone in Central Africa* was published posthumously, edited and abbreviated, in 1874.

And Stanley? Finding Dr. Livingstone was not his only moment of fame. He, too, went on to be a well-known explorer. In the late 1870s he explored the length of the Congo River, and on a third journey (1879–1884), he helped to organize what would become the Independent State of the Congo (now Zaire). The British government knighted him for his explorations, making him Sir Henry M. Stanley.

Sir Richard Burton

Explorer of the Holy Lands of the Muslims
and Discoverer of the Headwaters of the Nile River
1821–1890

A distinguished author and a noted linguist, Sir Richard Burton was one of Britain's outstanding explorers of the nineteenth century. He was particularly praised for his efforts to understand the holy lands of the Muslims—those who follow the faith of Islam—and to locate the headwaters of the Nile River. He was also a flamboyant, reckless, and unpredictable man.

Born in 1821, Richard Burton was the son of an army officer and his wealthy wife, who indulged his taste for a life of leisure and hunting. Colonel Burton moved his family around England, France, and Italy with such frequency that the children had no real home. Sir Richard Burton's biographers generally agree that the explorer was so ambitious and hardworking because he was determined to be everything his father was not, and not to be anything his father was.

Burton's father sent his son to Trinity College, Oxford, to study for the clergy in 1840. Burton was idolized by fellow students but disliked by the faculty for his independent ideas and outright disobedience. He was expelled in 1842 and joined the army of the East Indian Company in Sind, now in southern Pakistan. Dissatisfied with Christianity as it had been presented to him, he began a lifelong study of native languages and ways of life. Burton believed that by mastering the languages of the East, he would be able to understand the philosophies of life that are prevalent in that part of the world. He learned Arabic so that he could read the Koran, and he learned Persian to study the mystical doctrine of the Shiites. He studied the cultures from within, by disguising himself as an Arab and moving among the people, much to the disapproval of his fellow officers.

After a brief return to England, he decided on one of his most dangerous exploits—the penetration of Mecca, the holiest of Islamic shrines and a place forbidden to nonbelievers. The penalty for trespass was death, and several Christians and Jews had already paid that price. In 1853, Burton disguised himself as Mirza Abdulla, a Persian wanderer, and safely reached Mecca. There he visited the Kaaba—a cube-shaped building in the courtyard of the Sacred Mosque that holds Islam's most sacred object, the Black Stone. Burton recognized that the stone was a meteorite. For six days, he studied life in Mecca. When he left, his garments and luggage were stuffed with his notes; had they been discovered, he would have been killed.

His next expedition was to Harar, in what is now Ethiopia, another city sacred to Islam. Here he revealed his true identity to the Amir, or local ruler, believing that the Amir's need for friendship with Britain would protect him. His exploration of Islamic shrines resulted in the three-volume *Personal Narrative of a Pilgrimage to El-Medinah and Meccah*, one of the most popular of the forty-eight books he wrote. Burton was now a famous man, and such influential organizations as the Royal Geographical Society offered to finance his explorations.

He turned his attention to the exploration for which he would be best known and longest remembered. He determined to search for the source of the Nile, a question that had puzzled geographers for more than 100 years. His first expedition ended in disaster when warlike Somali tribesmen attacked his camp, killing and injuring many of the party. Having suffered a spear slash in both cheeks, Burton was forced to cancel the expedition. He returned to England at that time and served briefly in the Crimean War, in which Britain fought Russia for control of southeastern Europe.

In October 1856, he set out again to discover the source of the Nile, taking John Hanning Speke with him as second in command. The two men instantly became rivals rather than partners. By the time they reached Lake Tanganyika in central Africa in early 1858, both men were ill from tropical heat, insects, and the steaming jungle. Natives assured them that the lake was the source of the Nile, but they soon learned this was not the truth. They set out to return to Zanzibar but stopped in central Tanzania because Burton was still very ill.

Learning of a lake larger than Tanganyika, Speke suggested they look at it. Burton, to his lifelong regret, told him to go alone. Speke discovered Lake Victoria and presumed the Nile sprang from the northern shore of the lake, although he did not actually see the river. Burton was reassured that the source of the Nile had not been found without him. The two men returned to Zanzibar, where Burton rested to speed his recovery. Speke departed for England, promising not to reveal the discovery of Lake Victoria until they could announce it together. Instead, however, Speke announced his discovery to the Royal Geographical Society and persuaded them to finance another expedition, with himself in charge. The rivalry between the two explorers was now public.

On his second expedition, Speke discovered a break in the shoreline that he named Ripon Falls and claimed was the headwaters of the Nile. Burton argued that he had not explored the entire northern shore and could not be sure this was the only break in the shoreline. Public debate on the issue continued for five years, with Speke claiming to be the sole discoverer of the source of the Nile and Burton claiming Speke had not eliminated all other possibilities. The matter was to come to a head in a public debate on September 15, 1864, at a meeting of the British Association for the Advancement of Science. Unfortunately, Speke died the day before the debate in a hunting accident.

Much upset by his rival's death, Burton later issued a statement admitting that Speke had been right. And he was. The Nile does begin at Ripon Falls at the northern end of Lake Victoria.

Burton devoted the rest of his life primarily to writing countless books, including his classic translation of *Arabian Nights*. He had married at the age of forty, and his wife, Isabel Arundel, proved devoted and tolerant of his idiosyncrasies. Burton left the army to enter Britain's Foreign Service, and he was given a title in 1886. Sir Richard Burton and Isabel were in Trieste when he died in 1890.

Robert Edwin Peary

Arctic Explorer; First Person to Reach the North Pole
1856–1920

Arctic explorer Robert E. Peary was a genuine twentieth-century pioneer, exploring the jungles of Nicaragua to find the path of an inter-oceanic canal, dashing for the North Pole in the Arctic, pioneering new, revolutionary means of air travel. He was a civil engineer, explorer, and aviation advocate.

Born in Cresson, Pennsylvania, in 1856, Peary was raised in Maine, graduating from Bowdoin College in 1877. First hired as a surveyor for the town of Fryeberg, Maine, he became a draftsman for the Coast and Geodetic Survey and then joined the U.S. Navy Civil Engineers Corporation.

Peary's first field assignment was to supervise the building of an iron pier in Key West, Florida. Disliking the contractor's methods, Peary did his own diving to explore the harbor bottom and developed his own blasting techniques. Yellow fever kept him off the project for a while, and when he returned, he suspended the project because of a lack of progress. The Navy backed him up.

Peary then went to Nicaragua, where he explored possible routes for an inter-oceanic canal, hacking his way through tropical jungle, climbing mountains, and crossing canyons. But he was always more interested in polar regions.

In 1886, on a six-month leave from the Navy, he sailed to Greenland and spent three weeks exploring the ice cap. This trip confirmed his lifelong interest in Arctic exploration, though he did return to Nicaragua for a second survey. On this second trip, he took with him African-American Matthew A. Henson, who would become his close friend and the field manager of his later expeditions.

In 1891, Peary asked for and received an eighteen-month leave from the navy to return to Greenland. On this trip, his new wife, Josephine Diebitsch Peary, and six other men, including Henson, accompanied him. A trip made on sleds to the northern tip of Greenland—a journey of 1,300 miles (2,090 km)—confirmed that Greenland was an island. Two years later, Peary led another expedition to Greenland, and his wife, then pregnant, went along. She gave birth to a daughter, Marie Ahnighito, the first Caucasian child born that far north—and then returned to the United States with her infant. Peary remained behind but made little advance in his explorations. On return trips in 1896 and 1897, he vowed to reach the North Pole and decided the only way was from the north coast of Greenland.

In 1898 he led another expedition north. The group established a base at the edge of the polar sea, but Peary suffered frostbite, and eight of his toes were amputated. He later taught himself to walk without a limp. He stayed in the Arctic for four years and made his closest approach to the North Pole.

After the assassination of President McKinley, when Vice-President Theodore Roosevelt became president, it was easier for Peary to get leave from his naval duties with the Bureau of Yards and Docks, because Roosevelt was extremely interested in exploration of unknown regions. In September 1903, Peary was given a three-year leave to make another attempt to reach the Pole. He made one failed attempt in 1907 and then tried again in 1908. His ship made it farther north under its own power than on any previous expedition. By the end of March, the expedition reached the 88th parallel. Gradually, most of the party turned back, discouraged by the perils of the ice pack, which included "pressure ridges," where small, steep mountains of ice well up because of currents under the ice, and "leads," open lanes of water created when sections of ice are split apart. Anyone slipping into a lead drowns or freezes to death in minutes.

Peary and Henson along with four Inuit guides and forty dogs made the final dash for the Pole, reaching it on April 6, 1909. At the Pole, they did a sounding that revealed, to their surprise, that the ocean was more than 9,000 feet (2,740 m) deep at that point. The return trip found them exhausted, but they had carefully positioned igloos and supplies along their route. Pushing forward, they traveled 413 miles (665 km) in sixteen days and then collapsed in exhaustion.

An American surgeon, Dr. Frederick A. Cook, claimed to have reached the North Pole a full year before Peary's party, which diminished their triumph. But then Inuit who were interviewed testified that Cook never went more than 20 miles onto the icepack, and a sea captain later came forward to testify that he'd been paid by Cook to produce sextant readings consistent with the North Pole. Cook was discredited, but by the time Peary returned to the United States, Cook had already been internationally recognized for a discovery he didn't really make. Although the hoax was revealed, little public enthusiasm remained for the North Pole.

Congress, with more understanding than the general public, gave Peary the nation's thanks and retired him in 1911 with the rank of rear admiral.

But Peary was not ready to retire. He turned his attention to what next intrigued him—the airplane. Peary believed that an aeronautic department should be created, with weight equal to the Departments of War and Navy. As World War I approached, Peary stressed the importance of peacetime use of aviation and used his personal reputation as a valued explorer to raise $250,000 for the Aerial Coastal Patrol Fund. He was also named chairman of the National Committee on Coast Defense by Air and president of the Aero League of America.

Robert E. Peary died of pernicious anemia in 1920 at his home in Washington. His importance goes far beyond what we usually know him for—the first man to reach the North Pole. He revised maps of Greenland, developed important methods of Arctic travel, made scientific observations of the polar ice cap that benefited meteorology and hydrography, and helped scientists to understand the tides of the Arctic Ocean. His records of Inuit life were important to anthropologists.

Rear Admiral Peary was the author of *Northward Over the Great Ice* (1898), *Nearest the Pole* (1907), *North Pole* (1910), and *Secrets of Polar Travel* (1917). His wife published her experiences with Peary in *My Arctic Journal* (1893).

Matthew Henson

Accompanied Peary on His First Expedition to the North Pole;
Possibly One of the First African–American Explorers of the
Nineteenth Century
1866–1955

Matthew Henson holds the distinction of being one of the first people, with Robert Peary, to reach the North Pole and also being one of the first—if not *the* first— African-American explorer of the nineteenth century.

Henson went to sea as a boy of twelve in 1878. He had walked from Washington, D.C., to Baltimore, Maryland, to be a cabin boy. Captain Childs of the merchant ship *Katie Hines* did not want to take on such a young lad, but Henson explained that he was an orphan. His parents were freeborn black sharecroppers who had moved to Washington, D.C. When they died, Henson and his brothers and sisters moved in with an uncle.

Captain Childs took the boy on and taught him not only to be an able-bodied seaman but also the basics of math, history, and geography. As they traveled to China, Japan, North Africa, and the Black Sea, Childs also read the Bible to his cabin boy. When Childs died, Henson gave up the sea and took a job as a clerk in a furrier's company in Washington, D.C. There he met Robert Peary, who would go on to fame as leader of the first expedition to reach the North Pole.

Peary had brought Arctic furs back from an expedition and went to the furrier to sell them. He met Henson and, sensing that the younger man's interest in adventure matched his own, hired him as a personal assistant for his upcoming Nicaraguan trip. Henson spent two years in Central America with Peary, and Peary came to admire his skills as a mechanic, navigator, and carpenter.

In 1891, Peary, Henson and four others—plus the new Mrs. Peary—left for Greenland. When they set up base camp, Henson's ability as a carpenter was useful: he built a two-room house for their headquarters. The house was called Red Cliff House. When the party left to cross Greenland from west to east, seeking the island's most northern point, Henson soon had to return to Red Cliff House because of injuries. There he met racial prejudice from crew members who had stayed behind and who did not respect the native Eskimo population either. Henson quickly learned the Eskimo language, Arctic survival skills, and the local culture.

Henson spent the next eighteen years traveling with Peary. In 1895, they charted the Greenland ice cap and discovered the island's northernmost point. Over the next years, they tried for the North Pole several times and met with failure. On their 1902 attempt, six Eskimo helpers died, and food ran out. In 1906 they spotted a land mass they called "Crocker Land"; later expeditions proved it to be a mirage.

The two explorers made their final attempt in 1908. Henson was then forty and Peary was fifty. They were getting too old to explore the Arctic, and they knew they had to make it now. Peary had said from the beginning of this expedition, "Henson must go all the way. I can't make it without him." He knew that Henson was the best of all his assistants and the one he relied on most.

As a black man in those times, Henson did not receive the honors that Peary did when it was determined that their party was indeed the first to reach the North Pole. But in 1937, when he was seventy, Henson was made an honorary member of the famous Explorers Club in New York. In 1946 he was honored with a U.S. Navy medal, and he was later awarded a gold medal from the Chicago Geographic Society.

Matthew Henson married twice. In 1891, he married Eva Flint who asked for and was given a divorce in 1897, because of his continuous absence. In1907, he married Lucy Jane Ross. Henson died in 1955 and was buried in the Bronx, but in 1987 one of his biographers, S. Allen Counter, worked to have his remains and those of his wife moved to lie next to Robert Peary in Arlington National Cemetery. Counter's book, *North Pole Legacy: Black, White and Eskimo,* is now out of print and difficult to find.

Wilbur and Orville Wright

First to Fly Powered Aircraft
Wilbur (1867–1912); Orville (1871–1948)

Almost everybody knows that the Wright brothers first flew a controlled, powered heavier-than-air craft at Kitty Hawk, North Carolina in 1903. What many people don't realize is that the brothers did many earlier experiments before they achieved powered flight and that the work of several earlier men led to their success. There were the Montgolfier brothers who, in 1783, built an "aerostate" that consisted of a huge linen bag, lined with paper and heated by a small, straw-fed fire, and J. A. C. Charles who introduced the hydrogen balloon, also in 1783. In 1852, Frenchman Henri Giffard invented the *dirigible* (French for "steerable") airship, the first balloon with machinery. It was powered by a steam engine that drove three propellers, and steered by a triangular rudder. In the late nineteenth century, German Otto Lilienthal had a conical hill built near Berlin from which he could experiment with his gliders, which we call hang gliders today. After twenty-five years of experiments, Lilienthal made his first flight in 1891. He steered the vehicle by shifting his weight, but that did not provide any real control. Unfortunately Lilienthal was fatally injured in 1896 in a fall; by then he had completed almost 2,000 short flights.

The Wright brothers built on all the work that preceded their experiments but they were most influenced by Lilienthal. Wilbur Wright was born in 1867 on a farm in Millville, Indiana; by the time Orville was born in 1871, the family had moved to Dayton, Ohio. The boys had two older brothers, Reuchlin and Lorin, and a younger sister, Katharine. Their father, Milton, a bishop in the United Brethren Church, edited and published a religious newspaper.

Neither boy completed much schooling. Wilbur dropped out because he got hit in the head with a bat and because their mother had tuberculosis. Orville was more interested in the printing press that produced his father's newspaper. He invented a machine to fold the papers, and then he and Wilbur built their own press and published a neighborhood newspaper. Next they opened the Wright Cycle Company, a shop where they repaired and sold used bikes. It should be no surprise that they invented two types of bikes themselves.

When they decided they wanted to see if humans could fly, the Wright brothers watched birds for hours, studying the way they turned by lifting one wing tip up and turning the other down. In 1899, they built a model kite that had a "wing warping" system. It worked so well, they wanted a bigger model, and they wanted to test it somewhere that was very windy. The U.S. Weather Bureau recommended Kitty Hawk, North Carolina.

One of the Wrights's earliest experiments involved building a small wind tunnel at their bicycle factory. It consisted of a gas engine hooked to a small fan that blew air through a cardboard box. Using paper wings, they could observe how air currents affected wing structure. Eventually, after trying 200 pairs of paper wings, they built full-sized wings that would give their aircraft lift and balance. They also compiled the first useful tables for calculating lift and drag.

They learned to fly by doing experiments with gliders, and during those flights they learned that they needed a better method of steering than weight-control. When their glider crashed back to the soft dunes at Kitty Hawk, they learned that they needed to increase the air pressure under the wings to hold the craft up. They thought an engine would do it because the engine would make more wind go under the wings. Giffard had found steam engines too heavy and slow for practical use but had not tried an internal-combustion engine because of the danger of fire in combination with the hydrogen that lifted his dirigible off the ground. The Wrights now needed a lightweight, internal-combustion, gas engine. Since they were not using hydrogen, the danger of fire was not as great. But when they contacted engine companies, nobody wanted to sell the brothers an engine. They thought it would disgrace their engines to be attached to so foolish a project. So the brothers built their own engine.

In their first experiment, the glider did not fly because the engine was too heavy. They redesigned both the engine and the glider and then, on December 17, 1903, it flew 120 feet (36 m). The engine was a four-cylinder, twelve-horsepower, internal-combustion, gas engine. They tried again several times that day, and in the final flight of fifty-nine seconds achieved a distance of 852 feet (259 m). Only three or four men witnessed these short flights—and they were apparently not much impressed.

The Wright brothers were reluctant to share their triumph. Shy men who were happiest working in their garage workshop, they had no desire to become celebrities. Asked to make a speech, Wilbur said that he knew of only one bird—the parrot—that talks, and it didn't fly very high. They also did not want to let their competition know what they had accomplished. In the next few years they modified and improved their design and took out patents on everything in their machines. Maybe they wanted to perfect the design themselves, and maybe they were trying to protect their inventions. Whatever the reason, their attempts to beat the competition hampered the development and improvement of aircraft. And their actions did not win them public support.

In 1909, they established an aircraft manufacturing company in Dayton, Ohio, and began to turn out two airplanes a month. The Wrights negotiated with the U.S. government to produce military aircraft—at $100,000 per plane. After other pilots began flying their own planes, the Wrights's price dropped to $25,000. But if they were to remain leaders in aviation, they needed more than the military. Wilbur went to Europe, giving a series of demonstration flights in France. In 1908 he held the distance, altitude, duration, and speed records of the French Federation Aeronautique International, but these records were soon broken. Instead of creating a market for his planes, he inspired so many European competitors that, within five years, American aircraft would be outdated and incapable of competing with French machines.

In 1910, the Wright brothers took their father, aged eighty-two, up on his first flight. He kept calling out, "Go higher! Go higher!" Wilbur died in 1912, but Orville lived until 1948 and saw planes cross the oceans and fly faster than the speed of sound.

Roald Amundsen

First Man to Reach the South Pole
1872–c. 1928

Norwegian explorer Roald Amundsen was the first man to reach the South Pole. His 1911 expedition to the South Pole brought him fame, but he later wrote, "no man has ever stood at the spot so diametrically opposed to the object of his real desires." Roald Amundsen's real goal was the North Pole. In recent years, scientists have suspected that he may have indeed been the first aviator to fly over the North Pole, a record long attributed to Richard E. Byrd.

Amundsen was born in 1872 in Borge, a small town in southeastern Norway. From boyhood, he had only one ambition—to be a polar explorer. He read constantly about polar expeditions, studying in particular the journey of Sir John Franklin who set out to find the Northwest Passage in 1845 and never returned. Amundsen's parents, however, wanted him to study medicine, and he dutifully enrolled in medical school. Both his parents had died, however, by the time he was twenty-one, and he left medical school.

Convinced that polar expeditions usually failed because explorers did not know how to captain a vessel, Amundsen went to sea aboard a sealing vessel. His first polar trip came in 1897 when he was a crew member on a Belgian expedition to investigate the coast of Antarctica. The ship froze in ice off the coast and was isolated for thirteen months. The crew all developed scurvy— a disease that results from the absence of fresh fruits and vegetables in the diet—and the captain was too ill to command. Amundsen took charge. The ship broke out of the ice in March 1899, having set a record for the first winter spent in Antarctica. Of course, the crew set the record by accident.

Now a captain, Amundsen began to plan his own Arctic expedition, in search of the Northwest Passage—the same passage Columbus and other earlier explorers had sought in vain. Amundsen's expedition sailed from Oslo in June 1903 in *Gjöa,* a 47-ton, 70-foot (21-m) sloop (a kind of sailboat). They crossed the North Atlantic, sailed along the coast of Greenland, and crossed to Canada's northeast coast, beset by ice floes, strong winds, fog, and shallow waters.

The ship found a natural harbor on an island near Hudson Bay and remained there for two years, studying the magnetism of the North Pole. They built observatories and equipped them with precision instruments. Amundsen also carefully observed the Inuit, their food and clothing, and learned from them how to drive a dog team. In August 1905 the ship continued westward, spending three weeks crossing waters so shallow that less than 1 inch (2.5 cm) of water lay beneath the ship's keel. When the crew sighted a whaling vessel from San Francisco, they knew they had been the first ship to navigate the Northwest Passage.

Amundsen was now a famous explorer, and his goal of reaching the North Pole seemed closer. His plan was to drift across the Pole on a ship frozen in the ice. But in April 1909 he learned that American Robert Peary had reached the Pole; Amundsen immediately changed his plans and headed for the South Pole.

His expedition to the South Pole was a competitive race, because England's Robert F. Scott was making his second attempt to reach the Pole. Amundsen was determined to get there first. His crew established a base in the Bay of Whales and set up seven depots along the early parts of the route. Amundsen and four others departed in four light sleds, each pulled by thirteen dogs.

The surface of Antarctica is smooth in some places but covered with deep crevasses, ice ridges, and mountains in other places. "White-out" is common, a condition where a person loses his or her depth perception and the mind cannot distinguish between snow and sky. Fierce winds blow, blizzards are common, snow is deep, and frostbite is always a danger. Braving all these hazards, the group of five men reached the South Pole on December 14, 1909. Amundsen left a tent and a letter for Scott. Scott's expedition reached the Pole a month later and, unfortunately, they all perished on the way back. His expedition gave future explorers geological information as well as knowledge about what not to do.

Amundsen was still drawn to the North Pole, and in June 1918 his next expedition left Norway on the *Maud,* a ship designed by the explorer himself. The expedition was a disappointment geographically. For two years, the *Maud* lay frozen into coastal ice; once released, it had to sail to Seattle, Washington, for repairs. Next it was frozen in for five years. Always interested in aviation and its possibilities for polar exploration, Amundsen had taken two small planes on the *Maud.* Unfortunately, they both crashed early in the expedition. In spite of these failures, the expedition was called one of the most important research projects yet carried out in the Arctic.

In 1925, in New York for a lecture, Amundsen met an American millionaire named Lincoln Ellsworth, who offered to buy two "flying boats" and pay for parts of the expedition. The two planes left Norway for Alaska in May but both developed problems. A pilot managed to fly one plane carrying the men from both planes to a small island where the explorer and his party were rescued and returned to Norway.

Amundsen's next adventure was on the airship (blimp) *Norge*, with Lincoln Ellsworth, Italian Umberto Nobile, a pilot, and a crew of twelve. This time, they met with success. The men dropped the flags of Norway, the United States, and Italy over the North Pole. They also became the first men to fly from Europe to America. They had flown across uncharted polar territory and were able to see that there was no land. This observation truly completed the mapping of the world that had begun centuries earlier. Amundsen's triumph was diminished, however, by the fact that American Richard E. Byrd claimed to have flown over the Pole just three days earlier. Amundsen had been among those to congratulate Byrd when he landed.

Amundsen and Nobile had a quarrel, with Amundsen criticizing the *Norge*, which Nobile had built, and Nobile trying to diminish Amundsen's part in the historic flight. Nonetheless, when Nobile's new airship, the *Italia*, crashed in the Arctic, Amundsen volunteered to be part of the rescue team. Amundsen's plane took off but was never heard from again, and he was presumed lost at sea. The wreckage of Amundsen's plane was found on August 31. Nobile and his crew were rescued on June 22, 1928.

In the 1990s, at the Byrd Polar Research Center in Ohio, a scientist named Dennis Rawlins studied a diary belonging to Richard E. Byrd. From notes in the diary, Rawlins became convinced that Byrd's aircraft did not reach the North Pole. According to Rawlins, Byrd made a serious attempt but turned back because of an engine leak some 149 miles (240 km) short of the Pole. Thus Roald Amundsen was indeed the first man to fly over the North Pole.

Sir Ernest Shackleton

Antarctic Explorer
1874–1922

Although he never reached the South Pole, Ernest Shackleton is famous as perhaps the greatest of all Antarctic explorers. He is renowned not for his discoveries but for the qualities of leadership he displayed in the extreme weather conditions of that part of the world.

Shackleton was born on February 15, 1874, in Kildare, Ireland, the son of a well-known Quaker family. He was educated in London but left school to become a master mariner in the merchant fleet. Although he was with Robert Scott's 1901 expedition to Antarctica and himself led a 1907 expedition that came within 111 miles (179 km) of the South Pole, Shackleton is most famous for his two-year expedition on the *Endurance*.

With a crew of twenty-eight, he sailed from South Georgia, a small island in the southern reaches of the Atlantic Ocean. They reached the Weddell Sea, attached to the polar ice cap, in January 1915 and soon found themselves stranded in packed ice (sailors call it pack ice). Drifting helplessly with the ice, they believed that eventually the ship would free itself and they could sail again. Meanwhile, it was dark twenty-four hours a day. They survived on stored food, and Shackleton kept his men's spirits high.

The ship Endurance *was crushed by ice floes and eventually sank.*

But in October, the ship was crushed by the ice. The men salvaged what they could and camped on the ice. Then, on November 21, the ship sank. The men tried to haul the smaller boats across the ice but found that impossible, so they drifted with the ice as it moved northward. In April, the ice pack on which they camped reached the open water of the far south Atlantic. In the three small open boats they had saved, the men rowed and sailed north through drifting chunks of ice and temperatures that ranged from -10° to -30° Fahrenheit (-23° to -34° Celcius).

After a desperate week, they landed on the northeastern edge of Elephant Island, a spot where great cliffs rose above a tiny—and unsafe—beach. The next day they sailed west to a safer beach. Shackleton left twenty-two men on Elephant Island, under the command of Frank Wild, while he and a small crew sailed on the 22-foot (7-m) *James Caird*, the largest of their remaining small boats, to seek help. Winter had come again, and it took them sixteen days to sail 800 miles (1,287 km) through the rough seas back to South Georgia where they had started. Blown by the winds of a storm, they landed on the side of South Georgia that is not occupied, and Shackleton and two others, although weak from exposure and the effort of their voyage, started immediately to hike across the mountains of the island. Without sleep they walked for thirty hours into the whaling station at Stromness on May 20, 1916. The Norwegian whalers thought they were seeing ghosts since it was long since assumed that Shackleton and his party had perished.

Shackleton made four trips carrying supplies to the men he had left on Elephant Island. Finally on August 30, 1916, in a Chilean ship, the *Yelcho*, he reached Elephant Island to rescue them. The men, one by one, came out of their small shelters, and Shackleton watched carefully, counting them. All were safe and well. He had not reached the South Pole, but it was more important that he had not lost a man on his treacherous and difficult journey. The expedition had also done a great deal of important scientific work, contributing to the world's knowledge of Antarctica.

Shackleton set out on one more expedition in 1921, aboard a sealer called the *Quest*. On his two previous expeditions he took teenagers, encouraging them toward careers as mariners. This time, he arranged with the London *Daily Mail* to run a contest for Boy Scouts. Out of the 1,700 who applied, the Boy Scout leader Baden Powell narrowed the list to 10, and Shackleton selected 2. One was James Marr, an eighteen-year-old undergraduate zoology major from Aberdeen, Scotland, who later went on to make major contributions to the knowledge of the Antarctic.

The voyage on the *Quest* was Shackleton's last. The night the ship arrived at South Georgia, he suffered a heart attack and died. The crew buried him on the island, where his grave looks out across Cumberland Bay. Frank Wild, who had been on Elephant Island with the 1914 expedition, now took over and sailed south to the Weddell Sea and then to Elephant Island.

It has been said that the age of exploration died with Shackleton, and a new age began—that of political wrangling over territories and scientific research.

George Mallory and Andrew Irvine

Possibly the First Two Persons to Reach the Summit
of Mount Everest in 1924
Mallory (1886–1924); Irvine (1896–1924)

In 1924, referring to Mount Everest, in the Himalayas, George Mallory wrote, "The highest of the world's mountains, it seems, has to make but a single gesture of magnificence to be the lord of all, vast in unchallenged and isolated supremacy." Little did he know that within months the mountain would claim his life in such a single gesture. The disappearance of George Mallory and Andrew Irvine is one of the greatest unsolved mysteries of the twentieth century. At the heart of the puzzle is whether or not the two were the first to reach the summit of Mount Everest. If they died as they ascended, Sir Edmund Hillary's 1953 accomplishment as the first to climb Everest is intact, but if it could be proved that they died on their descent, the two Englishmen would have the honor of being the first to conquer the mountain, twenty-nine years before Hillary and his Sherpa companion, Tenzing Norgay.

In the 1920s, Mount Everest was unexplored and unknown. Before his fateful trip in June 1924, Mallory had made two previous attempts at the mountain. On the first trip, Mallory and his party, including ten Sherpas or guides, reached 23,108 feet (7,045 m). On his next expedition in 1922, Mallory and two other climbers—Edward Norton and Theodore Somervell—reached 26,575 feet (8,100 m), climbing without supplementary oxygen.

Six days later, two other British climbers broke their record, reaching approximately 27,560 feet (8400 m). However, they used artificial oxygen, starting a debate that dominated high-altitude mountaineering for decades.

In 1924, Mallory returned to Everest a third time. The thirty-eight-year-old schoolteacher was accompanied by Somervell and Norton again and by Andrew Irvine, a twenty-eight-year-old Cambridge student. A severe mid-May storm killed two of the Sherpa guides and weakened the rest of the party. But on June 4, Norton and Somervell set off for the summit, climbing without artificial oxygen. At 28,000 feet (8,530 m), respiratory problems forced Somervell to turn back. Norton struggled for another hour and climbed only an additional 125 feet (38 m). But doing so, he set a record that was not broken for fifty-four years.

Four days later, Mallory and Irvine set out. Mallory reported through a Sherpa that the day offered "perfect weather for the job." Both men carried 33-pound (15-kg) oxygen tanks, primitive and heavy by today's standards.

The two vanished. They were last seen by geologist Noel Odell at 12:50 p.m. on June 8. He reported seeing two tiny "objects" moving across a snow slope. Then the mist closed in, and they were lost to his sight. Odell was uncertain where on the mountain he had seen the two, and there was controversy over his interpretation.

In 1933, an expedition found an ice ax lying on a gently inclined ice slab, some 65 feet (20 m) below the slope. Markings on the ax identified it as belonging to Irvine. Later climbers have remarked that it was an unlikely place for seasoned climbers to fall. Perhaps the ax was lost or even discarded on the ascent. For some years it was thought that a piece of hemp rope and a tent pole found by the Chinese in 1960 were traces of the two lost climbers, but they were later proved to be remnants of the 1933 expedition.

In 1979 a party of Chinese and Japanese climbers attempted to climb Everest's north face. A Chinese climber named Wang Hongbao tried to tell Ryoten Hasegawa, one of the Japanese, that in 1975 a party of Chinese climbers had seen two bodies. One was easily identified as Maurice Wilson, an eccentric climber who had died trying to conquer the mountain alone in 1923. The second body, found at 26,575 feet (8,100 m) was puzzling. Wang Hongbao and Ryoten Hasegawa could not communicate easily—neither understood the other's language—but Hongbao kept repeating, "English, English." Hasegawa realized with amazement that his companion could be referring to Mallory or Irvine. Unfortunately, the mountain claimed the life of Hongbao the next day.

A 1997 expedition found a green canvas tent, wooden poles, pegs, and several food cans on the north ridge. This discovery spurred the Mallory and Irvine Research Expedition led by American Eric Simonson in early May 1999. This expedition found the body of Mallory, well preserved because of sub-zero temperatures and dry air and clearly identified by a name-tag sewn into his clothing. His leg was broken, and his shoulder injured, suggesting a fall. He was tied to a length of climbing rope, but his goggles—protection from the blinding glare of the snow—were in his pocket, suggesting he might have removed them once the sun went down or was obscured by mists. Mallory was found about 800 (243 m) feet below the summit, his face frozen to the ground. There was no sign of Irvine.

The expedition had hoped to find a camera with film that would clearly indicate whether or not the two had reached the summit before they perished, but no evidence was found, so the mystery remains. Most members of the 1999 expedition argue that the route was too long and hard—Mallory and

Irvine did not make it to the summit, but others disagree and think that the two were the first to conquer Everest.

The ridge and faces and steps of Mount Everest are well-known today by high-altitude mountaineers, in contrast to the utter lack of information available to Mallory and Irvine. Today, some claim the mountain has been commercialized. The thrill of an attempt is available to anyone willing to pay $65,000 or more to undergo the hardship of extreme temperatures, ferocious storms, oxygen deprivation, and primitive accommodations. So many people accept this challenge that the guides are getting rich, and the mountain is sometimes crowded with climbers. Garbage, including thousands of used oxygen bottles, litters the South Col route.

But those who want to climb it are wise to remember that Everest has claimed more than 500 victims over the years—one out of every four who attempt the summit die trying. The deadliest year ever was 1996 when twelve climbers, including two expedition leaders, were killed.

Recent triumphs have occurred on the mountain too. In May 1999, Lev Sarksov, a mountain guide from the former Soviet republic of Georgia, successfully ascended the mountain in 161 days. He was sixty years old, breaking the record of the previous oldest climber. There's always another record to be set, even on this vast and magnificent mountain.

Admiral Richard E. Byrd

Opened the Polar Regions of the Arctic and Antarctic to Modern Research

1888–1957

Admiral Richard E. Byrd is the one man credited with opening the polar regions of the Arctic and Antarctica to modern research. He pioneered the technology of navigational aviation and made modern exploration and investigation of those regions possible, and he drew popular attention to a previously unknown land.

Richard Evelyn Byrd was born in Winchester, Virginia, in 1888. A 1912 graduate of the U.S. Naval Academy, he made a name for himself first as a pilot, serving in the battleship fleet until forced to take medical retirement in 1916 because of a smashed ankle suffered while a midshipman. In 1918 he was recalled to active duty and won his wings as a naval aviator. During World War I he took NC-1 "flying boats" across the Atlantic to France. He was based in Nova Scotia, Canada, and responsible for two air bases there. After the war, he was called to Washington, D.C., where he held bureaucratic positions, making preparations for transatlantic flights, lobbying for pay raises for military personnel, and helping to establish the Bureau of Aeronautics.

Although Byrd had been interested in the polar regions since childhood, his involvement in their exploration did not begin until the mid-1920s. In 1924 he was appointed navigator for a proposed dirigible flight from Alaska to Spitsbergen, Norway. When a presidential order canceled the flight, Byrd organized a Navy flight to the Arctic. In 1925, linked to an expedition sponsored by the National Geographic Society, he completed the first flights over Ellesmere Island and the interior of Greenland.

In 1926, he organized a privately financed expedition to the Arctic, supported by Edsel Ford, John D. Rockefeller, Jr., *The New York Times*, and others. Byrd and his pilot, Floyd Bennett, claimed to have reached the North Pole on May 9, 1926, but scholars have since raised questions about their success. Nevertheless, both men received the Medal of Honor.

Byrd's next goal was to fly over the South Pole. The expedition that set out to accomplish this was the first of five major trips Byrd made to Antarctica. They accounted for the discovery of hundreds of thousands of square miles claimed for the United States. Byrd planned that first expedition carefully, asking experts to design clothing, huts, tents, and trail gear suited to the polar climate. He took a powdered fruit extract to prevent scurvy, the disease that had long plagued sailors who had little or no fresh fruit or vegetables.

Four ships and three aircraft departed for Antarctica but ran into various kinds of trouble. A storm damaged one ship and delayed the entire party; the seas were so rough that the men became violently ill; the dogs that were intended for dog-sled travel also became ill and some died. However, the group set up their base, called Little America I, some 800 miles (1,287 km) from the Pole on the Bay of Whales.

Antarctica is an almost spookily surreal land, frozen solid all year round, with mountains that rise abruptly out of the sea, thick glaciers that flow into freezing waters, and dangerous icebergs floating on the waters. All three would give Byrd difficulty. Byrd and other crew members made several flights to prepare for their major flight over the Pole. On November 29, 1929, after a dangerous flight in which an overloaded plane followed the narrow path of a glacier and had trouble rising above the mountains, Byrd and a small crew passed a note around the plane that said, "We have reached the Pole." They could not talk to one another because of the extremely noisy engines. At the Pole, they tossed out an American flag weighted with a stone. As a reward for his successful trip, Byrd, at forty-one, was made the youngest rear admiral in the U.S. Navy.

His second expedition lasted from 1933 to 1935, and included many scientific projects—studying meteors and cosmic rays, weather, geography, and the vibrations of the ice cap. In the winter of 1934, Byrd refused to leave base camp America II with the others. He spent the winter alone with his dog in a meteorological hut, some 100 miles (160 km) into the interior of Antarctica. He provided the first winter weather observations from the interior but he nearly died of carbon monoxide poisoning. Byrd was forced to abandon his third expedition—Little America III—in 1941 because of America's entry into World War II. After the war, Byrd became commanding officer of the U.S. Antarctic Service and the Navy put him in charge of Operation Highjump. That project, which studied Antarctica, included thirteen ships and 4,700 men. In 1946 and 1947, they explored 2 million square miles (5 million sq km) of land, and Byrd made his second flight over the South Pole. His final expedition, as head of Operation Deep Freeze, was undertaken in the middle 1950s and established Little America V. Byrd again flew over the Pole. His final service for his government was as Officer in Charge of United States Antarctic Programs.

Admiral Byrd died in March 1957. He was the author of five books: *Skyward* (1928); *Little America* (1930); *Discovery* (1935); *Alone* (1938); and *Exploring with Byrd* (1937). In 1985 the Institute of Polar Studies at Ohio State University acquired the first set of Admiral Byrd's papers. This led to an endowment to fund a research scientist in honor of the explorer and the renaming of the institute as the Byrd Polar Research Center.

Ormer Locklear

Daredevil Pilot
1891–1929

Texas native Ormer Leslie Locklear was a daredevil pilot who flew for the Army Air Service and for Hollywood in the 1920s and died tragically in a plane crash in 1929. Today he is considered the "father of aviation aerobatics."

Locklear was born in Greenville, Texas, in October 1891, raised in Fort Worth, and educated at the University of Texas. Young Locklear was always a daredevil, known first for trick-riding on a motorcycle. But he was most fascinated by aeronautics. At the age of twenty, he began taking private flying lessons and bought a monoplane (an aircraft with one set of wings).

In 1917 he joined the U.S. Army Air Service, training at San Antonio and Austin, and was then sent as a flight instructor to Barron Field near his hometown of Fort Worth. One source suggests that Locklear showed such extraordinary abilities as an aerial gunner and navigator that the army assigned him to safe teaching duties in the United States rather than risk losing him in a World War I dogfight. Another source suggests he flew in stunt-flying shows in order to recruit pilots for the military.

After the war, Locklear, like many military pilots, became a barnstorming stunt pilot, flying at state fairs and exhibitions. He was in partnership with Milton Elliott, another former army pilot. Elliott flew their biplane (an aircraft with two sets of wings, one above the other) while Locklear performed tricks such as walking on the wings without a parachute. He stood on the top wing with his feet in strong leather straps fastened securely to the wing. His hands and arms were free, and he smiled and waved to the crowd as Elliott buzzed a field where spectators watched in awe. The two also flew through barns and crashed into demonstration houses as part of their routine. Locklear once said he did those stunts not for the thrill of danger but because he wanted to demonstrate what could be done. "Someday we will all be flying," he predicted.

Locklear and Elliott were both hired by Universal Film Company as stunt pilots for motion pictures. Their second feature film in 1929 was *The Skywayman*. They were to simulate the crash of a burning airplane by attaching torches to their plane so that it would look like it was in flames. Locklear attached the torches at 8,000 feet (2,400 m), and they nosed it into a shallow dive. But then the plane caught fire and went into a tailspin. At 200 feet (60 m), the out-of-control aircraft plunged to the ground in flames and both men were killed instantly. The scene was shot at night, and the bright lights used for night filming may have blinded the pilots. The crash was recorded on film and used in the movie's final scene. Later, Fox Film released the sequences of the crash as a newsreel.

For Locklear's funeral, 50,000 mourners lined Fort Worth's Main Street. He will be recognized in an Aviation Heritage Museum planned for Fort Worth, a city that was home to several aviation pioneers, including astronaut Alan Bean and men whose efforts led eventually to the development of American Airlines.

Amelia Earhart

Known as "America's Most Famous Woman Pilot";
First Woman to Fly Across the Atlantic Solo and the
Only Person to Fly it Twice
1897–c. 1937

Amelia Earhart is America's most famous woman pilot and the subject of one of its most enduring mysteries. On a round-the-world flight in 1937, Earhart and her navigator, Fred Noonan, disappeared in the South Pacific. No trace of them or their plane has ever been found, though many rumors and theories have surfaced over the years.

Earhart had a rocky and uncertain childhood. Born in Atchison, Kansas, in 1897, Earhart spent her early years in the home of her wealthy grandparents. They considered her father, lawyer Edwin Earhart, a ne'er-do-well because he provided neither social status nor a generous income for his family. For some time, Amelia's mother, Amy, lived in Des Moines, Iowa, with Edwin, while Amelia and her younger sister, Muriel (Pidge), stayed in Kansas. In 1909, Edwin Earhart, working for the Rock Island Line Railroad, received a promotion and the girls went to live with their parents. Edwin unfortunately began to drink heavily, and Amy left him for a brief period, taking the girls to stay with friends in Chicago. A trust fund provided for the girls' education.

In 1917, Amelia trained as a nurses' aide in Toronto, Canada, and served as a volunteer in a military hospital until the end of World War I in 1918. She enrolled in medical school in 1919. But in 1920, she dropped out to join her parents in California.

There she became passionately interested in flying. Earhart had seen her first airplane at the Iowa State Fair when she was quite young but had not been much impressed. Now, at an "aerial meet" in Long Beach, California, she was so intrigued that she took a ten-minute flight in an open-cockpit biplane. From then on, she knew she had to fly.

Neta Snook, Earhart's flying instructor at Kinner Field near Long Beach, California, taught her in a restored Canadian training plane. That year Earhart bought her own plane and named it "The Canary." (Later she sold the plane and bought a bright yellow car she called "the yellow peril.") Planes were unreliable in those days which may account for Earhart's several accidents. Snook, however, had private doubts about her pupil's skill as a pilot, and those doubts were later shared by Earhart's contemporaries.

In October 1922, Earhart set a women's altitude record of 14,000 feet (4,267 m), which was broken by another woman only a few weeks later. She was hooked on record-breaking flying, but she still had to support herself. The fall of 1925 found her employed as a social worker in Boston, where she joined the local chapter of the National Aeronautic Association and worked with a company that built a small airport and sold planes. She was now a frequent subject of newspaper articles, and famous enough to actively promote aviation for women.

Aviator H. H. Railey was so struck by Earhart's resemblance to famed pilot Charles Lindbergh that he called her "Lady Lindy." When New York publisher George Putnam asked Railey to find a woman to make a trans-atlantic flight, Railey immediately thought of "Lady Lindy." He called her with the proposal in April 1926.

Earhart met Putnam and agreed to be part of the flight, but only as a passenger because she had no experience with multi-engine or instrument flying. Pilots Wilmer Stultz and Louis Gordon agreed to fly the tri-motor Fokker named *Friendship*, and Amelia was listed as the commander of the flight.

The *Friendship* left New York for Nova Scotia on June 3, 1928—less than ten years after Earhart had begun flying. From Nova Scotia, they flew to the British Isles, landing in south Wales instead of Ireland, as they had planned. Reporters ignored Stultz and Gordon, focusing on Earhart, whom they called "the girl."

Once back in the United States, Earhart flew solo from the Atlantic to the Pacific Coast to attend the national air races. After that, she was a celebrity, invited to lecture and always in the newspapers. George Putnam, who had become her benefactor, worked hard to keep her name before the public and to publicize the book she wrote about her transatlantic flight, *20 Hours, 40 Minutes.*

George Putnam, supposedly happily married, also accompanied Earhart on many of her speaking trips. In addition to aviation, they had discovered mutual interests in the outdoors, books, and sports, and gossip about the pair began. Both denied any romantic attachment, but in December 1929 Putnam's wife divorced him. Apparently he proposed to Earhart several times before she accepted; they were married in February 1931.

Meanwhile, Earhart was appointed assistant to the general traffic manager at Transcontinental Air Transport, which later became TWA. Her job was to attract women passengers. In 1929 she helped organize a cross-country air race for women pilots. When humorist Will Rogers called it "The Powder

Puff Derby," it had a lifetime name. Earhart also was instrumental in starting the "Ninety-Nines," an organization of professional women pilots, and she served as its first president. The group took its name from the number of applicants for charter membership—ninety-nine. Earhart wrote regular articles for national magazines and continued to speak across the country.

Several women pilots were planning solo trips across the Atlantic, and George Putnam knew that his wife would have to be the first if she was to keep her position as America's premier woman pilot. In early 1932, no one had successfully duplicated Lindbergh's flight five years earlier. Earhart took off on May 20, 1932.

She landed in an open field in Ireland, somewhat off course from her intended destination. When she asked where she was, a man said, "In Gallagher's pasture. Have you come far?" "From America," she said.

Earhart was not only the first woman to fly the Atlantic solo, she was the only person to fly it twice. She also held the record for crossing the ocean in the shortest time and for the longest nonstop flight by a woman.

A proud George Putnam joined his wife as she toured Europe. They came back home to a tickertape parade in New York and she received countless honors: President Franklin D. Roosevelt presented the aviatrix with a gold medal from the National Geographic Society, numerous cities gave her their keys, and she was named "Outstanding Woman of the Year."

A trans-Pacific flight seemed the next logical adventure, even though ten male pilots had died trying to make that crossing. Earhart would pilot a civilian plane and carry a two-way radio. She flew from Wheeler Field in Hawaii to Oakland, California, in January 1935. President Roosevelt sent congratulations: "[You have] shown even the 'doubting Thomases' that aviation is a science which cannot be limited to men only."

Earhart flew to Mexico on a goodwill visit; accepted an appointment at Purdue University in Indiana to consult on a study of careers for women;

and began to plan her around-the-world flight. She wanted to be the first to travel around the world at its widest part.

Frederick Noonan, a former Pan American Pacific Clipper navigator who knew the Pacific, would accompany her. They left Oakland for Hawaii on March 17, 1935. As she took off from Luke Field in Hawaii, the plane's right wing dropped. Earhart overcompensated, and the plan swung out of control, collapsing to slide along the runway. There was no fire but the plane was badly damaged. It was shipped back to California, and Earhart started planning another try at a round-the-world trip.

This time, she reversed her original flight plan and headed east instead of west. In the rebuilt Electra, she left Los Angeles for Florida on May 21, 1937. She and Noonan flew out of Miami on June 1, headed for San Juan, Puerto Rico. From there they would fly around the northeast edge of South America, then on to Africa and the Red Sea.

No one had flown from Karachi, Pakistan, to India before. Earhart set that record, landing in Calcutta, India, on June 17. From there, it was on to Rangoon, Bangkok, Singapore and Bandoeng, Indonesia. In Bandoeng, the aviatrix and her navigator stopped while she recovered from a bout of dysentery and while repairs were made to the long-distance instruments of the plane. On June 27, they left for Australia, then on to New Guinea. They were headed home, having traveled 22,000 miles (35,400 km) with only 7,000 miles (11,250 km) to go. Earhart was tired and still sick.

The Electra left New Guinea on July 2 with enough fuel to fly slightly over twenty hours. Seven hours later, Earhart radioed a position report that showed them about to cross the Nukummanu Islands, headed for Howland Island where a U.S. Coast Guard cutter, the *Itasca,* stood ready to act as radio contact. No one in the Nukummanu Islands saw or heard the plane fly over. Eight hours after takeoff, she made her last radio contact—she was on course for Howland, flying at 12,000 feet (3,600 m). Several brief radio transmissions were too short to fix the plane's location. Earhart radioed the *Itasca* nineteen hours after take-off, saying fuel was running low and she thought they must be close to the ship but could not see it. One brief transmission followed and then, nothing. At 21 hours after her takeoff, the crew of the *Itasca* presumed she had ditched at sea and began search operations.

The search was large, long, and expensive. Nine naval ships and sixty-six aircraft, sent by President Roosevelt, searched for over two weeks at a cost to taxpayers of $4 million. After the government search was discontinued, Putnam continued a private search. In October, he too gave up hope. It has been determined that the aircraft went down between 35 and 100 miles (56 and 161 km) off Howland Island. A life raft on board was never found.

Many theories have been advanced over the years to account for her disappearance. Some of the most popular are: she was captured as a spy for the U.S. government; she deliberately drove her plane into the ocean (though no one can say why); she was captured by the Japanese; she lived for many years on an island in the South Pacific with a native.

What do we know for sure? Bones discovered on Saipan were not those of Earhart and Noonan as first suspected. They belonged to Saipan natives. More helpful is the physical evidence found by four archaeological expeditions to the uninhabited Pacific atoll once known as Gardner Island and now called Nikumaroro. (An atoll is a small round coral reef, usually with a lagoon in the middle.) Physical evidence suggests that Earhart's plane landed there after failing to find Howland Island.

Will we ever know beyond a doubt what happened to Amelia Earhart? Probably not, but she remains one of our most intriguing explorers and the subject of one of our greatest mysteries.

Charles A. Lindbergh

First Pilot to Fly Alone and Nonstop Across the Atlantic Ocean
1902–1974

Charles A. Lindbergh was the first pilot to fly alone and nonstop across the Atlantic Ocean, an achievement that made him a national hero in the 1920s. Unfortunately he gained another kind of notoriety when his infant son was kidnapped and killed. That criminal act resulted in a federal anti-kidnapping law known as the "Lindbergh law."

Lindbergh was born in Detroit, Michigan, on February 4, 1902, the son of a lawyer who served in the U.S. Congress. Young Charles was raised on a farm in Minnesota and showed an early aptitude for mechanical skills. He enrolled in the University of Wisconsin to study engineering but found himself so fascinated by the new field of aviation that he dropped out of school and became a barnstormer—a pilot who performed daredevil stunts at fairs and other public events.

At that point, Lindbergh had pretty much taught himself to fly, but he wanted formal training. He got it by enlisting in the U.S. Army, graduating in 1924 as an army reserve pilot from flight school at Brooks and Kelly Fields in Texas. He then went to work for a St. Louis corporation as the pilot of a mail plane.

For several years, a $25,000 prize had been offered for the first pilot to fly nonstop between Paris and New York. Hotel owner Raymond Orteig had offered the prize in 1919, and several pilots had been killed and injured trying to win it. No one had succeeded by 1927, when Lindbergh decided that the way to win was to have the right plane. He worked on the design of the plane with engineers from the Ryan Aeronautical Company in San Diego. The cost was borne by several St. Louis businessmen, and Lindbergh appropriately named the plane *The Spirit of St. Louis*.

In early May 1927, Lindbergh flew from San Diego to New York City to test the plane. On this test, he allowed himself the luxury he would not have on the overseas flight—an overnight stop in St. Louis. Without the stop, he flew coast to coast in twenty hours, twenty-one minutes, which set a record.

On May 20, 1927, the *Spirit of St. Louis* took off from Roosevelt Field near New York City. Lindbergh landed 33 hours later at Le Bourget Field near Paris where a crowd of thousands cheered his arrival. He had flown over 3,600 miles (5,790 km), and he had won the $25,000 prize. Lindbergh was honored in Europe and, once back in the United States, he was awarded the Congressional Medal of Honor and the Distinguished Flying Cross. The Daniel Guggenheim Fund for the Promotion of Aeronautics sent Lindbergh across the United States to raise interest in aviation. Lindbergh persuaded the fund to support the experiments of pioneer rocket scientist Robert H. Goddard, whose experiments eventually led to the development of missiles, satellites, and space travel.

On a 1927 goodwill tour of Latin America, Lindbergh fell in love with Anne Morrow, the daughter of the American ambassador to Mexico. They were married in 1929, and Anne Lindbergh soon caught her husband's passion for flying. She learned to fly, and together they traveled throughout the world, charting new routes for airlines.

By March 1932, the Lindberghs were living in New Jersey and were the parents of a twenty-month-old infant named Charles Augustus, Jr. On March 1, Charles Jr. was kidnapped from the family home. His body was found about ten weeks later but it took two long years to arrest and charge a German carpenter, Bruno Richard Hauptmann. He was convicted in 1935, and after the trial, the Lindberghs left for Europe, trying to avoid the public attention that had surrounded the kidnapping and the trial. As a result of the tragedy, Congress passed the "Lindbergh law" which makes kidnapping a federal offense if the victim is taken across state lines or if the mail service is used for ransom demands. Bruno Richard Hauptmann was executed in 1936.

In 1938, Lindbergh paid a state visit to Germany that caused controversy to swirl around him for some time. He had been touring aircraft factories in both France and Germany and was most impressed with the highly developed industry in Germany. Hermann Goering, a high-ranking Nazi official, presented Lindbergh with a German medal of honor. Many Americans criticized the hero-pilot for accepting a medal from the Nazis, and he would later be accused of being a Nazi sympathizer because he did not return the medal.

Lindbergh's politics were the subject of much criticism in the next several years. In 1941, living again in the United States, he joined the America First Committee, an organization that opposed America's entry into World War II. He was outspoken in his criticism of President Franklin Delano Roosevelt and went so far as to claim that British, Jewish, and pro-Roosevelt groups were leading America into war. His status as a hero gave him more influence over the public than most people enjoy. After Roosevelt publicly denounced him, Lindbergh resigned his Army Air Corps commission.

When the Japanese attacked Pearl Harbor on December 7, 1941, Lindbergh's politics changed. No longer preaching noninvolvement, he tried to re-enlist, but was refused. He spent much of World War II serving as an advisor to the Ford Motor Company and United Aircraft Corporation, but in 1944 he went to the Pacific war area as a civilian advisor to the U.S. Army and Navy, flying about fifty combat missions.

After the war, Lindbergh avoided public attention until 1954 when President Dwight D. Eisenhower restored his commission in the army and appointed him a brigadier general. He also worked as a consultant for Pan American World Airways and helped design the Boeing 747 jet.

In the 1960s, Lindbergh became interested in Africa and the Philippines, and he spoke out on behalf of the conservation movement. He campaigned for protection for the humpback and blue whales—both endangered species—and he opposed the development of supersonic planes because of their possible effect on Earth's atmosphere.

Charles Lindbergh died at his home on Maui, Hawaii, in 1974. He had published two books about his record-setting Atlantic Ocean flight. *We* was published just after the 1927 flight; the "we" of the title being Lindbergh and the *Spirit of St. Louis*. In 1953 he published *The Spirit of St. Louis,* an expanded account of the flight. In 1970 he published *The Wartime Journals of Charles A. Lindbergh*. In 1978, *The Autobiography of Values,* a collection of his writings, was published posthumously.

Jacqueline Cochran

First Woman to Break the Sound Barrier
c. 1910–1980

On May 18, 1953, Jacqueline Cochran broke the sound barrier, traveling 625.5 miles (1,006 km) per hour in an F-86 Sabre jet. She was the first woman to join the previously all-male "supersonic club," and the story of how she became the most famous woman test pilot is a real rags-to-riches story.

Cochran was born in a poor mill town in northern Florida. The family consisted of her parents, two older brothers, and two older sisters. No one paid much attention to the youngest child, and she longed to escape from the crowded poverty of their shack on the edge of a swamp. She slept on the floor, didn't have enough to eat, and was always being scolded. Accidentally, she learned that she was not the child of these parents, but they had promised someone to raise her and never tell the story to anyone. Who?

When Cochran started the first grade, the teacher whacked her hands with a ruler. Cochran fled and did not go back for a year. The next year, however, the teacher took a great interest in her and paid her to bring firewood to her room. She taught the young girl to love books, and showed her how to fix her hair with a ribbon. She bought her the first ready-made dress the child had ever had. After two years, however, the teacher left for Ohio, and Cochran never went back to school.

At eight years old, she accepted a job doing housework and looking after children. She was such a good worker that family after family hired her. When the sawmill where her foster father worked closed, her family climbed into a railroad caboose for a free ride to Columbus, Georgia, where the mills were hiring. Cochran worked from six o'clock in the evening until six o'clock in the morning for six cents an hour. The conditions were hard—she pushed a heavy cart carrying bobbins of thread until her bare feet ached. Lint in the air made her cough, and there was no place to sit down during her short lunch break. With one of her early paychecks, she bought her first pair of shoes. By the time she was ten, she was in charge of fifteen other children. When she told them she would be rich someday, they laughed.

When the workers went on strike, Cochran left with them. She went to work at the home of a woman who owned beauty shops. She helped fix meals and do housework in the mornings and evenings. During the day she cleaned floors and sinks in the beauty shops and mixed shampoos and hair dyes. When the workers went back to the mill, Cochran did not go. By the time she was thirteen, she could operate the permanent-wave machine and was earning $35 a week. She gave her family a little from each paycheck and saved the rest. By the time she was fourteen, she had saved several hundred dollars. When a shop in Montgomery, Alabama, wanted someone who could operate a permanent-wave machine, Cochran left Columbus and her family behind.

In Montgomery, she made friends, bought a Model T Ford, and began to go to parties. Her next career move was to study nursing. After three years of training, she moved to a small mill town in Florida. She knew how poor the people were in these towns, and how badly they needed care. After some time, however, nursing was not enough; she wanted to help people, and she needed money to do it. For two years, she tried various jobs and found she liked selling products and working in beauty shops. At the age of twenty or thereabouts, she was working in an expensive salon in New York City and, during the winters, she worked in that salon's Florida location.

One night at a dinner party she was seated next to a man named Floyd Odlum. He was quiet, friendly, and had a sense of humor. She found herself telling him she wanted to work for a cosmetic company selling beauty aids across the country, so that she could travel from store to store. When he said, "You would need wings to do that!" the idea of flying caught her imagination. On a three-week vacation, Cochran learned to fly, although no one thought she could do it in so short a time.

Cochran decided that having her own business would leave her time to fly, so she started a cosmetics company and flew all over America getting it underway. Floyd Odlum encouraged her, and by now they were good friends. During this time, she also became a better pilot, learning to read the stars and understand Morse code.

In 1934, now a skilled pilot with a successful business, she decided to enter an air race. She and her co-pilot, a man named Wesley Smith, were flying from London to Melbourne, Australia, but in Bucharest, Hungary, they had to give up because their plane was giving them so much trouble that they knew it was not safe. When Cochran tried to enter the Bendix Transcontinental Air Race the next year, she was told women were not invited. However, after every male pilot participating signed a paper agreeing to allow a woman to enter the race, she was permitted to participate. An electrical storm and an overheated engine defeated her, but she knew the Bendix race would never again be closed to women. In 1937 she came in third in that race, and in 1938 she won it. Meantime, in 1936, she and Floyd Odlum were married.

Both Cochran and Floyd did well in business, and they soon owned a new airplane and three homes. They spent most of their time on a farm in the California desert. Cochran continued to send money to her family, and she continued to fly, entering races, testing new products, trying out new engines, fuels, instruments, and propellers. She had several close calls, but she found testing the most satisfying aspect of flying because of the information she acquired from it.

Even before the United States entered World War II, Cochran wanted to find a way to help in the European war effort. General H. H. "Hap" Arnold, chief of the Army Air Corps, told her about men who were flying American planes from Canada to Britain for use by the British air force. When he suggested she fly one, she accepted the opportunity. Male pilots protested, but eventually Jackie took off on her first flight with a male pilot as navigator, which soothed the other men somewhat. They flew all night and landed in Scotland safely, in spite of being strafed by bullets that may have come from the enemy or may have been "friendly fire" from a U.S. ship. Back in the United States, she was invited to lunch with President Franklin Delano Roosevelt. A few days later, General Arnold suggested she organize a group of American women pilots to fly in Britain. She recruited and trained twenty-five women who eventually flew planes from factories to airports and from airport to airport in Britain—it was a dangerous job, but it freed British pilots for combat.

When the United States entered the war, Cochran was called back to America to organize a training program for women pilots. She was in charge of the Women's Auxiliary Ferrying Squadron, which later became the Women's Air Force Service Pilots (WASP) with Cochran as director. By the end of the war, 1,800 women had entered the training program, and more than 1,000 had graduated. Cochran received the Distinguished Service Medal for her work.

Meanwhile, Cochran's cosmetic business was losing money, so after the war she focused on reorganizing it. She also developed an interest in politics, but she continued to fly in races and as a test pilot. In 1952 she was a consultant for the Canadian company that built the F-86 Sabre jet. She flew from Edwards Air Force Base in California, where the weather was good and a speed course for timing was already established. The company hoped she would break some women's records. She hoped she would break some men's records.

Colonel Chuck Yeager encouraged her. During her third flight, Yeager flew nearby as an observer. He knew she planned to reach the speed of sound, Mach One, that day. She flew the plane to 45,000 feet (13,716 m)—nearly 9 miles (14 km) above the earth—and then pointed it straight toward the ground. She reached Mach 1.01 before pulling out of the dive. Before the plane was returned to Canada, Cochran set three world speed records and broke the sound barrier three times. She would go on to be the first woman to take off from and land a jet on an aircraft carrier, the first to reach Mach 2, and the first to pilot a jet across the Atlantic. Cochran's list of accomplishments is now displayed in the Dayton, Ohio, Aviation Hall of Fame. In 1971, she was admitted to the Society of Experimental Test Pilots. The society's president told the assembled pilots, "Jacqueline Cochran has done more for aviation than many of you men."

She received the International Flying Organization's gold medal for outstanding accomplishment, and in later years received the Distinguished Flying Cross and the Legion of Merit. She was also voted Business Woman of the Year, but she sold her Jacqueline Cochran line of cosmetics a few years after her famous flight. In 1954 she published an autobiography, *The Stars at Noon*. She died in 1980.

Jacques-Yves Cousteau

Undersea Explorer; Inventor of the Aqualung
1910–1997

Jacques-Yves Cousteau is known to many television viewers as an undersea explorer, the man who produced the famous television series, *The Undersea World of Jacques Cousteau.* Cousteau was also a resistance fighter in World War II; he invented the aqualung, which allows human beings to spend great amounts of time deep in the ocean, and was instrumental in the planning of the submersible submarine; he explored the Amazon River and studied the culture of the area's inhabitants; he was a pioneer underwater photographer; and he was a strong environmental activist, the recipient of many honors and awards.

Cousteau was born in St.-André-de-Cubzac, France, in June 1910. In his youth, he had two passions—the water and machines. At the age of eleven, he built a model crane; at thirteen, he built a battery-operated car; in his teens, he saved his money to buy a home-movie camera.

The adventurous young man was not a good student, because school bored him. When his parents sent him to a strict boarding school, however, he did much better in his studies. After graduation from high school, he entered the *École Navale* (the French Naval Academy). In 1933, he joined the French Navy as a gunnery officer. Seriously injured in an automobile crash, he began swimming in the Mediterranean Sea to regain strength in his arms. When a fellow officer gave him a pair of fisherman's goggles to keep the saltwater from stinging his eyes, Cousteau's life was changed. Submerged and wearing the goggles, he saw a jungle that could not be seen from the surface. Wanting to spend more time in this environment and share it with others, he began working on a machine that would enable divers to breathe underwater.

During World War II, Cousteau fought for the French underground or, as it was called, the "resistance." He was a spy and later received several medals for his work. In 1943, he and French engineer Emile Gagnan perfected the aqualung, which allowed divers to stay underwater for several hours. Divers used this device to remove enemy mines from the ocean after World War II.

Cousteau was named a captain in the French Navy in 1948 and later became president of the French Oceanographic Campaigns. In 1950 he bought the *Calypso*, the ship he used on explorations until it sank in Singapore Harbor in 1996. By the 1950s he was producing films and publishing books to finance his trips. Two films, *The Silent World* and *World without Sun* won Academy Awards in the documentary category. His books include *The Living Sea, Dolphins,* and *Jacques Cousteau: The Ocean World.* In 1957 he became director of the Oceanographic Museum of Monaco and headed the Conshelf Saturation Dive Program which experimented with men living and working underwater for long periods of time.

In 1968 Cousteau began the television series that brought him international fame. Calling Earth the "water planet" he reminded viewers that three-fourths of Earth is covered by water and introduced the public to a world of sharks, whales, dolphins, sunken treasure, and coral reefs.

Cousteau returned to the Mediterranean, where he had first become intrigued with underwater explanation, in the early 1970s. The beauty that had moved him earlier had disappeared, destroyed by humanity's careless treatment of the oceans. Cousteau began a campaign to call attention to coral-reef destruction, oil spills, overfishing, garbage dumping, and sea-floor dredging for sand and gravel. If the oceans die, he warned, all other plants and animals, including man, would be in grave danger. In 1974, he founded the Cousteau Society to protect ocean life.

Cousteau's concern for preserving nature in its original state led him to take a major expedition down the Amazon River. His expedition flew, hiked, dived, and even climbed trees to survey the land. They took the *Calypso*, along with inflatable boats, kayaks, jeeps, a hovercraft, a riverboat, a helicopter, an amphibious airplane, and a truck. They studied animal life and plant life, insects, monkeys, bats, the pink river dolphin, and other amazing creatures. More importantly, they studied the life and culture of the native Indians—the way they lived and used the jungle even while preserving it.

By the 1990s, Cousteau was speaking out on the danger of the population explosion, which he saw as the main cause of such problems as pollution, depletion of the ozone layer, the warming of the planet, the elimination of some living species, and even the danger of nuclear accident.

Cousteau's many awards include the Distinguished Peace Leadership Award from the Nuclear Age Peace Foundation, the U.S. Medal of Freedom, and membership in the French Academy. Cousteau died in June 1997, at the age of eighty-seven.

Thor Heyerdahl

Sailed a Balsa-log Raft over 4,000 Miles from Peru to Polynesia 1914—

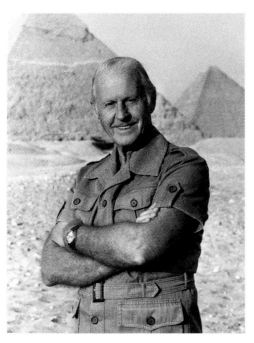

Ask Americans who were reading the news in the 1940s and 1950s who Thor Heyerdahl is, and they're likely to say, "The name is familiar, but. . . ." Ask them if they remember *Kon-Tiki*, however, and they'll almost certainly say, "Sure. The raft." In 1947, Thor Heyerdahl and five other men sailed a balsa-log raft slightly over 4,000 miles (6,400 m) from Peru to Polynesia. He was testing his theory that primitive South Americans could have traveled to the Pacific Islands 1,500 years earlier.

Today, Thor Heyerdahl is Norway's greatest national hero, known for his "diffusionist" theories. This means that he does not accept such ideas as the Bering land-bridge theory, which claims that the North American continent was once connected to Asia by a bridge of land that the ancestors of Native American and Canadian Inuit peoples traveled across. Heyerdahl believes that people diffused or scattered themselves across the world by water travel—in boats that many contemporary anthropologists claim are too frail for the voyages Heyerdahl thinks they made. His theory, he suggests, accounts for cultural similarities between areas of the Old World—Europe—and the New World—North, South and Central America and the Pacific Islands—during the fourteenth and fifteenth centuries.

Heyerdahl has long been preoccupied with finding out what links various races and ethnic groups, rather than joining most anthropologists who want to study what makes each race and nationality different. He believes there was a common cultural heritage, probably 5,000 years ago in Egypt and Pakistan's Indus Valley, and he thinks Azerbaijan may be the clue to the origins of our various cultures. The ocean, he claims was only a barrier to our ancestors as long as they were bound to dry land. Once the boat was invented, civilizations diversified and cultural contact between various civilizations was common. Heyerdahl has been quoted as saying "Man hoisted sail before he saddled a horse."

Heyerdahl was an unlikely candidate to demonstrate man's prowess on the open waters. Until *Kon-Tiki*, he had never sailed a boat, much less a raft. And as a child, he almost drowned in an accident. The fear of water did not stay with him, fortunately. Speaking of reed boats like the one used later on the *Ra* voyage, Heyerdahl has admitted that a single reed of papyrus is fragile but points out that tied together in bundles, they make a seaworthy vessel that is safer than any canoe or ship. When breakers surge over the boat, the water runs out through the thousands of tiny openings between reeds.

Heyerdahl first became interested in migration across oceans when he visited the Polynesian islands in the late 1930s. Trained as a biologist, he had studied plant and animal life, but he noted that plants and dogs appeared to have spread to Polynesia from South America before the Europeans arrived. Living on a South Sea island he noticed that the prevailing winds always blew from east to west. Listening to the myths and legends of the Polynesian people, he saw a cultural similarity to the people of Peru.

Heyerdahl could not test his theory until the end of World War II. Then he built his balsa-log raft and recruited fellow anthropologists to join him on the journey. The raft's design was based on an authentic design found in petroglyphs, etched or painted on ancient walls, burial crypts, and ancient seals. Heyerdahl also used the memory of

Heyerdahl and crew drift aboard the balsa raft Kon Tiki *during their historic journey.*

people who still use such craft. The *Kon-Tiki* was named after a voyager, the "Peruvian sun-god," who, Heyerdahl believed, made a similar voyage 1,500 years earlier. Was Heyerdahl ever afraid? He admits there were moments when he was deathly afraid, but he got used to the "friendly partnership between the dancing ocean and its gentle playmate . . . our flexible, wash-through aboriginal raft-ship."

His successful *Kon-Tiki* journey proved that it was possible for primitive peoples to travel great distances across the oceans of the world, on craft previously considered unseaworthy. The book he wrote about this adventure, *Kon-Tiki,* has been translated into sixty-seven languages and is still available in bookstores and read all over the world. The movie he made with a primitive camera won an Oscar for the year's best documentary. Heyerdahl became famous himself, and he brought international recognition to Norway. But he was also criticized by traditional scientists in the fields of archaeology, ethnography, and anthropology, who disliked his combination of practical, theoretical, and non-traditional research.

Heyerdahl went on to lead an expedition to the Galapagos Islands in 1954, where he found remnants of the Inca culture, and to Easter Island in 1955 and 1956, where he investigated the island's large and mysterious stone sculptures. In 1969, Heyerdahl constructed a papyrus-reed boat, the *Ra*, on which he and six crew members crossed the Atlantic to the Canary Islands from Morocco—3,000 miles (4,827 km) in eight weeks. In 1971, Heyerdahl commissioned Native Americans from Bolivia to construct a second version of the ship—the *Ra II*—which crossed the Atlantic from Morocco to Barbados in fifty-seven days. His fourth vessel, the *Tigris,* a 60-foot (18 m) reed vessel, began its journey in 1978 at the convergence of the Tigris and Euphrates Rivers and sailed 4,200 miles (6,760 m) in about five months to arrive at the Red Sea.

In the 1990s, Dr. Heyerdahl's most recent project was directing archaeological excavations in Tucume, Peru, at South America's largest complex of pyramids—twenty-six large structures and numerous smaller ones. Art on the site shows boats built of reed bundles and rafts made of balsa logs. While he worked on this project in the mid-1990s, the Norwegian government, with Heyerdahl, sponsored a project to equip the town of Tucume with running water, a sewer system, schools, bridges, irrigation channels, and dams.

Despite his focus on ancient history, Heyerdahl has always been an environmentalist. On his voyage in the 1960s, he saw oil slicks and chemical pollution in the oceans, and he sent a report to the United Nations. He believes the world should be spending money on environmental concerns rather than funding destructive global wars, which are, he says, a form of global suicide.

In 1994 when the Winter Olympics were held in Lillehammer, Norway, the voice that welcomed the world was that of Thor Heyerdahl. His accomplishments are honored at the Kon-Tiki Museum in Oslo, Norway.

Sir Edmund Hillary

First to Climb Mount Everest (1953)
1919—

Sir Edmund Hillary is famous for being the first, along with his Sherpa companion, to climb Mount Everest, the world's highest mountain. Mount Everest lies between Tibet and Nepal. It's summit is 29,028 feet (8,848 m) above sea level.

Between the 1920s and the 1950s, several major expeditions tried to reach the summit but failed. Today some mountaineers claim that a pair of British adventurers may have reached the top in 1924. George Mallory and Andrew Irving were spotted about 900 feet (274 m) from the peak but then disappeared and were never seen again. A 1999 expedition searched for evidence to indicate whether tragedy struck them on the way up or on the way down.

Either way, mountaineering is as much about getting back down safely as it is about reaching the top. Sir Edmund Hillary and his companion, Tenzing Norgay, did both.

Hillary was born in 1919 and grew up in Auckland, New Zealand. He remembers a fairly lonely childhood because he was younger than his classmates. When he went through a growth spurt—six inches (15 cm) in one year and 5 inches (13 cm) the next—he gained the respect of his classmates and had more friends. In his teen years he went with a school group to a national park where he saw volcanic mountains, and his first snow. He thinks skiing and scrambling around those hills was the origin of his fascination with mountains and snow and ice. Although he made his living as a bee-keeper, he was always an avid mountain climber.

Hillary has described himself as a rugged, robust, and physically strong type, rather than having the eye and balance of an athlete. He first climbed mountains in the southern Alps of New Zealand and later in the Himalayas, where he climbed eleven peaks over 20,000 feet (6,000 m). He joined Everest expeditions in 1951 and 1952. Then, in 1953, he joined an expedition led by Sir John Hunt and sponsored by the Joint Himalayan Committee of the Alpine Club of Great Britain and the Royal Geographical Society. The expedition reached the South Peak in May but all except Hillary and Norgay were forced to turn back from exhaustion due to the high altitude. Norgay had been part of several previous attempts to climb the mountain.

The two reached the summit at 11:30 A.M. on May 29, 1953. Their success was announced to the British public on the eve of the coronation of Queen Elizabeth II, and Hillary was later given the title of Sir Edmund Hillary by the queen. He and Sir John Hunt published *The Ascent of Everest* (published in the United States as *The Conquest of Everest*). Hillary later said, "We didn't know if it was humanly possible to reach the top of Mount Everest. And even using oxygen as we were, if we did get to the top, we weren't at all sure whether we wouldn't drop dead or something of that nature."

Hillary next turned his attention to trans-Antarctic exploration and participated in the first mechanized expedition to the South Pole. He continued to organize mountain-climbing expeditions and in 1977 led an expedition on the Ganges River to its source in the Himalayas. His 1979 book, *From the Ocean to the Sky,* is an account of that expedition. In 1975 Hillary published his autobiography, *Nothing Venture, Nothing Win.*

Over the years he became increasingly interested in the welfare of the Nepalese people. In 1958 he went to Nepal to build clinics, hospitals, and schools. Hillary was also a concerned environmentalist. Airstrips built to aid in the country's development soon brought too many tourists and would-be mountain climbers to Nepal. The Nepalese began to cut down too much of their forests to provide fuel for the tourists. Hillary persuaded the government to pass laws protecting the forest and to protect the the area around Mt. Everest as the Sagarmatha National Park. At his urging, the government of New Zealand provided financial aid for these projects.

Today Hillary devotes his time to environmental causes and the welfare of the Nepalese people. He says he was trained by his mother to be interested in the welfare of others. Like many mothers, as she fed him a large meal, she often said to her son, "Remember the starving millions in Asia."

When a fan tried to compare Hillary to a great sports hero and suggested Mickey Mantle, Hillary gently corrected him, "More like Neil Armstrong." The first man to conquer Everest might indeed be compared to the first man to walk on the moon.

John H. Glenn, Jr.

First Man to Orbit the Earth
1921—

John Glenn, Jr., was the first man to orbit the Earth in space. On February 20, 1962, he piloted the Mercury-Atlas 6 *Friendship 7* spacecraft on a three-orbit mission around the Earth, traveling at 17,500 miles (28,160 km) an hour. The time from takeoff to landing near Grand Turk Island in the southeastern Caribbean was four hours, fifty-five minutes, and twenty-three seconds. Glenn, who already had an impressive military service record before the flight, went on to serve in business and then in the United States Senate for almost twenty-five years. In 1998, he returned to space as the oldest person to fly on a NASA mission.

John Herschel Glenn, Jr., was born in 1921 in Cambridge, Ohio, the state where he was raised. He graduated from New Concord High School (now renamed John Glenn High School) and attended Muskingum College. He entered the Naval Aviation Cadet program in 1942. In 1943 he enlisted in

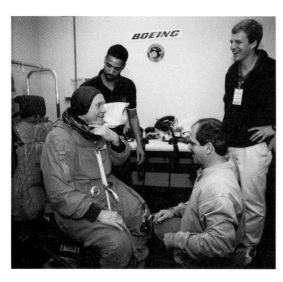

At the Johnson Space Center in Houston, John Glenn gets a suit fit check in preparation for his 1998 shuttle mission.

the Marine Corps and, after advanced training, joined Marine Fighter Squadron 155, flying F4U fighters in the South Pacific for a year. During World War II, he flew fifty-nine combat missions, and afterwards was on patrol duty in Guam.

From June 1948 to December 1950 Glenn was an instructor in advanced flight training at the Corpus Christi Naval Air Station in Texas. He then attended amphibious warfare training at Quantico, Virginia, and flew ninety fighter missions during the Korean War. Glenn went on to test-pilot school at the Naval Air Test Center at Patuxent River, Maryland, and was assigned to the Navy Bureau of Aeronautics from 1956 until 1959. That year he was assigned to the NASA Space Task Group and selected as a Project Mercury Astronaut. After his orbit of the Earth, Glenn wanted to remain active in the space program, but he had become a national hero. President John F. Kennedy believed it was not in the country's best interests to allow a national hero to become engulfed in the Cold War, and Glenn was not allowed to risk further space flights.

Two years after his flight, Glenn resigned from the Manned Spacecraft Center and resigned from the Marine Corps a year later. From 1965 until 1974 he was an executive with Royal Crown International. In 1974, he was elected to the U.S. Senate, carrying all Ohio counties. He was re-elected in 1980 with the largest margin in Ohio history and returned twice after that with a substantial majority. Glenn was a leading senate expert on technical and scientific matters, widely respected for his work to prevent the spread of weapons of mass destruction.

In 1998 Glenn was selected to participate in another NASA shuttle mission, flying as a payload specialist on STS-95. His selection for the crew brought praise for an appropriate honor bestowed on the former astronaut— and criticism for an unjustified reward for a politician. Glenn ignored the criticism and prepared for the mission. On board the STS-95, he participated in experiments designed to study the relation between aging and the body's ability to adapt to weightlessness. Back on Earth, Glenn was reported to have survived well with few complications, except more difficulty in regaining his balance than was experienced by younger crew members. He also took part in scientific follow-up studies after the mission. Although Glenn admitted it was unlikely he would return to space one more time, he showed no intention of settling down to a quiet retirement.

John Glenn has received numerous honors, in addition to the re-naming of his high school in his honor. A highway near his boyhood home has been re-named Friendship Boulevard, and Muskingum College has re-named its athletic building the John Glenn Gymnasium. Also, a replica of the *Friendship* 7 Mercury Capsule is on permanent display in the college's Boyd Science Center. A portion of Interstate 40 near New Concord has been designated the John H. Glenn Memorial Highway. The town of New Concord and Muskingum College plan a museum in John Glenn's name.

In addition, he has received honorary degrees from Muskingum, Nibon University in Tokyo, and Wagner and New Hampshire colleges. When his fourth term as a U. S. senator ended in 1998, he did not seek re-election.

Chuck Yeager

America's "Most Famous" Test Pilot Ever;
First Person to Fly Faster than the Speed of Sound
1923—

Chuck Yeager is the most famous American test pilot ever. He was the first person to fly faster than the speed of sound, but there's a lot more to Yeager's story. He was, for instance, shot down over enemy territory in 1943 during World War II. But with the help of the French resistance he evaded capture and made his way to Spain, which was then a neutral country. And he broke the sound barrier for the last time when he was in his seventies.

Charles Elwood Yeager was born in Myra, West Virginia, in 1923 and raised in the town of Hamlin, population about 600. The town was rural, depending on agriculture, timber, coal mines, and natural gas. His father drilled for natural gas, and Yeager credits his father with his early interest in mechanics. "I got to overhaul engines, and run big gasoline pumps and water pumps," he told one interviewer.

Yeager also credits his family for fostering his own sense of duty and commitment. For him, breaking the sound barrier was not a matter of competition or wanting to be the first. "I was assigned as a test pilot on it [the X-1 plane with which he broke the barrier], and it was my duty to fly it." Yeager remembers that discipline was strong in the family home, and the children were taught to finish a job once started. For him, all his life, flying was a matter of doing the best job he could and not of being twice as good as anyone else.

As a child, Yeager had no interest in airplanes. "We didn't even know what an airplane was," he once recalled. When he was in his mid-teens, a small plane made an emergency landing in a cornfield near his home, and he bicycled over to look at it. He was not impressed—he looked for a minute, and then turned around and went home.

When Yeager graduated from high school in 1941, the world was at war and it was, he said, a natural thing for boys to enter the armed forces. He isn't sure why he chose the Air Force—known then as the Army Air Corps—but he enlisted intending to be a mechanic. His early training with his father would give him an advantage there. But then he read a notice that high-school graduates, eighteen or older and able to pass a physical, could apply for pilot training under the flying sergeants program. "Flying sergeants" meant they would still be enlisted men when they finished the program—not officers. But he did it, "just to be doing something."

His first ride in an airplane was not a success. He was chief of a crew working on a twin-engine bombardier training plane. After he had overhauled the engine, the engineering officer prepared to take it up and check it out. He invited Yeager to go along. So Yeager got in, sat down, and fastened his seat belt. The pilot started doing touch-and-go landings, and Yeager started vomiting. He later recalled that he felt woozy the first few times he flew, as long as someone else was piloting the plane. But once he started flying the airplane himself, that feeling went away.

Yeager trained in the United States and was sent to Britain in the fall of 1943. Within days he was flying dog-fight missions (air-to-air combat) and "really learned to fly." He was, he claims, no better than any other pilots, but he had good eyes. And all his life he had good hand-eye coordination. In a daylight raid over Berlin, he downed his first enemy plane.

The next day, Yeager was shot down. He bailed out of his burning plane with bullets in one leg, fragments in his hands, and cuts on his head—all minor. He landed in occupied France, with Germans all around. Digging into the woods as deep as he could, he hid until the Germans appeared to move on and he could find a French farmer. The resistance forces helped him, and he reached Spain in about a month. After another month in Spain, he caught a ride on a British plane and returned to his squadron.

At that time, a pilot who had any contact with the French resistance was sent home—primarily to protect the resistance movement. Yeager didn't want to go home, and he worked his case all the way up to General Dwight D. Eisenhower, commander of Allied forces in Europe (and later president of the United States). Eisenhower let him go back to flying. He flew sixty-four combat missions and downed thirteen enemy aircraft.

Flying slower than the speed of sound was a problem for World War II pilots. It meant that their planes encountered strong turbulence. After the war, the Air Force knew it had to solve the problem. As a result, it developed the X-1 plane. With thin wings and rocket-powered, it was at least twice as strong as the planes flown during the war. At that time, no one knew if a fixed-wing plane could survive flight faster than the speed of sound, but Yeager did not think about whether or not it was possible. He was a military test pilot with an assignment, and it was his duty to complete it. Yeager broke the sound barrier on October 14, 1947, flying with two broken ribs sustained in a riding accident just days earlier. Five years later, Yeager set a new speed record, flying at twice the speed of sound.

Yeager's career has not been without moments of intense danger. Once, pushing a plane beyond Mach 2—twice the speed of sound—Yeager found himself in an airplane that was out of control, spinning twice per second as it went around. "I just pretty well rode it," he said later. Finally it flipped into a normal spin, and he was able to recover control. The incident lasted fifty-one seconds, but that, he says, can seem a long time.

Yeager became a squadron commander in Europe in 1954 but eventually came back to the United States commanding an F-100 squadron and flying a dozen different planes every week. In 1960 he went through the War College and was promoted to full colonel, assigned to Edwards Air Force Base in charge of the test-pilot school. The name was soon changed to Aerospace Research Pilots School, and Yeager was training astronauts for the Gemini, Mercury, and Apollo missions. He was instrumental in setting up the first space mission simulator and introducing advanced computers to the program. Yeager taught astronauts until the mid-1960s, when the program was transferred to NASA because the government had decided space missions were for peaceful, not military, purposes. In the years since, Yeager has been an outspoken critic of NASA.

On December 12, 1963, Yeager was flying the experimental NF-104A Lockheed Starfighter at over twice the speed of sound, and at more than 100,000 feet (30,400 m), when the plane went into a spin that he could not control. He deployed the drag chute on the plane but it sheared off and the plane began to fall. At 6,000 feet (1,828 m), Yeager ejected, but his ejection seat had separated from the parachute and became entangled in the chute lines. It had burning propellant on it, and his suit—filled with 100 percent oxygen—ignited. He was badly burned on the neck and shoulder, and breathing was difficult because of the smoke. Fortunately, a helicopter with a surgeon aboard picked him up within minutes of his landing. He survived, he says, because he was intimately familiar with his pressure suit, ejection seat, and parachute.

Yeager was promoted to brigadier-general in 1968, the first enlisted man to rise to the rank of general in the Air Force. In 1976, he was awarded the Congressional Medal of Honor for bravery, the only American to earn this honor for peacetime service. His other awards include the Purple Heart, the Bronze Star, an Air Force Commendation medal, a Silver Star with oak leaf cluster, the Distinguished Flying Cross, and the Air Medal. He has also won civilian awards and in 1973 he was the youngest military pilot inducted into the Aviation Hall of Fame.

Chuck Yeager retired from the Air Force in 1975 but continued to consult as a test pilot for many years. The 1979 Tom Wolfe book, *The Right Stuff,* and the subsequent movie, starring Sam Shepard, were based on Yeager's life and made his story known to thousands of Americans who were unaware of his achievements. In October 1997, on the fiftieth anniversary of the flight in which he broke the sound barrier, Chuck Yeager made his last flight as a military consultant, breaking the barrier again in an F-15 fighter. He was then in his mid-seventies.

Dr. Robert Ballard

*Led the Expedition in 1985 that Discovered
the Wreckage of the* Titanic
c. 1940s—

Dr. Robert Ballard gained worldwide attention in 1985 when he led the expedition that discovered the wreck of the *Titanic*, the famed luxury liner that hit an iceberg on April 14, 1912, and went down, taking with it approximately 2,200 people. But Ballard had a long and important career as an underwater explorer before the *Titanic* discovery. Now the President of the Institute for Exploration and chairman of the JASON Foundation for Education, he was senior scientist and director of the Center for Marine Exploration at the Woods Hole (Massachusetts) Oceanographic Institution for thirty years. Still, he is a twentieth-century man who thinks of himself primarily as an explorer and refers to himself as a "high-tech, modern-day Captain Nemo (referring to the hero of Jules Verne's *20,000 Leagues under the Sea)* who is doing exactly what he always wanted to do.

The sea has always fascinated Ballard. He collected seashells and driftwood even as a young boy in southern California; he studied the creatures in the tidal pools, and he read everything from *The Travels of Marco Polo* to Jules Verne's *20,000 Leagues under the Sea*. In college he majored in geology and chemistry, but in graduate school his atten-

Ballard used underwater submersibles such as this one to discover and explore sunken ships and ancient artifacts in the deep sea.

tion focused on oceanography, and he received his Ph.D. in Marine Geology and Geophysics from the University of Rhode Island. While in graduate school in Hawaii, he worked at a marine park teaching dolphins to perform tricks. Ballard served in the Vietnam War and is a commander in the U.S. Naval Reserve.

Ballard has participated in more than 100 deep-sea expeditions, many using deep-diving submersibles such as the *Alvin*, a three-person submarine. In addition to the *Titanic*, his discoveries include the German battleship *Bismarck*, eleven warships from the lost fleet of Guadalcanal, the luxury liner *Lusitania* torpedoed by the Germans in 1915, the hospital ship *Britannic*, and the World War II aircraft carrier *Yorktown*.

As interested in education as he is in exploration, Dr. Ballard took approximately 200,000 students to the bottom of the Mediterranean Sea by telepresence in 1989. The students saw underwater volcanoes, artifacts, and the remains of ancient trading vessels. The JASON project allows thousands of students to share the excitement of live exploration. Ballard founded the program after he discovered the *Titanic* and received thousands of letters from schoolchildren wanting to know how he had found the ship.

A spokesman for underwater exploration, Ballard has written for popular magazines such as *National Geographic,* in addition to his scholarly publications, and has been part of numerous TV programs for the BBC, National Geographic Educational Films, German television, public television, and various specials. He is the author of a novel, *Bright Shark;* a children's pop-up book, *Explorer;* and two autobiographies, *Explorations* and *Exploring the Lusitania,* as well as the 1997 title, *Lost Liners.* He has received numerous awards.

Ballard says that higher education taught him to think and to develop a plan. "If you can plan it out, and it seems logical to you, you can do it. And that is the secret to success." He believes strongly in problem-solving and in learning to organize your thoughts. "I discovered the power of a plan," he told an interviewer.

Ballard's latest discovery is an archaeological treasure. In 1999, on an expedition sponsored by the National Geographic Society, he discovered in the Mediterranean Sea, more than a fifth of a mile down, the hulls of two ships believed to be more than 2,500 years old. These ships, probably Phoenician, are from the classic age of Homer, the Iron Age. The wreckage site contains a stone anchor and numerous ceramic containers, indicating that the ships had perhaps carried wine. For Robert Ballard, the seas still have many secrets to reveal.

Shannon Lucid

Set the World Record for a U.S. Astronaut in Space
1943–

In 1996, when she spent 188 days aboard the Russian space station *Mir*, Shannon Lucid set a world record for a U.S. astronaut in space. She was the first woman to receive the Congressional Space Medal of Honor and was also awarded the Order of Friendship Medal by Russia's President Boris Yeltsin. The National Aviation Club selected her to receive its first annual Achievement Award, the award that would have been presented to Amelia Earhart upon the completion of her around-the-world flight. Lucid, the mother of three grown children, called the space experience her "great adventure." She currently holds the international record for the most flight hours in orbit for any non-Russian and the most flight hours for any woman in the world—223 days in space.

Shannon Lucid was born to missionary parents in Shanghai, China, and considers Bethany, Oklahoma, her hometown. However, as a child, she lived briefly in the Texas Panhandle. In an article on her experience, she called the *Mir* a "cosmic tumbleweed" and likened it to the tumbleweeds she had seen in Texas as a child. She graduated from Bethany High School in 1960 and earned a bachelor's degree in chemistry from the University of Oklahoma in 1963, and a master's and a Ph.D. from the same university in 1973. At that time, few women had careers in the sciences or aviation, but Lucid pursued her dream.

Before entering the space program, Lucid was a graduate assistant in the University of Oklahoma's Department of Biochemistry and Molecular Biology and taught in the Department of Chemistry. She also worked for the Oklahoma Medical Research Foundation and for Kerr-McGee in Oklahoma City. She was licensed as a private pilot at the age of twenty and is now rated as a commercial, instrument, and multi-engine pilot.

Lucid was selected as a candidate for the astronaut-training program in 1978 and became a member of the first astronaut class to admit women. She completed training in 1979, qualifying for assignment as a mission specialist on shuttle flights. In addition to her experience on *Mir*, she has been in space in 1985, 1989, 1991, and 1993.

For the *Mir* flight, she trained for one year in Star City, Russia, (where her husband was able to visit her), and became fluent in the Russian language. Her journey began with liftoff from the Kennedy Space Center in Florida on March 22, 1996.

In an article written for *Scientific American* magazine, Lucid described her six-month experience on *Mir*, which means "peace " in Russian. She shared the shuttle with two Russian cosmonauts, Onufriyenko and Usachev, whom she remembers for their spirit of cooperation. She conducted various experiments while the two men worked to maintain the now-aging space station. They ate Russian and American dehydrated food—reconstituted with hot water. She especially liked the Russian soups—borscht and vegetable—and their meat-and-potato casseroles.

The aspect of space life Lucid liked best was the scientific experimentation. In effect, she had her own lab and worked independently, and, in her words, before one experiment became dull it was time to start another. She was in constant contact with the National Aeronautics and Space Administration (NASA) about her work, which included studying embryos in fertilized Japanese quail eggs and studying the effect of a microgravity environment on wheat. She also observed and photographed Earth under various seasonal and light conditions and described watching ice break up in spring and seeing the entire Northern Hemisphere suddenly glow green with spring.

The aspect of space life she liked least was the need to exercise to prevent her muscles from decreasing in the weightless environment. The station had two treadmills and a bicycle, plus bungee cords, which the astronauts could pull against to simulate Earth's force of gravity. She found the exercise boring, and the treadmills were so noisy she could not talk to her companions.

Lucid returned to Kennedy Space Center on September 26, 1996. She is still an active-duty astronaut and hopes to be assigned to another NASA space flight.

The Balloonists

It was the last frontier in aviation—circling the world nonstop in a hot-air balloon. Author Jules Verne had fantasized about such a flight in a novel called *Five Weeks in a Balloon,* written in 1889. It wasn't until the 1990s, however, that such a flight became an obsession with several teams of balloonists, all seeking the $1-million prize offered by an American brewing company. Teams from around the world poured millions of dollars into the race to be first. On March 20, 1999, an unusual team—41-year-old Swiss psychiatrist Bertrand Piccard and 51-year-old English balloonist Brian Jones—successfully completed the 25,401-mile (40,879-kilometer) trip in a record-breaking nineteen days, one hour, and forty-nine minutes. They landed in the desert area north of Mut, Egypt, about 300 miles (482 km) southwest of Cairo.

Until then, American Steve Fossett had been one of the leading contenders for the title. Fossett is chairman of Lakota Trading, Inc., a Chicago-based marketing company, and president of Marathon Securities, Inc., a member of the New York Stock Exchange. Ballooning is only his most recent interest. Fossett also holds seven world records in sailing, including the

Balloonist/entrepreneur Richard Branson (center) prepares to depart on a world tour with his team.

fastest crossing of the Pacific Ocean, both solo and with a crew. He swam across the English Channel, placed forty-seventh in Alaska's Iditarod Dogsled Race, drove the twenty-four-hour Le Mans sports-car race in France, and competed in the Ironman Triathlon, which requires participants to run the twenty-six-plus miles of a marathon and then swim and bicycle.

In 1995 Fossett made the first solo balloon crossing of the Atlantic Ocean, going from Canada to Germany. The next year, he crossed the Pacific Ocean alone. In January 1997 he flew from St. Louis to Sultanpur, India, setting a world distance record of 10,360 miles (16,670 km) and the world duration record of six days, two hours, and forty-four minutes. Fossett flies the *Solo Spirit*, a fairly small balloon with an unpressurized capsule.

Fossett took off from St. Louis, Missouri, on January 5, 1997. He was forced to land 60 miles west of Krasnodra, Russia, because of the faster winds of the subtropical jet stream. A malfunctioning heater and increased fuel consumption also figured in the decision.

Both Fossett and British entrepreneur Richard Branson had bigger budgets, bigger balloons, and better publicity than the team who finally made it. But Piccard and Jones had some advantages that the others did not, including favorable winds and permission to fly over China, a route that saved them important time. (Fossett had been hindered by refusal of access to Libyan air space.)

Piccard and Jones flew the Breitling *Orbiter 3* (named for the Swiss watchmaking company that sponsored them), a smaller balloon than those of other adventurers. The *Orbiter 3* was a combination helium and hot-air balloon, fueled by propane rather than the kerosene used by its predecessors. Propane is a heavier fuel—a weight problem for the balloon—but a more reliable fuel. The balloon itself was 180 feet (54 m) high, but the pressurized capsule, where the two men lived for 20 days, was almost 18 feet (5.4 m) long and just over 9 feet (2.7 m) high—the size of a small camper van. It contained a small water heater, a toilet, and a bunk. Electricity for navigation and communication came from solar-charged lead batteries. The problems encountered by the explorers included ice slabs on the outer layer of the balloon which, they admitted, caused them sheer panic; winds that died over the Pacific and, later, with even more severe consequences, over the Caribbean; difficulty in breathing at high altitudes; a heating system that failed, forcing them to put their drinking water under their seats to keep it from freezing and to huddle together in chilling 40° F (4.4° C) temperatures.

In the sky, often 7 miles up, Piccard and Jones did little actual navigation. They took instructions from an extremely talented mission-control team of meteorologists on the ground in Switzerland. These scientists plotted the jet streams and told the pilots where to go.

The *Orbiter 3* took off from the Swiss Alps and drifted south to North Africa to pick up the jet stream across the Arabian Desert. Crossing the Pacific Ocean took six days, until, east of Central America, they were trapped in deeply frigid but unmoving air. Here they developed breathing problems. Then the balloon caught another jet stream and was propelled across the North Atlantic toward North Africa. They remained aloft after crossing the finish line, because it was Piccard's hope to land near the pyramids of Egypt. Ultimately he had to settle for a remote desert short of that goal—and they had to wait for several hours to be rescued by helicopter from their landing site. They had flown nonstop around the world in nineteen days, one hour, and forty-nine minutes.

Piccard and Jones had tried twice before to set the record and were turned back. Their triumph this time was an emotional experience for both men. Piccard, fighting back tears, said, "I am with the angels and just completely happy."

Christa McAuliffe

First "Teacher in Space" on the Space Shuttle Challenger
1948–1986

By the mid-1980s, the American space-shuttle program had become almost routine. Humans had landed on the moon, and many Americans thought there couldn't be much more. Where once they had hung on every moment of a shuttle flight, they now lost interest in space exploration. In order to revive that interest, NASA decided to send a civilian—"an ordinary citizen"—into space. They wanted that person to be someone who could talk freely—and on camera—about his or her experiences preparing to go into space and actually going on the flight—the excitement, fears, things learned, things questioned. President Ronald Reagan decided that the first average American to travel in space should be a schoolteacher. It was a perfect choice—a good schoolteacher knows how to interest and excite listeners.

NASA announced it was conducting a nationwide search for the first

Teacher in Space, the one who could do the best job of describing the experience of being on the shuttle to most of the people on Earth. Almost 12,000 people completed the eleven-page application, including many authors, scholars, and doctors. Out of all those applications, NASA chose McAuliffe, a social studies teacher at Concord High School in Concord, New Hampshire.

McAuliffe was born on September 2, 1948, in Framingham, Massachusetts, the oldest of five children born to Edward and Grace Corrigan. In high school, Christa met Steve McAuliffe. She went on to Framingham State College and received her degree in history in 1970. She and Steve were married and moved to Washington, D.C., so that he could attend law school.

McAuliffe taught school until her son, Scott, was born. Then she earned a master's degree in school administration, and the family moved to Concord. Their daughter, Caroline, was born in Concord. McAuliffe settled down to domestic life in an old, three-story house, but she was soon back in the classroom. In addition to teaching, she was active in community life—she belonged to a tennis club, took part in the life of her church, belonged to the local playhouse and the YMCA, was a Girl Scout leader, a jogger and a swimmer, and a volunteer at the local hospital.

McAuliffe was reluctant to apply for the Teacher in Space program, but so many of her friends urged her that she sent in the application at the last minute and then forgot about it. Even when named a finalist, she was quite sure she would not be chosen because others were more qualified than she was. At her school, students talked about McAuliffe's field trips, because she believed strongly in "hands-on" experience as the best way to learn. When she was chosen for the *Challenger* mission, she called it the "ultimate field trip."

In space, McAuliffe's duties would be to introduce each flight member, explain his or her role, show the cockpit with its dials and switches, and talk about daily life in the shuttle—how the crew ate, slept, and exercised in microgravity. She would also discuss why people explore space, how the shuttle flew, and what technological advances were expected in the future. It was her mission to help people understand the space program and feel the thrill of it. She was also asked to keep a journal, just as westward-moving pioneer women in America's nineteenth century kept journals of their experiences. McAuliffe believed that space was the twentieth-century frontier, just as the American West had been 100 years ago.

McAuliffe began space training at NASA's Houston facility in 1985. Worried that she would be considered a freeloader and not serious about training, she worked hard to prove that she understood the challenges and responsibilities of her assignment. Crew members readily accepted her.

On January 28, 1986, the space shuttle *Challenger* roared into space. Just seventy-three seconds later, it exploded, killing all seven astronauts aboard. Those who watched the shuttle launch on television that day will never forget the sight of it exploding or the poignant camera shot of McAuliffe's mother, Grace Corrigan. It was a day of heartbreak for the United States.

Christa McAuliffe's urge to teach is alive today in the Christa McAuliffe Planetarium in Concord, New Hampshire. The planetarium is dedicated to showing youngsters the possibilities and excitement of space science and astronomy. It welcomes them to the "ultimate field trip." Ten years after the *Challenger* disaster, the planetarium unveiled an exhibit about McAuliffe. The permanent exhibit will highlight McAuliffe as a person and as an astronaut. Her hometown wants to be sure everyone knows the answer to the question, "Who was Christa McAuliffe?"

Sally Ride

First American Woman in Space
1951—

Sally Ride was the first American woman in space, part of the 1983 *Challenger* crew, and her experience opened the door to space exploration for many American women who would follow in her footsteps. She was not, however, the first woman in space—the former Soviet Union had already put two women in space. The first, Valentina Tereshkova, was part of a crew in 1963; the second, Svetlana Savitskaya, flew exactly one year before Ride.

Sally Kirsten Ride was born in Encino, California, in 1951. Her father was a political science professor and her mother was a volunteer counselor at a women's correctional institution. Her sister became a Presbyterian minister. As a child, Ride was most noted for her athletic ability. While still quite young, she became interested in tennis and eventually earned a place on the U.S. junior tennis circuit. At Westlake School in Los Angeles, she also developed an interest in science—but tennis came first.

In 1968 she enrolled at Swarthmore College in Pennsylvania to study physics but dropped out in her second year to become a tennis professional. After some time, she knew she would never be good enough to be a top-ranked player, and she returned to school, this time to Stanford University. As an undergraduate, Ride double-majored in physics and English literature. She was so interested in the work of William Shakespeare that she considered an English lit graduate-school program but finally settled on astrophysics.

A Ph.D. candidate in 1977, she was looking for post-doctoral work and read NASA's call for astronauts in the Stanford University paper. More than 8,000 men and women applied to be mission specialists, and she was one of 208 finalists. In the end, 35 were accepted, 5 of them women, including Sally Ride; the other women were a biochemist, a geologist, a surgeon, and an electrical engineer. NASA was then developing projects for private industry and needed scientists and technicians—mission specialists—almost more than it needed pilots.

Ride's year-long training program included parachute jumping, water survival, adaptation to gravitational pull and weightlessness, and radio communications and navigation. Once she earned her pilot's license, flying became a hobby. Ride was assigned to a project that designed remote mechanical arms to be used in deploying and retrieving space satellites.

During the second and third flights of the *Columbia* shuttle, Ride was a ground-based communications officer, handling messages between the crew and ground control. Finally in 1982 she was chosen as a crew member for the *Challenger* shuttle. Ride does not believe she was chosen because she is a woman, but feminists throughout the United States celebrated her appointment as a victory for women.

When the shuttle lifted off at 7:00 A.M., June 18, 1983, from Cape Canaveral, Florida, many spectators were wearing T-shirts emblazoned with "Ride, Sally Ride," a line from an old popular song. On the mission, Ride deployed two communications satellites, conducted trials of the mechanical arm she had helped to design, and performed and monitored about forty scientific experiments. The communications satellites were from Canada and Indonesia. Ride was in space six days and called the flight "the most fun that I'll ever have in my life." She flew again in October 1984, and has a total of more than 340 hours in space.

Ride next acted as a liaison officer between NASA and private companies doing work on the space program. When the *Challenger* exploded after its launch in 1986, killing all aboard including civilian teacher Christa McAuliffe, Ride was a member of the presidential commission charged with investigating the accident. In 1986 she moved to Washington, D.C., to become assistant to the NASA administrator for long-range planning. In this capacity, Ride created NASA's Office of Exploration and produced a report on the future of the space program, "Leadership and America's Future in Space."

In 1987, Ride, by then married to a fellow astronaut, retired from the space program to become a science fellow at the Center for International Security and Arms Control at Stanford University. Two years later, she was named Director of the California Space Institute and professor of physics at the University of California, San Diego. She continues to be a spokesperson for space exploration and to encourage young women to study science and math.

Eileen Collins

First Woman to Pilot a Space Shuttle
1956—

The first woman ever selected to pilot a space shuttle, USAF Lieutenant Colonel Eileen Marie Collins became the first woman to command a shuttle when she and her crew took the *Columbia* into orbit on July 23,1999. The *Columbia* carried the Chandra X-ray Observatory, a $2.5-billion telescope to be deployed in space to help scientists study exploding stars, quasars, and black holes. The Chandra was the heaviest payload ever carried by a shuttle—over 50,000 pounds (22,600 kg)—and presented unusual problems for Commander Collins. If she had been forced to abort the flight, she would have had to deal with making an emergency landing carrying that heavy telescope. As it was, the mission was almost flawless, marred by only two minor problems—leaking fuel on takeoff that slightly altered the arc of the shuttle's flight but did not endanger the crew; and a brief electrical short circuit that flashed warning lights within seconds of blastoff and knocked off controllers on two engines. Backup controllers immediately kicked in. But if an engine had shut down, Collins would have had to make the first emergency landing of a shuttle flight.

Eileen Collins was born on November 19, 1956, in Elmira, New York. She has two brothers, a sister, and two parents who, she says, were very supportive of everything she wanted to do. She attended Elmira Free Academy, graduating in 1974, and has said that in high school she began to read about famous women pilots. "Their stories inspired me. I admired the courage of these women to go and fly into dangerous situations."

While in college, Eileen took flying lessons and earned her pilot's license. After she graduated from Syracuse (New York) University with good grades, she was one of the first women to go straight into the Air Force pilot-training program from college. It was then that she set her heart on becoming an astronaut.

She graduated from the Air Force Undergraduate Pilot Training program in 1979 and spent several years as an instructor on different aircraft. She has flown more than 5,000 hours in more than thirty types of aircraft. In the mid-1980s she studied at the Air Force Institute of Technology and then served as an assistant professor in mathematics and a T-41 instructor pilot at the U.S. Air Force Academy in Colorado Springs, Colorado. In 1990 she graduated from the Air Force Test Pilot School at Edwards Air Force Base in California and was chosen for the astronaut program. She joined the program in July 1991. In 1995 she was the first woman to serve as co-pilot on a shuttle flight, and she knew that people were watching her, mainly women around the country.

Collins is not only a pilot but also a wife and mother. Her husband is Pat Youngs, a San Antonio pilot she met when they flew C-141s together. They were married at the Air Force Academy chapel and have one young daughter.

Command of the *Columbia* brought Collins a great deal of publicity—and stress. Beginning in March 1998 she was at the center of a media blitz. She spoke at ceremonies in the White House with the president and first lady at her side and did interviews with television and newspaper reporters from around the country. She told the nation, "When I was a child, I dreamed about space. I admired pilots, astronauts, and I've admired explorers of all kinds. It was only a dream that I would someday be one of them." As the shuttle liftoff approached and media attention increased, Collins demonstrated that she was right when she told a reporter, "I think I work well under stress, and sometimes I work better under stress."

While Collins did not expect the *Columbia* flight to make her a national heroine, she did hope that it would inspire all children—boys and girls—to reach for their dreams. After the flight, she said she most looked forward to a vacation and time with her husband and daughter. In her free time, she enjoys running, golf, hiking, camping, reading, and photography.

Mae Jemison

First Black Woman Astronaut in Space
1956–

Although she was thrilled by the Gemini space flights in the mid-1960s, Mae Jemison probably never dreamed of being an astronaut as a child. At that time, astronauts were selected from among military test pilots. That meant they were all white males. But by the 1990s, many changes had taken place. In 1992, Jemison became was the fifth black astronaut and the first female black astronaut in the history of NASA.

Jemison was born October 17, 1956, in Decatur, Alabama, but her family moved to Chicago when she was three years old. Mae was the youngest of three children born to Charlie and Dorothy Jemison, a maintenance worker and schoolteacher. After an uncle introduced her to science, subjects such as anthropology, archaeology, and astronomy fascinated her throughout her childhood.

During high school a research project led her to visit a local hospital, and she developed a strong interest in sickle cell anemia, a disease that affects

African-Americans. She decided she wanted to dedicate her life to bio-medical engineering. But she also pursued her interests in dancing, art, and archaeology. In her senior year in Chicago's Morgan Park High School, Jemison applied for a number of scholarships. She graduated from high school in 1973 at the age of sixteen. With a National Achievement Scholarship, she was able to attend Stanford University in California.

At Stanford she was one of few females and minorities in the engineering program, but she called attention to herself by working hard and making good grades. In 1977, at the age of twenty, she graduated with a double major in chemical engineering and African-American studies.

By that time, Congress had amended the Civil Rights Act of 1964 to forbid federal agencies from discriminating on the basis of sex, race, religion, or national origin. That meant Jemison could apply for the NASA program, but she did not feel she was ready. She knew she lacked some of the qualifications. Instead, she attended medical school at Cornell University, graduating in 1981. While in medical school, she was part of teams providing basic medical care to people in Cuba, Kenya, and Thailand. After graduation, she volunteered briefly at a Cambodian refugee camp.

Jemison next entered the Peace Corps, a government agency dedicated to promoting world peace by improving health and living conditions in underdeveloped nations. She was named the medical officer for Sierra Leone and Liberia, West Africa. She was twenty-six, one of the youngest doctors to work in Sierra Leone. She supervised pharmacy, laboratory, and medical staff personnel, provided medical care to local residents, wrote self-care manuals, and developed guidelines for health and safety issues. She also worked with the Centers for Disease Control on research for the hepatitis B vaccine.

Dr. Jemison left the Peace Corps in 1985. Her sights were now set on the space program, because she felt she had the necessary qualifications. She submitted her application. Meanwhile she worked as a general practitioner with the CIGNA Health Plans of California in Los Angeles while taking graduate classes in engineering to further prepare for the space program. After the 1986 crash of the space shuttle *Challenger,* NASA suspended its recruitment program, and Jemison's application was put on hold. She resubmitted her application in October 1986, and in February 1987 was notified that she had passed the first phase of the selection process. She was one of fifteen candidates accepted out of some 2,000 applicants.

She flew to Houston for extensive medical exams and personal interviews to determine if she was physically and emotionally strong enough to be in the program.

For instance, during an emergency, she might have to stay inside a small survival ball for days, alone, in the dark. NASA wanted to be sure she could handle this kind of stress.

After she was accepted into the program, Jemison began the difficult one-year training program. She had to overcome her fear of heights, because she had to parachute from an airplane over both land and water. She studied rocket propulsion, astronomy, aerodynamics, meteorology, and physics. She learned the jobs of everyone on the crew, although she would be a science mission specialist. She practiced survival techniques in both water and wilderness areas. All astronauts in training spend hours at a mission simulator or model of the shuttle, learning all its gauges, switches, and warning lights, practicing liftoffs, ascents, orbiting, reentry, and landing. They also are exposed to weightlessness, so they will know what to expect in the zero gravity atmosphere of space.

Jemison completed the NASA training program in August 1988, one year after her acceptance. Many astronauts wait a long time between completing the program and their first flight, but as quickly as September 1992 she was named to the crew of the shuttle *Endeavour.*

The *Endeavour* was a joint U.S. and Japanese mission. One of Jemison's experiments was to see whether frogs would grow normally from eggs fertilized and hatched without gravity. They did. She also did research on calcium loss from bones in space. This would help determine how long a person could safely stay in space. She also researched the effects of biomedical feedback on space sickness, using herself as the experimental subject. Biomedical feedback techniques include relaxation and controlled thought processes.

In 1993, Jemison felt she had fulfilled her obligation to NASA. She also believed she could make other contributions to society. She resigned from the space program to teach space technology at Dartmouth University. She also founded The Jemison Group, Inc., a private company that explores the influence of advancing technology on developing countries. The company, for instance, studies the way solar power can work in place of traditional fuels in tropical areas. To encourage African-Americans to prepare for careers in science and engineering, the company sponsors an international science camp for students from underdeveloped countries.

Today, Dr. Jemison divides her time between Houston, home of The Jemison Group, and Dartmouth University where she still teaches. She believes her participation in the space program demonstrated that all peoples of the world can be astronomers, physicists, and explorers.

To Find Out More

Books

General
Russell Bourne. *The Big Golden Book of Christopher Columbus and Other Early Adventurers.* Racine, WI: Western Publishing Co., 1991.
Discoverers of the New World. By the editors of *American Heritage, the Magazine of History.* New York: American Heritage, 1960.
Joyce A. Grosseck and Elizabeth Attwood. *Story of America: Great Explorers.* Grand Rapids, MI: The Fideler Company, 1962.

John and Sebastian Cabot
Henry Kurtz. *John and Sebastian Cabot.* New York: Franklin Watts, 1973.

Christopher Columbus
Isaac Asimov. *Christopher Columbus, Navigator to the New World.* Milwaukee: Gareth Stevens Children's Books, 1991.

Núñez Cabeza de Vaca
Mary Wade. *Cabeza de Vaca: Conquistador Who Cared.* Houston: Colophon House, 1995.

Henry Hudson
Isaac Asimov and Elizabeth Kaplan. *Henry Hudson.* Milwaukee: Gareth Stevens Children's Books, 1991.

Lewis and Clark
Rhoda Blumberg. *The Incredible Journey of Lewis and Clark.* New York: William Morrow, 1995.
Christine A. Fitz-Gerald. *The World's Great Explorers: Meriwether Lewis and William Clark.* Chicago: Children's Press, 1991.

The Wright Brothers
Walter J. Boyne. *The Smithsonian Book of Flight for Young People.* Smithsonian Books, 1987.

Admiral Richard E. Byrd

Richard Byrd. *Little America*. New York: G. P. Putnam's Sons, 1930.

——————— . *Discovery*. New York: G. P. Putnam's Sons, 1935.

Amelia Earhart

Blythe Randolph. *Amelia Earhart*. Chicago: Franklin Watts, 1987.

Jacqueline Cochran

Marquita O. Fisher. *Jacqueline Cochran, First Lady of Flight*. Champaign, Illinois: Garrard Publishing, 1973.

Edward Jablonski. *Ladybirds: Women in Aviation*. New York: Hawthorn Books, 1968.

Jacques-Yves Cousteau

The Cousteau Society. *An Adventure in the Amazon*. New York: Simon & Schuster, 1997.

Jacques-Yves Cousteau: Exploring the Wonders of the Deep. Chatham, NJ: Raintree/Steck Vaughn, 1997.

Thor Heyerdahl

Thor Heyerdahl. *Kon-Tiki*. Amereon, Ltd., 1993; Washington Square Press, 1995.

Sir Edmund Hillary/Mount Everest

Broughton Coburn. *Everest: Mountain without Mercy*. New York: Random House, 1997.

Jon Krakauer. *Into Thin Air*. New York: Anchor Books, 1998.

Christa McAuliffe

Colin Burgess and Grace George Corrigan. *Teacher in Space—Christa McAuliffe and the Challenger Legacy*. Bison Books, 2000.

Grace George Corrigan. *A Journal for Christa*. Bison Books, 2000.

Robert T. Hohler. *I Touch the Future: The Story of Christa McAuliffe*. New York: Random House, 1986.

Laura S. Jeffrey. *Christa McAuliffe—A Space Biography*. Enslow Publishing, 1998.

Sally Ride

Jane Hurwitz and Sue Hurwitz. *Sally Ride: Shooting for the Stars*. New York: Fawcett Columbine, 1989.

Karen O'Connor. *Sally Ride and the New Astronuats: Scientists in Space*. Chicago: Franklin Watts, 1983.

Sally Ride. *To Space and Back*. New York: Lothrop, Lee & Shepard Books, 1989.

Mae Jemison

Della A. Yanuzzi. *Mae Jemison: A Space Biography*. Springfield, NJ: Enslow Publishers, 1998.

Web Sites

Hercules
http://www.perseus.tufts.edu/Herakles
    Relates the story of Hercules and the Giants and provides links to a map tracing the travels of Hercules

Alexander the Great
http://www.1stmuse.com/alex3/alex-text.html
    Home page for a multimedia project about Alexander, with links to other sites, including one that summarizes his life

Brendan the Navigator
http://www.ptialaska.net/~mboesser/voyager.html
    This rather brief discussion contains the best information available on Brendan
http://www.mariner.org/age/intro/aoe.html
    General information about very early exploration; links to pictures of Saint Brendan and Venice; maintained by the Mariner's Museum

Leif Eriksson and the Vikings
http://www.mariner.org./age/vikingsdisc.html
    The Mariners' Museum page on Viking discoveries

Marco Polo
http://www.forham.edu/halsall/source/polo-kinsay.html
    A complicated discussion of the value of Polo's record and an analysis of the places he claimed to have visited

John and Sebastian Cabot
http://www.optonline.com/comptons/ceo/00765-A
    Encyclopedia entry
http://www.win.tue.nl/cs/fm/engels/discovery/cabot.html
    A biography of John Cabot
http://www.heritage.nf.ca/exploration/bristol ex.html
    A recounting of English voyages to Newfoundland and Labrador before Cabot

Christopher Columbus
http://www.mariner.org/age/columbus.html
    Introductory page on the explorations of Columbus, with links to pages on each of his voyages, his death, and pictures
http://www.caller.com/attract/colum.html
    The replica ships at Corpus Christi, Texas

http://metalab.unc.edu/expo/1492.exhibit/Intro.html
 "1492: An Ongoing Voyage," an exhibit at the Library of Congress, with links to many sites related to Columbus

Amerigo Vespucci
http://www.newadvent.org/cathen/15384b.html
 Biographical entry from *The Catholic Encyclopedia*

Ponce de León
http://www.infoplease.com/ce5/CE041650.html
 A brief biography

Giovanni da Verrazzano
http://www.win.tue.nl~engels/discovery/verrazzano.html
 Traces Verrazzano's voyage to the East Coast of what is now the United States, with a complete list of sources

Cabeza de Vaca
http://www.archeologyinc.org/narvaezvaca.html
 A discussion of the Narvaez expedition and Cabeza de Vaca's survival
http://www.pbs.org/weta/thewest/wpages/wpgs610/cabeza.html
 Cabeza de Vaca's narration of his journey, translated in 1905

Jacques Cartier
http://www.win.tue.nl/~engels/discovery/cartier.html
 An overview of his expeditions, with links to several related sources, including some in French

Hernando de Soto
http://www.cr.nps.gov/delta/desoto.html
 A brief sketch with links to related sites
http://www.newadvent.org/cathen/04753a.html
 A detailed entry from *The Catholic Encyclopedia*

Francisco Vásquez de Coronado
http://www.win.tue.nl/cs/fm/engels/discovery/coronado.html
 A very brief discussion; list of other sources

Sir Francis Drake
http://www.mcn.org/2/oseeler/voy.html
 A synopsis of Drake's voyage on the *Golden Hind*
http://www.mariner.org/age/drake.html
 The Mariners' Museum main pages, with links to several sites with information about Drake

Sir Walter Raleigh

http://www.nps.gov/fora/sirwalter.html
    A summary of Raleigh's career, maintained by the Fort Raleigh National Historic Site
http://www.luminarium.org/renlit/ralegadd.html
    Links to many biographical sites

Samuel de Champlain

http://www.lcweb.loc.gov/exhibits/treasures/trr009.html
    Champlain's 1607 map; site maintained by the Library of Congress
http://www.optonline.com/comptons/ceo/00923 A.html
    An encyclopedia entry with links to Lake Huron and Lake Champlain

René Robert Cavelier, Sieur de la Salle

http://www.plpsd.mb.ca/amhs/history/sdls.html
    A brief biography
http://www.csn.net/advent/cathen/09009b.html
    A biography from *The Catholic Encyclopedia*
http://www/infoplease.com/ce5/CEO29702.html
    A brief biography with bibliography

Vitus Bering

http://www.horsensmuseum.dk/flenk/bering/ber en.html
    A brief summary of his explorations, with maps

Captain James Cook

http://www.geocities.com/TheTropics/7557/
    An overview of his life and voyages

Daniel Boone

http://www.berksweb.com/boontext.html
    A brief overview of Boone's life, with a link to the Daniel Boone Homestead page; maintained by the Berks County Conservancy
http://www.nationalcenter.inter.net/BoonebyRoosevelt.html
    An article about Boone written by Theodore Roosevelt

The Franciscan Friars of California

http://www.californiamissions.com/morehistory/background.html
    Historical background on the missions
http://library.advanced.org/3615/
    Home page for the Spanish Missions of California with links to tours, information about authors, history, people who lived in the missions, and more
http://www.pressanykey.com/missions
    An index of California mission information

Lewis and Clark

http://www.lewisclark.net/biography/index.html
   Biography of Meriwether Lewis and William Clark, with links to site displaying maps, a timeline, journals, the South Dakota Trail, and contact information
http://www.cp.duluth.mn.us/~tmcs/lewsclrk1.html
   A brief overview with a good map

Davy Crockett

http:www.infoporium.com/heritage/crockbio.shtml
   A brief biographical sketch

Sir John Franklin

http://www.ric.edu/rpotter/SJFranklin.html
   "The Fate of Franklin," with links to resources about Franklin and Arctic exploration
http://www.cronab.demon.co.uk/frank/html
   Thorough coverage of Franklin's life, written to mark the 150th anniversary of his death

Hamilton Hume

http://www.win.tue.nl/engels/discovery/hume/html
   A brief sketch

Charles Wilkes

http://www.south-pole.com/p0000079.html
   An overview of Wilkes's expeditions, with a recommended reading list and bibliography

"Kit" Carson

http://www.tombtown.com/bios/carson.html
   A brief sketch of Carson's life

John C. Frémont

http://www.kcmuseum.com/explor09.html
   A biographical sketch, maintained by *Compton's Encyclopedia*

Dr. David Livingstone

http://www.home.vicnet.au/~neils/africa/livingstone.html
   A biographical overview

Sir Henry Morton Stanley

http://www.vicnet.au/~neils/africa/livingston.html
   Mentions Stanley's role in finding Livingstone
http://www.kirjasto.sci.fi/hstanley.html
   A brief biography but has suggested readings and selected works

Robert Edwin Peary

http://www.cbcph.navy.mil/museum/peary.html
  A good biography maintained by the Civil Engineer Corps and Seabees Museum
http://www.bowdoin.edu/dept/arctic/peary.html
  A biography of Peary, maintained by the Peary-MacMillan Arctic Museum, with links to other sites maintained by the museum

Matthew Henson

http://unmuseum.mus.pa.us/henson.html
  A thorough discussion of Henson's life, his explorations with Robert Edwin Peary, and the belated recognition he received; includes a map of their route to the North Pole

Roald Amundsen

http://www.www.mnc.net/norway/roald.html
  Links to several pages about Amundsen
http://www.mnc.net/norway/Amundsen.html
  A thorough overview of his life and career

Sir Ernest Shackleton

http://www.expedition-freight.co.uk/shackleton.html
  A brief discussion of his 1914 Imperial Trans-Antarctic Expedition and the Shackleton Rowett Expedition of 1921
http://www.south-pole.com/p0000097.html
  Two pages presenting a thorough biography, links to related sites, a list of staff members and the shore party, and pictures

George Mallory and Andrew Irvine

http://www.mountainzone.com/everest/99/history.html
  Presents the mystery of Mallory and Irvine and whether they reached the summit of Mt. Everest before they died; links to other sites about Mt. Everest

Richard E. Byrd

http://www-bprc.mps.ohio-state.edu/
  Home page of the Byrd Polar Research Center
http://www.firstflight.org/shrine/richard/ byrd.html
  A biographical sketch

Amelia Earhart

http://www.ionet.net/~jellenc/ae eyrs.html
  Biography of Earhart's early years, with links to site covering her later career and last flight; final site has links to many pages about Earhart and a list of references

Charles A. Lindbergh
http://www.worldbook.com/fun/aviator/html/av6.html
   A biography, divided into early life, his historic flight, goodwill ambassador, the Lindbergh kidnapping, and World War II

Jacqueline Cochran
http://www.firstflight.org/shrine/jacqueline_cochran.html
   A brief biography

Jacques-Yves Cousteau
http://www.ecomall.com/activism/emag.html
   An interview with Cousteau, published posthumously in *The Environmental Magazine*
http://www.ecoscape.com/coousteau.html
   Discussion of Cousteau's beliefs, especially concerning environmentalism and the nature of man
http://www.aguanet.com/ocean/topics.coustea.html
   A brief biography with links to related sites

Thor Heyerdahl
http://www.nrk.no/undervisning/p2/heyerdahl/heyerdahl.del1.html
   Answers to a quiz about Heyerdahl, with links back to the quiz page

Sir Edmund Hillary
http://www.achievement.org/autodoc/page/hil0bio-1
   A biography with links to an interview and a brief profile

John Glenn, Jr.
http://www.lerc.nasa.gov/persons/astronauts/e-to-h/GlennJ.H.html
   Biographical data from the John H. Glenn Research Center, Lewis Field, Cleveland, Ohio; link to the NASA home page

Chuck Yeager
http://www/achievement.org/autodoc/page/yea0int-1
   A lengthy interview with Yeager, plus a link to a biographical page

Robert Ballard
http://www.jasonproject.org/ballard.html
   Discussion of Ballard's work with the JASON Foundation project to involve students in live exploration; links to the Institute for Explorations and other pages about Ballard

Shannon Lucid

http://www.sciam.com/1998/0598issue/0598lucid.html
   Text of Lucid's *Scientific American* article about her experience on *Mir*
http://www.greatwomen.org/lucid.html
   Brief sketch of Lucid's career
http://www.jsc.nasa.gov/Bios/htmlbios/lucid.html
   Biographical data from NASA

Balloonists

http://www.westl.edu/
   Home page for Washington University in St. Louis, with numerous pages about
   Steve Fossett's attempt to circle the world

Sally Ride

http://www.quest.arc.nasa.gov/women/bios/sr/html
   Biography, with further readings suggested
http://www2.lucidcafe.com/library/96may/ride.html
   Biography, with links to books by and about Ride as well as related sources

Eileen Collins

http://www.jsc.nasa.gov/Bios/htmlbios/collins.html
   Biographical data from NASA
http://www.womeninaviation.com/eileen.html
   Brief biography; site is maintained by Women in Aviation
http://www.flatoday.com/space/explore/stories/1998/030798a.html
   Short feature article from *Florida Today*

Mae Jemison

http://www.lib.lsu.edu/lib/chem/display/jemison.html
   An overview of Jemison's life with a bibliography, an address for the Jemison Institute,
   and links to NASA documentation of the *Endeavour* mission
http://www.apple.com/applemaster/maejemison/index.html
   This brief article focuses on the goals and interests of the Jemison Group and the
   Jemison Foundation

Index

Numbers in *italics* represent illustrations.

Photo Credits

Photographs © AP/Wide World Photos: back cover bottom center, front cover bottom left, 4, 5, 8, 40, 42, 108, 224, 242; Archive Photos: 8, 229 (Archive France), 136 (Blank Archives), 8, 236 (Express Newspapers/Z856), front cover bottom center, 1, 4, 66, 197, (Popperfoto), back cover bottom left, 8, 247 (Reuters), 3, 4, 5, 6, 7, 30, 49, 98, 122, 128, 147, 171, 186; Art Resource, NY/The Pierpont Morgan Library: 4, 69; Bridgeman Art Library International Ltd., London/New York: 3, 24 (British Library, London, UK), 6, 159 (Private Collection); Corbis-Bettmann: 7, 182 (H.S. Capman), 8, 212 (Museum of Flight), 8, 232 (Reuters), 7, 193 (George Rinhart), back cover bottom right, 9, 71, 260 (UPI), 248 (Ralph White), back cover top center, back cover top right, 3, 4, 5, 6, 7, 9, 20, 36, 46, 55, 67, 72, 75, 87, 109, 112, 115, 134, 137, 140, 150, 163, 168, 176, 201, 202, 208, 257; Culver Pictures: front cover top center, 3, 4, 5, 6, 7, 8, 10, 13, 58, 105, 130, 190, 220; Liaison Agency, Inc.: 8, 254 (Thierry Boccon-Gibod), 118, 234 (Hulton Getty), back cover top left, front cover bottom right, 8, 9, 240, 250, 263, 266 (NASA); North Wind Picture Archives: 6, 103, 126; Stock Montage, Inc: 3, 4, 5, 6, 27, 52, 61, 64, 90, 119; Superstock, Inc.: 4, 33 (Bibliotheque Nationale, Paris/AKG, Berlin), 79 (The Huntington Library, Art Collections, and Botanical Gardens, San Marino, CA), 8, 214 ("Dick" Whittington Collection, Huntington Library, Art Collections, and Botanical Gardens, San Marino, CA), front cover top left, 5, 95, 101 (Stock Montage), front cover top right, 5, 8, 81, 239.

About the Author

Judy Alter's recent books for young readers include *Extraordinary Women of the American West* (named a Notable Social Studies book for Young Readers for 2000 by the Children's Book Council), biographies of Christopher Reeve and Laura Ingalls Wilder, and numerous first readers on subjects ranging from Wild West shows to beauty pageants. Her awards include Best Juvenile Novel of 1984 from the Texas Institute of Letters, Best Western Novel from Western Writers of America, and two Western Heritage (Wrangler) Awards from the National Cowboy Hall of Fame for short stories.

She is also the author of seven novels for young people and several adult novels. She regularly writes book reviews for the *Fort Worth Star-Telegram* and a column about Texas writers for the *Dallas Morning News*.

When not writing, Alter is the director of TCU (Texas Christian University) Press in Fort Worth, Texas, a small but respected academic press. The single parent of four now-grown children and the grandmother of one baby girl, she presides over a household that includes two large dogs and two cats. Her hobbies are reading and cooking.